COUNTRIES

CIVIC ARTS

ERIC·R·KUHNE·&·ASSOC

15-27 GEE ST·CLERKENWELL

LONDON·UK·EC1V 3RD

T + 44 (0)20·7549·8499

F + 44 (0)20·7549·8449

www·civicarts·com

MIDDLE EAST

First published in Great Britain in 1999 by Fusion Press, a division of Satin Publications Limited.

Fusion Press,
a division of
Satin Publications Limited
20 Queen Anne Street
London W1M 0AY
E-mail: sheenadewan@compuserve.com

Cover Image: ©1999 Nickolai Globe
Layout: Justine Hounam
Map illustrations: Hamish Sanderson
Printed and bound by The Bath Press Ltd.
Front cover image: Lotfollah Mosque, Esfahan, Iran.
©1999 Andrew Dowling
ISBN: 1-901250-79-2

The Godless Pilgrim

Andrew Dowling

AUTHOR

A writer, film maker and visual artist, Andrew Dowling was born in 1969. He was educated at the University of Sydney, Australia, and has since remained in the city, living there with his wife and travelling companion, Kirsty Albert. Godless Pilgrim is his second book.

To Kirst, for various reasons.

And to my parents,
who never receive the thanks they deserve.

The first rule for understanding the human condition is that men live in second-hand worlds. They are aware of much more than they have personally experienced; and their own experience is always indirect. The quality of their lives is determined by meanings they have received from others. Everyone lives in a world of such meanings. No man stands alone directly confronting a world of solid fact. No such world is available. The closest men come to it is when they are infants or when they become insane: then, in a terrifying scene of meaningless events and senseless confusion, they are often seized with the panic of near-total insecurity. But in their everyday life they do not experience a world of solid fact; their experience itself is selected by stereotyped meanings and shaped by ready-made interpretations. Their images of the world, and of themselves, are given to them by crowds of witnesses they have never met and never shall meet. Yet for every man these images - provided by strangers and dead men — are the very basis of his life as a human being... Every man interprets what he observes – as well as much that he has not observed: but his terms of interpretation are not his own.

Cecil Wright Mills

Contents

PREFACE

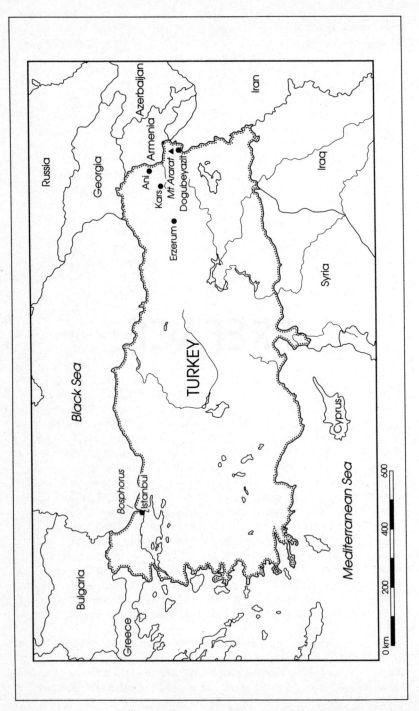

TURKEY

"Allaaaahu akbar allaaaaahu akbar! Allahu akbar allaaaahu akbar..."

God is great. God is great.
The sound is thin, forlorn. The voice drifts down from the ancient stone tower, blows through us, and is quickly lost to the vast empty spaces that have threatened to crush us all morning. The words are familiar but the sound is not. In Cairo, Damascus, Beirut, even Dar Es Salaam, the words have come as brutal, scratchy noise, rousing visitors, breaking their dreams. Calling the faithful to prayer. It is a sound heard countless times before, but never like this.
Here there are no loudspeakers, no hissing static. Just a single voice, the sound carved into the wind thirty feet above us. The attraction of early Islam is cradled somewhere in this fragile sound; even to a non-believer it is inspirational. To have heard such a thing in Mecca a thousand years ago must have been awesome. Listening to it now, to that pale voice far above us, it comes as no surprise that Islam should have spread as spectacularly as it did.
Come to prayer. Come to salvation. There is no God but Allah.
The two Turks who have remained on the ground – heavy men, in polyester suits, their noses hooked like scimitars – applaud their friend's performance, laughing. His head pokes through a gap in the blistered old rock, framed by ancient lichens: a window high in stone that was once a church steeple, is now a minaret. He grins, waves. Kirst and I wave back.
When he climbs back to earth, we wander together – a strange troupe, struggling to communicate, smiling at ourselves – to the next stone ruin. We are at a place known as Ani, a ruined city sitting uncomfortably on the border between Turkey and Armenia. Ani was, for a long time, the capital of Armenia. Now it is nothing more than a pile of stones in an empty landscape: a handful of ruined buildings, ancient churches, basilicas ravaged by ice and wind and Turkish neglect. There is a brooding atmosphere about the place, one almost of ritual murder.
The land around is vast and green and without trees. Utterly horizontal, it is empty of everything, rolling hills are carpeted only with stern grass and black rocks, all grim beneath the low sky. The landscape has been like this – bleak, lifeless – all the way from Kars, the nearest Turkish town. Our road, flanked on either side by snow-capped mountains that are only just higher than we are, has brought us through a world green and grey, wide and open, where nothing dares to raise its head into the sky. No trees, no towns, no people.
At the gates of Ani, a few buildings huddle together, the only settlement for miles. I cannot see them any more: the scale of this place is too huge. We have walked so far that the stone wall encircling the site has vanished. Between earth and sky there is only us, among the ruins. The low swirling

clouds press on us, and I wonder if there can be any place in the world more desolate than Ani today.

A thin wind blows.

I turn slowly to face Armenia. Observation towers, across the river which cuts the landscape behind Ani, are reminders of just how strongly the Armenians hate the Turks. We have been warned that if we take photographs of the Armenian side we risk being shot.

The history of this area is as grim as the land itself. It was here that one of the worst massacres this century took place, of the Armenian population of eastern Turkey in the dying days of the First World War. Then, as now, the Turkish government denied it ever happened. It denies that this almost uninhabited area was once full of Armenian Christians, denies that it had once ordered the elimination of up to a million of such people. Today it is wary of all evidence of the land's previous inhabitants, declaring that the church we have just left was really the country's first mosque. We are told that these are Muslim lands, that Christianity can only be found on the other side of the river.

We stand in a zone of confrontation, between two bitter enemies. Between Turkey and Armenia, between Islam and Christianity. Here, on this tiny strip of lonely land high in the mountains, two religions, two histories, collide with utter animosity. It is here that my journey into Islam begins.

Islam's foundations were laid over a thousand years ago, at the beginning of the Seventh century. It was then that an Arab merchant named Muhammad received the first of a series of visions which would etch his name into history as the Prophet of Islam.

Muhammad ibn Abdullah lived in the central Arabian town of Mecca, in the region known as the Hijaz. He was a member of the Quraysh tribe, the most powerful tribe in Mecca and one that had turned the city, in just a few generations, into the most important trade centre in Arabia. The wrenching social change that had accompanied such success had made many uncertain about the future, uneasy about a culture of greed which had eroded traditional tribal values.

In the year 610AD, Muhammad took his family to Mount Hira just outside the city for a spiritual retreat, a common practice among the Arabs of the region. It was here, on the seventeenth night of the Arabic month of Ramadan, that Muhammad was torn from his sleep and confronted by a shining vision of what he later identified as the archangel Gabriel. "Recite!" commanded the angel. Muhammad at first refused, believing himself to be no prophet. Such activities were the province of soothsayers and madmen. Only after the third command did Muhammad open his mouth. And as he did, the words of a new scripture rushed from his lungs, words not his own, words beyond his control. Muhammad had received the word of God.

Over the next two decades, Muhammad received many such revelations, and proved himself a man of exceptional talents. By the time he died in

632AD, he had united the fractious tribes of Arabia into a single united community, and had brought them a new religion that was uniquely suited to their way of life and view of the world. More importantly, he had set in motion a dynamic faith, a fledgling empire which would, only decades after his death, stretch from India in the East to the Atlantic in the West, from the Aral Sea in the North to the deserts of Nubia in the South. A mere century later, the Islamic empire would be greater than Rome at its zenith, conquering the world as though it truly was the will of God. It would institute modes of learning and thought so far advanced that western civilisation would be considered barbarian. It would twice threaten to take Europe itself, and would remain the dominant world civilisation for almost a thousand years.

Today, while Islam's dominance has vanished, its importance has not. No other religion has the potential to shape the world as much as Islam in the next few decades. It is the world's second largest religion, behind Christianity, with one billion adherents, one-fifth of the world's population. Moreover, it is the fastest growing of all major religions. With the highest birth rates in the world, the Muslim population will double in twenty years. Even in the US, Islam grows faster than any other religion; for the first time, Muslims outnumber Jews.

Islam also represents more of a challenge to Western civilisation than any other religion or culture. A claim often made in the last few years is that since the end of the Cold War, it is Islam that has emerged as the West's main ideological rival. This claim is limited in its outlook. The pedigree of confrontation between Islam and the West extends right back to the Seventh century, when the religion of the crescent moon stormed out of the deserts of Arabia, sweeping the known world before it. In comparison the challenge posed by Communism was brief indeed. And today, in a shrinking world, afflicted by war, poverty, and a resurgence of Islamic extremism, the issue of Islam is more important than ever.

Despite this importance, however, obtaining a balanced view of both the religion and the cultures it represents can be difficult. Much of the dramatic news of the past two decades has been news of 'Islam'. The Iranian Revolution, the Arab-Israeli conflict, both Gulf Wars, Afghanistan, Lebanon. Confrontation with Libya, ethnic strife in Bosnia, civil war in Tajikistan, rebels in Kashmir, assassinations in Egypt and Algeria, the bombing of the World Trade Centre. As a result, the images of Islam prevalent in the West are negative. They are of fanaticism, violence, brutality, and chaos; of little regard for human life; of misogynist societies whose laws spring directly from the Dark Ages.

These images, of course, present a huge problem to anybody who wishes for an understanding of Islam, and of the societies it stands for, which is based on anything more substantial than sensationalism. And compounding this problem is the fact that 'Islam' is a necessarily vague term, dangerously vulnerable to misinterpretation. No other concept can be used to denote such a wide set of beliefs, cultures, histories, politics and peoples. Islam, as is so often said, goes beyond religion: it is a complete way of life. For a believing Muslim, Islam covers everything from politics to prayer, from justice to sex, from the meaning of life to the way one should wash. And because of this, when 'Islam' is used to describe any single aspect of Islamic society, such as extremist violence in one country, or regressive social reform in another, its use distorts the way we see Islam as a whole.

Several years ago, I travelled to the Middle East for the first time. What I found surprised me. I was confronted by complex, vibrant societies, ones I knew I could never perceive through the narrow glare of the Western media. And to my surprise, most of my experiences were positive. What was significant about this was not that my experiences should have been positive, but that this should have come as a surprise to me. I had to ask myself *why* I was unprepared for normal and friendly societies, for an accepting attitude toward the West, for overwhelming hospitality. And I knew then, that the only way for me to approach an understanding of Islam was to experience it myself.

For some time, I considered how this might be done. As a non-Muslim myself, my experience of Islam would inevitably be a vicarious one. And in aiming for an understanding not just of the religion itself, but of the various cultures which are so readily identified with it, my experiences were destined to take the shape of a journey. A journey into Islam.

For a few years I rolled the idea of such a journey around in my mind, slowly allowing it to gather a shape and life of its own. I knew from the beginning that I wanted to turn my encounter with Islam into a book, the kind of which I had been unable to find in my own study of the religion. I wanted to experience – and portray – the naked experience of an Islam that consisted of far more than either simplistic fundamentalist interpretations of faith or sensationalist images of fanaticism and cruelty. I wanted to experience Islam as it was lived and breathed by millions of believers. I wanted, essentially, to find a fundamentally balanced view of the religion, if such a thing could be found.

All this is why, now, I gaze out at crushing clouds, at the very beginning of an Islamic journey. This time, however, the journey is not through the Middle East, not through Arab lands at all. This time, the journey is into Asia.

The choice of Asia may seem strange for Islam is, after all, an essentially Arab religion. The liturgical, holy language of Islam is Arabic; the holiest sites of Islam lie in the Arab world; Arab cultural superiority is implicit in the religion itself. Yet the key to understanding the changes affecting the Islamic world lies not in Arabia, but in Asia. Only one Muslim in five is an Arab, while two in every three live in Asia. Asia contains the largest Muslim country in the world, Indonesia. One Asian country, Iran, is an inspiration to the movement of Islamic revivalism that is sweeping the world. Islam is growing faster, spreading faster, in Asia than anywhere else. Islam in Asia is no longer dormant, with the orthodox, fundamentalist call being heard louder and clearer from Mecca than ever before, with poverty driving more and more Asian Muslims in search of an alternative. As a result, nowhere else offers a better insight into the growing strength of Islamic radicalism throughout the world. And no other readily identifiable region contains such a variety of religion, custom and race as the countries between Turkey and Indonesia. Only Asia can provide the broad, sweeping view of the religion I require, an impression of the entirety, the diversity, the reality that is Islam.

It is this knowledge that has led me here, to this grey place of ghosts long dead. It is here that the journey begins, a journey through the curving arc of unknown territory, the invitation and mystery that is Asia.

Monday 22nd May
Dogubeyazit

Muhammad's preaching, when he first returned to Mecca after receiving his visions, was modest. He did not see himself as founding a new religion, merely as bringing the old religion of the One God to his tribesmen, the Quraysh. Like many Arabs at the time, Muhammad had come to believe that the High God of the ancient Arab pantheon, whose name was simply *al-Lah*, "the God", was the same as the God worshipped by the Jews and the Christians. He felt his revelations were simply an updated version of those given by God to the prophets Abraham, Moses and Jesus. Certainly, his preaching did not offend the Quraysh, who initially offered no opposition to him. Many Quraysh were quite willing to listen to Muhammad, as his views did not necessarily collide with their own.

The Quraysh, at that time, worshipped not only al-Lah, or Allah, but also numerous other, lesser deities. Muhammad's message in his first years was not overly monotheistic, and people seemed to accept that they could go on worshipping these lesser gods as they had always done. But when Muhammad began to condemn such worship as idolatrous and blasphemous, detracting from the unity of Allah, the attitude of the Quraysh changed. To them, the old gods were in many ways responsible for their new prosperity, and Muhammad and his followers became a persecuted minority.

As the opposition hardened, Muhammad's message became more and more confrontational, and more unacceptable to the ruling Quraysh clans. He preached mainly about the evils of idolatry, the imminence of divine judgement, against pride and arrogance. Muhammad's message condemned not only the beliefs of the Meccans but also their greed, their hypocrisy, their way of life. The focus of his new creed was on absolute submission to God. Indeed, Muhammad's religion would eventually be known as *islOm*, a name signifying the act of submission or complete surrender to God, and his followers known as *muslOms*, those who submit. To the Quraysh clans or families – proud, accustomed to their idols – such concepts were an abomination. They were horrified to witness their brethren supplicate themselves to God twice a day; they found it unacceptable that Arabs of their status and history should have to grovel in the dust like slaves. Eventually their opposition became too much to bear, and in the summer of 622AD, Muhammad and his followers set off for the oasis town of Yathrib, which would later become known as Medina, "the City".

Muslims today date their era not from Muhammad's birth (he emphasised that he was an ordinary man), nor from his first revelations (there was nothing particularly new about a revelation from God), but instead from the date of this migration to Medina, this *hijra*. This was the year Muslims first began to implement God's divine plan, by making Islam a political reality. In Mecca Muhammad could only preach Islam, but in Medina he could practise. This change was reflected in the revelations Muhammad continued to receive from God. In Mecca their emphasis was pure theology, while those received in Medina paid much more attention to the legislation of Islam: to the forms of the religion; to laws of divorce, laws of marriage, laws of inheritance.

The early Muslims remained in Medina for ten years. Their numbers were at first small – in an early battle with the Meccans, Muhammad fought alongside only 300 men – but their faith was strong. Fighting for Islam, believing God was behind them, they won almost every major battle. Muhammad continued to receive his revelations, which became more and more relevant to contemporary events as God seemed to comment on the situation as it developed, explaining the significance of battles, answering some of Muhammad's early critics, and helping resolve conflicts in the fledgling community. Helped by a significant Jewish community in Medina, Muhammad's message became more firmly rooted in scripture, drawing on the age-old traditions of the earlier religions but sewn together with a distinctive Arabic thread.

By the time Muhammad returned triumphantly to take Mecca without any bloodshed, he was accompanied by an army of 90,000. The gathering that received him was about 124,000 in number. It was a spectacular triumph. Muhammad entered the massive cube-shaped shrine at the centre of Mecca known as the Ka'ba, and destroyed all the idols of the Quraysh. The Muslims would rule the city.

Muhammad died in 632, after a short illness, having achieved a great deal. He had brought a new religion to the pagan peoples of Arabia, a religion of staunch monotheism and strict ethical doctrines which, in terms of both its system of principles and its insight into Arabian society as a whole, stood on an incomparably higher level than the paganism it replaced. He had unified the tribes into a single community, or *ummah*. He had provided revelations which would guide countless believers in the centuries that would follow. It took the ancient Israelites seven centuries to break with their old customs and accept a pure monotheistic faith, but Muhammad had managed to bring such a system to the Arabs in a mere twenty-three years. And Muhammad's system was uniquely Arabic.

Shortly before his death, Muhammad made what has been called the Farewell Pilgrimage, in which he Islamised the old pagan rite of the *hajj*, which in the past had seen Arabs from all over the peninsula make an annual pilgrimage to the Ka'ba. Muhammad sanctified the *hajj* as a fundamental part of his new religion, one of the five pillars on which Islam was founded, along with faith in God, daily prayer, fasting during the month of Ramadan, and alms to the poor. It was a vital step, providing a distinctly Arabic character for Islam which remains in place today.

In social terms, Muhammad revolutionised Arab society. During the pre-Islamic period Arabia had preserved the backward attitudes towards women which had prevailed for centuries. Polygamy was common, and wives remained in their father's household as little more than property. Some women enjoyed power and prestige – Muhammad's first wife, Khadija, was a successful merchant – but most were little more than slaves. They had no political or human rights. Female infanticide was common, and an Arab family would express dismay when a female child was born. Muhammad was a great social reformer, and the welfare of women had been part of his agenda. His teachings forbade, time and again, the killing of female children as a sin against God. The Arabs were reprimanded by God himself for their attitudes to women. Muhammad even gave women legal rights of inheritance and divorce, both staggering advances at the time. Their inheritance was inferior to that given to men, but in a society where women were no more than property, the effect was revolutionary. At the time, Western Christendom had lapsed into a highly misogynistic view of the world, heavily influenced by Saint Augustine's doctrine of the Original Sin, with woman seen as 'Eve the temptress', passing the contagion of the Original Sin to the next generation like a disease. Western women would not receive anything comparable to that granted by Muhammad until the Nineteenth century.

Islam heralded many other changes. A strong egalitarianism was fundamental to the Islamic ideal. Compassion for others and alms for the poor were both enshrined in basic Islamic doctrine. Muhammad had urged Muslims to seek knowledge, and his encouragement of science and free thought would drive Islamic scholarship for centuries. Islam was also characterised by extreme tolerance of other religions. Muhammad had repeatedly stressed that both Jews and Christians were part of a religious tradition involving worship of one and the same God:

> "Do not argue with the followers of earlier revelation otherwise than in the most kindly manner – unless it be such of them as are set on evil doing – and say: 'We believe in that which has been bestowed upon us, as well as that which has been bestowed upon you: for our God and your God is one and the same, and it is unto him that we surrender ourselves.'"
> *The Qur'an*, 29:46

Most importantly of all, Muhammad had bequeathed a holy book, the collection of his revelations which would become known as *al-Qur'an*, the Recital. Unlike the holy books of Judaism and Christianity, the Qur'an is not a set of stories, the work of men. It is written in the first person, and is the word of God in the Arabic language, spoken directly to Muhammad and the Arabs. It was outside the experience of any at the time, and was the greatest sign to the Arabs that God had spoken. Time and again, verses in the Qur'an allude to its own existence as sufficient proof of the existence of God, a creation beyond the capabilities of an ordinary mortal. It would be this book – untranslated, unchanged from the original Arabic – that would guide Muslims all over the world through their lives for the next thirteen centuries.

For me, sitting in our decrepit hotel in Dogubeyazit, a vision of Mount Ararat filling our window, such a brief knowledge of the history of Islam raises more questions than it answers. How did such progressive views towards women develop into one of the most misogynistic religions of the modern world? What in Muhammad's original message meant that countless Muslim women would be condemned to wear the kind of veil we see in the streets outside? How did a religion with a positive attitude towards knowledge produce Islamic scholars who, only twenty years ago, could still declare the earth was flat? How did the early unity shatter, dividing Islam into the countless sects of today? And above all, how could any religion that stressed tolerance towards other religions come to be characterised by hatred and disdain towards infidels?

I hope that this journey will be able to answer all of these questions. I do, however, know that the way in which Islamic doctrine developed, in the years after Muhammad's death, played a major part in the transformation of many Islamic practices. In a way reminiscent of Christianity, much of the official documentation of Islam did not begin until several generations after the death of the Prophet. The Qur'an delivered the will of God during Muhammad's lifetime, but soon the problems of governing a rapidly burgeoning empire brought the Arabs face to face with difficulties which had never arisen under his rule. In response, the early Arabs established the principle that not only should the Qur'an be viewed as the authoritative guide to conduct, but also the entire collection of the practices and utterances of the Prophet throughout his lifetime. This collection was known as the Traditions, the *hadith*.

The collection and analysis of the *hadith* did not take place until a century after Muhammad's death. Each individual *hadith* was attested by a chain of verification, taking the form "I heard from... who heard from... who heard from... who heard the Prophet say". A society-wide game of Chinese whispers, spread over several generations: verbal histories like this are difficult to trust in the best of circumstances. But there were also motives for deliberate distortion. The century following Muhammad's death was one of vigorous social change, as the expanding empire came into contact with a series of new social, political, and religious customs from its conquered people. Supporters of a particular point of view, or of a particular political group, or of a clan vying for power, could find no better way than to project their beliefs back in time, producing a *hadith* attributed to the Prophet and expressing a suitable opinion. Pre-Islamic customs re-emerged, new ones were adopted. As Islam grew, Islam changed.

This process of change, of a religion severed from many of its original customs and ideals, was by no means ended when the *hadith* were finally recorded in official form. Islam was a living religion, and the further it travelled, the further it changed. And nowhere was the change more significant than when Islam, the word and sword of an Arab God, conquered and then delivered itself to people of non-Arab lands.

Dogubeyazit, spread at the feet of Mount Ararat, lies in one of these lands. Tomorrow marks the beginning of our journey to another. Iran, ancient Persia, land of pitiless antiquity, was one of early Islam's most significant conquests. Its culture and history and language would influence the heart of Islam for ten centuries, and even today its place in the world of Islam is unique. As a place synonymous with the revival of Islam, I sense that if we are to understand the Islam of today then Iran holds the key.

I can scarcely imagine, however, what the country will bring. My childhood images of Iran were of desert warfare, of rockets in the desert. I am of a generation barely old enough to remember the Iranian Revolution. I have no memory of the Shah, no idea of the country as an erstwhile ally of the West. My impressions of Iran have been fully formed by the Western media in the last sixteen years: as a place of crazed Islamic fundamentalism; of anti-West sentiment; of guns and war and injustice; of cruelty to women; a backer of international terrorism; a guiding light to Islamic revolutionaries the world over. And despite having researched, interviewed, even having spent six months learning the language, I still feel I know nothing about the country. Tomorrow looms large in my mind.

The scratchy call to Maghrib prayer wails over the town as dusk washes Ararat with azure. I look down from our balcony to the street below, where children taunt a man whose feet point backwards, tied in hessian sacks. Supreme and dry and desolate he looks, standing with his back to the death of the sun. Tomorrow, then. Iran, where Revolutionary Guards remove lipstick from women with razor blades; where tourists are so rare that Iranians take photographs of them; where to look at a man's wife could get us killed; where we can hope to confront utter animosity to all things Western. Apocryphal stories, perhaps, but stories nonetheless. Stories vivid enough to dwell on as I contemplate what tomorrow will bring.

PART ONE
WEST

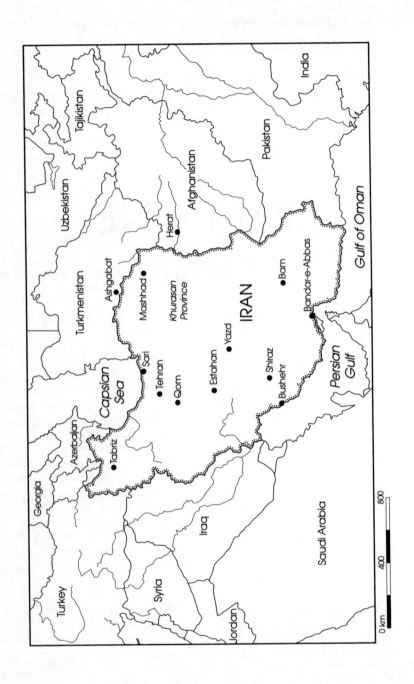

IRAN

The Turquoise Bridge

Tuesday 23rd May
to Tabriz

We wake with the dawn prayer. In dim light – which, according to Muslim tradition, is just enough to distinguish black thread from white – Kirst vanishes beneath a black shroud. This is her *Çar☐af*, a black polyester veil shaped like a nun's habit, bought three days ago; without such Islamically proper clothing she will be denied entry at the border. This is how Kirst will be seen for the next month and a half.

The *Çar☐af* is thick and heavy; it consists of a hood that fits over Kirst's head, with a hole for her face, and a loose-fitting polyester skirt. No hair shows, no skin apart from her face and her hands. The woman I know and love is suddenly transformed into a shuffling shadow, a pale non-entity. The denigration of women seems implicit in her appearance. Even to me, Kirst becomes another person, meek and invisible, beneath it. And if this is my reaction, I cannot imagine the power such symbols hold for those who live their entire lives with them, people whose societies have owned such traditions for over a thousand years. At least we know we will gain more of an appreciation of what it is like to suffer as a woman under Islam, to glimpse the other side of the gendered Muslim coin.

I look at Kirst as she parades before me, eyes downcast, with a demure smile on her lips that retains a hint of mischief. When she smiles, her lips retreat to reveal both sets of teeth; when she laughs her tongue presses out between them. Even in Australia the paleness of her skin is extreme; here it attracts attention wherever we go. Muslim men praise her beauty, Muslim women covet her hair. I had hoped that hiding her brown mane beneath the *Ça☐raf* would make her seem less noticeable as a foreigner, but I realise now there was little chance of that. With her light blue eyes and pale Anglo-Saxon skin, she is never going to be mistaken as a native.

I look forward to her company on this journey, and not just for the female perspective of Islam she will provide. She is my long-time travelling companion, more suited to me than anyone I know. On long trips like this one, her companionship keeps me sane. She is too close for me to describe her character honestly – to do so would be like describing myself – but nobody could dispute she has an effervescent spirit, an enthusiasm for life, so to see her before me now, ghostly and subdued, feels very strange indeed.

Old men, rough and puckered, are already planted in the dust outside our hotel when we emerge. They laugh good-humouredly at the sight of Kirst: it is clear where we are heading. We find a bus to the border, wait while the driver tours the town searching vainly for other passengers, and then we are off. Iran is not a popular destination.

A boy stands, shifting, trespassed, down the malted street
all angled impatience and slanted fear,
eyes an artful whiteness.
Shouts   sighs
             hands   commerce,
Guessing glances and crusted looks:
these are the things he sees.

Gruntled encounter, hay in a cart,
diligent horse, (mad art);
everything balanced on bone.
And the street, the street
(of marigold light and burnt earth, dusty dusty words)
happens anyway:
a street
of stores and mud and maleness and action,
Of sun and trucks and rumble and motion.

And always
over everything
hangs the mountain.

Border crossings will always remain the most dislocating of experiences, times of unseizable transition. Mind set on the unknown future, unprepared to deal with the chaos of the present, the traveller is plunged into a limbo world of illusion, where the only constant is confusion. This time is no different. When we squeeze through a side gate to the Turkish border compound, I am too occupied to pay attention to the dusty buildings or the long line of trucks. I can think only of how we are edging closer to a precipice. The attentions of money-changers, of wiry children trying to attach themselves to our bags, are nothing but annoyances.
We stagger under loads into a small room, cement floored, made dark by the brightness outside. Kirst and I have ceased to communicate. We have never been very supportive in situations of stress, and instead tend to retreat inwards, following our own trains of thought. Having her clothed in black and almost unrecognisable only makes things worse.
The room is full of bodies, pale and cringing shapes all bearing piles of red passports. They are so different from the darkened Turks and the sun-ravaged Kurds that I wonder where they have come from. Surely not Iran. They are Muslims all: the women clutching white veils, the men topped with white skull caps.
I push through the crowd to a metal grill, hand over our passports. The assumption that I will take charge is implicit in our attitudes now. That a mere garment holds such power is frightening. Kirst feels compelled to conform to all the veil suggests, while I have assumed the protective role befitting the husband of a Muslim woman. Every encounter today has

contained the expectation that she is my responsibility – the passports, paying for our hotel, finding the mini-van – while only yesterday this was not so. The inference from all this gender-oriented behaviour, an inference that comes from the veil itself, is that she needs me to take care of her, that she is not as capable herself. We have both detected it; the feeling is no doubt shared by those around us. It suddenly seems so much less convincing to claim that this woman, my wife, is a lawyer. My wife, my wife. For she is my wife as long as this journey lasts: we nurse carefully-forged marriage certificates, and Kirst's finger bears a gold plastic ring. "Cheap wedding," spat the jeweller in Istanbul.

Our passports are stamped almost immediately. I have no time to think, to get a sense of what is happening as it happens. Heavy steel doors at the far end of the room open, and I can only follow Kirst as we blunder into a private version of hell. A sound, hard, hollow and condemning, as the door clangs shut behind us.

Inside, the overwhelming impression is of yellow: yellow light, yellow dust filling the air, a yellow taint to the skin and hair of all I can see. The room is large, but not large enough to comfortably house the two hundred or so lost-looking souls who now fill it. They are the same bodies and faces of those outside, only here they are so many that they quickly become faceless. The men are blonde, with close-shaved heads and heavy beards; the women are white ghostly shrouds. I feel surrounded by patients in a mental ward. They shuffle around, as lost as we are. They are clad in old track-suit pants, T-shirts, sand-shoes with the heels kicked in. The women line the walls or crouch in huddled groups in the centre of the room. A soft mumbling, or perhaps a moaning, fills the air like the yellow dust itself.

At the far end of the room a digital clock blinks out the time in bright crimson, while above our resolutely closed door hangs a picture of Atatürk, frowning at those foolish enough to leave his country. Turkey already has the quality of remembered experience.

I glance around once more. Confusing us both, there seems to be no way out, no doors other than the one through which we have just come. We haul our bags to one side of the room. Guard them as we might, the shuffling insane persist in clambering over them, leaving footprints of dust. In a gap in the wall is an anguished man clad in combat fatigues. He is shouting into a telephone, and at the listless zombies crushed up against his window. I push through, receive a white card, but can wring from him no explanation, no description of what we are to do. My grasp of basic Farsi syntax has palsied.

We wait. I have a sense of time congealed, that the outside world no longer exists.

After an age measured only by the blinking of the red clock, a door opens. A hidden portal, a crack in the world, an escape route to reality at the other end of the hall. The crowd is slow to respond – the scramble does not begin for several seconds – but we are not. The tension and frustration and adrenalin of the last few hours is released, and we clamber over bodies, wrestling with the crowd, just to reach this salvation. Kirst trips a small woman with her bag, knocking her over. Another time, I might have cared. Only ten people make it through the half-open doorway; we are among them.

The world outside, if not sane, is at least one we can understand. A queue, a cursory baggage check. I expected something more thorough from a country that bans alcohol and all things Western: music, posters, videos and literature. And then we stagger, somewhat stunned, into the bright sunlight of the Islamic Republic of Iran.

Four hours later, we are on a bus to Tabriz.

The blond lunatics, it seems, were an aberration. Around us now, as it has been all afternoon, is the Iranian blood of my imagination: black hair, eyes so dark they look bruised.

It has been an afternoon of rapid action and bewilderment. Complete strangers paying for our ride through the six-kilometre Iranian border zone. A man, smiling and wordless, bundling us into a taxi to Maku, the first town, twenty kilometres away; then, feeling worried that we might not find the bus station, taking another taxi to follow us. In Maku, businesslike, he organises our tickets to Tabriz. A handshake, a brief wave, and he returns in the same taxi, back to the border, charity complete. An afternoon of kindness so outlandish that our first reaction has been shameful suspicion.

Now we sit sweltering on an ancient bus, as families from seats in front bring us iced water to slake our thirst. Iran is a land of unrelenting heat, and in my drooping state my heart goes out to Kirst, to all the women for whom such clothes are an injustice and a trial. At the terminal in Maku, a Kurd took us behind a parked bus, out of sight, to complain about the Iranian government, about its oppression of women. His brother's wife, dark-eyed, stood close by. At his request she removed her black cloaked veil – unveiling in public, an offence punishable by flogging – to show us her traditional Kurdish costume. A shimmering image of cobalt and cadmium, a butterfly emerging from a black chrysalis. And like a true butterfly, her freedom did not last long: the cloak returned in minutes. For her, like Kirst, the veil was an unwanted imposition from an unjust regime.

Shapes with no shape, dark and cindery, sail through the streets in the few towns we pass. Heavy tents of black fabric, clutched beneath the chin or held in place with the teeth. These are *chadors*, the Iranian version of the Islamic veil. Chador means both "veil" and "tent" in Persian. They are hot and heavy, difficult to manage, and are an Iranian tradition dating back to before the time of Islam. They are by far the most popular type of veil in the rural villages we pass, but not the only one: many of the younger girls wear what are known as *magneh*, circles of fabric a little like the wimples worn by nuns, hoods that settle around the necks and shoulders, with a round hole cut out for the face. Iranian sensibilities are satisfied as long as all hair remains hidden. In Iran, contrary to what I believed for years, 'veiling' does not imply a hidden face, the archetypal pair of eyes peering through a slit in black cloth. This is an Arab innovation. Indeed, in many Muslim societies, all that is required is a simple head covering, a scarf no different from those worn by suburban British housewives half a century ago. But not all societies are so flexible: elsewhere in the Muslim world, the restrictions are as cruel as they are unusual. Our first day in Iran may not be the time to consider the issue of women in Islam, but as we pass compounds of mud brick, walled and secluded like the women they contain, I hope that some of what we see on the rest of the journey will reveal the shape of life for the women of Islam today.

All colour has drained from the sky by the time we are dropped on the outskirts of Tabriz. Disoriented, confused and with little money, it is a relief to be taken under the wing of Iranian hospitality within minutes. Meten, a stranger passing, asks us if he can be of any assistance. He is a compact man, wound like a spring, with a fierce beard and teeth the colour of stale cheese. I find the intensity of his gaze, his complete disdain for all that he sees, and his claims that Tabriz is a dangerous place somewhat unnerving, but for the moment this hardly matters. He finds us a taxi, finds us a hotel, buys us dinner in the hotel restaurant. An angel of mercy with an angry glare.

Meten leaves us late. We have seen nothing of Tabriz, almost nothing of Iran. I am confused and relieved, and quite alarmed by Meten's stories of violence and intrigue, his instructions that we trust no one. I cannot yet taste my new surroundings, cannot yet believe we have touched earth. I am given nothing more than a hotel room, a broken mirror, a few sounds impossible to identify from beyond our shuttered window, and the sense of dislocation is strong. I spend the night half awake. The dark is liquid and dreamless; the ceiling fan rattles as it turns.

Wednesday 24th May – Friday 26th May
Tabriz

> Do not spurn any infidel, for it may be hoped that he will die a Muslim.
> Jalal ad-Din Rumi

The market in Tabriz is a place of spirits, of ghosts without name. It is a labyrinth of stone arches and quiet shop fronts, one that takes us from carpet weavers to gold sellers to spice merchants to tea stalls. We are back in time, three hundred, seven hundred years. This is no Westernised Grand Bazaar in Istanbul, Turkish touts screaming at tourists, idling up to them to wheedle them into their stores.

"No, no, no. That would be impolite," explains Nasser. His is a bunched up punching-bag face, blunt and heavy, and his eyes are smiles in swollen flesh. A watch repairer, he has entertained us in his store all morning. "You must not forget – you are in Iran now."

We are in Iran now. Difficult to comprehend last night, this fact is impossible to forget now. All morning we have been trying to orient ourselves to this city, to this country. Trying to avoid meeting the glances of the women we pass. Trying to walk through crowds of sailing black without pushing into women. Trying to adjust to the fact that the Latin alphabet has vanished from sight, and I must read all signs for both of us. Trying to reconcile the thick Farsi spoken here with anything I can understand.

"But we are not Farsi. Yes, I *speak* Farsi, but I am Turkish. Everyone in Tabriz is Turkish."

Fluent in five languages, well-acquainted with half a dozen religions, Nasser makes an interesting companion. He strolls with us through the bazaar, waving at spice stalls, snatching dried fruit for us to chew, attempting to introduce us as well as he can to Iran. The process of learning, or unlearning, is going to be a slow one.

Nasser's overwhelming passion is religion. This should not surprise us: in one of the world's few theocracies, religion is difficult to escape. Nasser's views, however, might not find a place in the confrontationalist attitudes of his government. All morning he has lectured us on the closeness of the three great monotheistic religions, on the impossibility that we will encounter any animosity from his fellow Iranians, and he is staggered that we might think of Iran as a place of anti-West resentment. Nasser's only ire is reserved for Buddhists. To a Muslim, the religion of fierce iconoclasm, Buddhism is depraved: Nasser cannot bear the thought of worshipping the statue of a single man, one who never claimed to be divine. Views like his were responsible for the virtual eradication of Buddhism from the Indian subcontinent under Muslim rule.

Nasser leads us to his favourite chai stall, an atmospheric nook in this place of dark and dust and stone. Men with origami faces, as though constructed of folded brown paper, sit at a single table, cups of tea before them. Their mouths are no more than single creases; from the corner of each protrudes a coloured tube, flexed and filled with smoke. The soft bubble of water in dozens of glass chambers is the only sign that they are breathing. Smouldering piles of honey-drenched tobacco, cradled in ceramic bowls and set alight with hot coals, provide sustenance to these men of papery antiquity. These are the most universal of Middle Eastern devices, known as *nargilye* in Turkish, in Farsi as *ghalian*, and the hookah to us, a linguistic gift from India. To Nasser, they are the "hubble-bubble".

"You want to smoke hubble-bubble?" he asks as we squeeze around the table. I have ridden the beast before; it is not an experience I wish to repeat. We will, however, have chai. In Iran this is not a matter of choice; already Nasser has served us three cups in his store.

Iranian tea habits are unique. Their tea is dark and strong and tannin-rich, and requires sugar to render it palatable. Iranian sugar, however, is not dissolved into the drink, but instead comes in rock-hard lumps that one must lodge between one's teeth, straining the hot liquid through it into one's mouth. After a morning with Nasser we are beginning to develop the skill, but it still results in garbled conversations, in crumbled messes of dissolved sugar.

A lined face watches me, watches us both. Our only outside light comes from a gap in the brickwork far above us. A few cuts of light slant down at us, dust specks rotating in them. The feeling is subterranean. The man inhales every breath through his hookah, the soft gurgling unceasing. Nasser mumbles something to him. The man's face brightens, and nods to us with genuine warmth and a half-toothed smile. And still the water bubbles.

"I told him you were foreigners from America," says Nasser. "He is a peasant – he would not know Australia, so I have to say America."

This is not what I would have wished: the media would have us believe we are in a country populated purely by a hatred of that Great Satan, the US. Kirst has an "Australia" badge sewn on to her bag in order to avoid precisely such confusion. But it does not seem to matter. The man is happy for us no matter where we are from. He mutters something briefly to Nasser, who then turns to us. "He wants to know if you are Muslim. You are Christian, I think, yes?"

A teasing question. It is religion I find interesting, not God. To me religion is a fascinating part of the psychology of man, a driving force behind history and art, an inspiration to philosophers. But it is not a fundamental part of my world view. In Australia, I am content to describe myself as an atheist, but I am no longer in Australia. I am in Iran, and the concept of atheism sickens most Muslims. On past occasions it has only produced confusion, outrage, and even abrupt termination of newly-formed friendships. During the next nine months I will be asked this question many times, and my answer is always going to have to be the same.

"Yes. We are both Christian." The old man nods, satisfied, and sits back in his chair.

The conversation loiters on this topic. "I have read about all the religions, you know. I have read the Torah and the Bible. I think it is good you are a Christian." A tea-drenched lump of sugar plays on Nasser's tongue. "But to me, it is Shi'a that makes the most sense."

"What makes it different from Sunni Islam?" Kirst knows the answer as well as I, but the question needs to be asked.

Nasser smiles a sideways smile. "The difference is between politics and God. Sunnism began with men who wanted power, but the Shi'a were always worshipping God. Sunnism is not true Islam."

The division of Islam into its two main sects, Sunni and Shi'a, is the most important one to make when examining the religion. The result of an early schism, the split has kept Islam deeply divided for the last thirteen centuries. The Sunnis are the dominant sect, and account for 85% of the Islamic world. Accordingly, most literature on Islam focuses on the religion from the Sunni point of view. Many Islamic writers do no more than briefly mention the Shi'a, as though the fact of the schism is enough to explain it. Few Sunnis are concerned with an honest analysis of the mentality of such a religion; to the Sunnis, Shi'ism is an aberration. None offer sufficient insight to impart the full texture of Shi'ism, to explain the faith of a country that has helped spark an Islamic revival around the world. And while most of the significant work in Islamic scholarship now springs from Western sources, Western writing is often just as cursory, particularly when it is intended for public consumption. The week before we left, an Australian newsprint article dismissed Shi'ism as a "fundamentalist" sect. This is worse than misleading oversimplification and generalisation: it is just plain wrong. Such interpretations are widespread, and demonstrate the lack of understanding of the religion as a whole. The problem with learning about Shi'ism from the Shi'a themselves, of course, is that it is likely to be as biased as Sunni versions of Islam, but I hope that six weeks in Iran, in the only country in the world where the Shi'a are the majority, will allow me to judge for myself.

Nasser stands. "Now I must excuse myself. I must go and make prayer." He rests his gaze, sombre and earnest, on me. "But you must come back this evening. My friend Majid would like to meet you, to make you welcome. We will buy you ice-cream."

There is no question that we might refuse Nasser's Iranian hospitality. Kindness and generosity to travellers is repeatedly stressed in the Qur'an; it is a duty of the religion. Nasser, with his squat face of hard putty, with his narrow smiling eyes, is inscrutable: we cannot tell if his kindness is his own or because his faith demands it. For the moment, it does not matter. We follow him out through the stone corridors, thankful, on our first day in Iran, that such hospitality exists at all.

Outside, in sunlight so jagged it hurts, it is difficult to feel as threatened by Tabriz as we did last night. We walk back to our hotel through crowded streets that no longer taste of menace.

Opposite our hotel is a park bearing a black and white portrait of Khomeini the size of a small building. We cross to it, wander through the struggling trees, sit and watch Iranian families. My surprise at what I see is an indication of how narrow my perception of Iran has been. Surrounding us are families picnicking on the grass, men and women laughing together. Couples stroll; no one hurries. Fathers play with their young daughters, smiles are painted on almost every face we pass. Young men sleep or sit contemplatively on the grass. The air is completely one of ease. I am disturbed that scenes of happiness, images of normal family life, should surprise me so much. An overwhelming sense of peace pervades everything; if it was not for the shapes of ghostly black everywhere, it would be a sense of freedom.

Traffic beyond the edge of the park, while completely chaotic and without rules, moves so slowly it cannot be called dangerous. The Iranians drive as they walk; traffic resembles not so much a jostling crowd as a bunch of families out for a relaxed stroll. We can almost believe we are in a tamer, safer version of Turkey, not in that dark and feared place on the map known as Iran.

The atmosphere of innocence continues into the night. Coloured globes hang in strings over the streets, fountains spurt over bright coloured lights. Families stroll the streets until late in such number that it feels like a carnival. By the time we leave Nasser, late at night, we feel comfortable enough to walk these streets alone, streets which only twenty-four hours earlier had filled us with fear.

However I imagined Iran, it was not like this. Nothing, in anything I have read, has prepared me for such a happy welcome.

Partisans of Ali

Saturday 27th May – Monday 29th May
to Esfahan

We spend a few days on our way to Esfahan, on a circuitous route that takes us close to the Iraqi border. The desert is sad and empty, and an air of loss and death hangs around the region. Half a million Iranians were killed in what they now call the "Iraq-imposed war", and the desert is steeped in their agony. In the border areas painted slogans and government-sponsored art still portray the tragedy. Roses, martyrs, blood and doves decorate lonely walls. Pictures of Saddam Hussein with knives at his throat, of Iranians dying. Slogans blaze even on the sides of villagers' houses. Not all pictures are anti-Iraq: "Down With USA" accompanies murals of burning American flags. But the most anger, the most regret, is devoted to the war. Ruined tanks dot the countryside, some set on pedestals in the villages we pass.

The Iran-Iraq war, the senseless conflict fought between 1980 and 1988, shaped not only the landscape of this region, but how both modern Iranians and the West have come to view Iran's place in the world. The conflict was begun less than a year after the Iranian Revolution, when an opportunistic Saddam Hussein invaded the Iranian province of Khuzestan, hoping to capitalise on the unstable political situation in Iran. At the time, sections of the Western media focused on what was termed the "martyr complex" of Shi'a ideology. Iraq, backed by both the US and the Soviets, faced an opponent riding a wave of Islamic fervour: while its war was one of dirty conquest, Iran's was one of religious righteousness. Half a million Iranians died: the government declared every single one of them martyrs. Twelve-year-old children were sent into mine fields ahead of soldiers to explode the mines.

They were dressed in white robes, and given plastic keys that they were told would open the door to Paradise. They knew they would die; they simply believed that this would guarantee their way into heaven. It is hardly surprising, with such stories, that the martyr complex has come to

23

be associated so strongly with Shi'ism in recent years. Iran is a Shi'a nation; Iraq is predominantly Sunni.

Yet martyrdom is not only a Shi'a obsession. Martyrs have been part of all strands of the Islamic faith from the very beginning. A Quranic passage reads: "Those who are slain in the cause of Allah are not counted among the dead. They are living in the presence of their Lord and are well provided for." Martyrdom is, admittedly, particularly important to the Shi'a, and does indeed influence what might be called a Shi'a mentality, but the association is far more complicated than a simple desire to give one's life in the cause of Allah, something shared by many Muslims throughout history. It is an association rooted in time, in the history of Shi'ism, and to understand it we need to understand a passion that has been kept alive for over a thousand years. Age-old emotions, base and atavistic, feelings difficult for an outsider to grasp: to understand the Shi'a passions of today, one must understand the Shi'a passions from the beginnings of Islam.

The origins of the Shi'a faith were established soon after the death of the Prophet, when the critical issue of succession arose. Muhammad had left no provisions to help decide the matter, although some had claimed that in a declaration shortly before his death he had proclaimed Ali his chosen successor. Ali was one of the earliest converts to the new religion, and was not only the Prophet's cousin, but was married to Muhammad's daughter, Fatima. Muhammad had left no male heirs, which meant Ali was the Prophet's closest male relative.

The powerful clans of Mecca had been forced to accept Muhammad's rule, but upon his death (demonstrating perhaps the limitations of their conversion to the new faith) began to prepare the way to elect one of their own to the leadership of the community. This crisis was averted by three of Muhammad's colleagues – Abu Bakr, Umar, and Abu Ubayda – who quickly installed Abu Bakr as ruler in place of the Prophet. It was a swift and necessary move, but one which ignored those who claimed Ali should rule.

Abu Bakr, like Ali, was one of the first converts of the religion. He was also related, indirectly, to the Prophet: his young daughter, A'isha, was one of Muhammad's last and most influential wives. This fact was chiefly responsible for a lingering resentment between Ali and Abu Bakr: Fatima had taken great exception to A'isha's influence over her father, and A'isha and Ali had become bitter rivals. Nevertheless, Ali accepted Abu Bakr's instatement with good grace. The title *Khalifat Rasul Allah*, or "the successor of the messenger of Allah" was bestowed upon Abu Bakr, a title that would become shortened to *Khalifa*, Caliph. It would come to designate the rightful ruler of Islam.

Abu Bakr was already an old man at his accession and soon died a natural death, to be replaced without serious opposition by Umar. The empire, at the time, was expanding rapidly, defeating Byzantine forces to take Damascus. Under Umar the expansion continued, and Iraq, Egypt and

Persia were added to the Muslim domain. The position of Caliph became one of immense political and military might, far beyond the simple position of the spiritual leader of a burgeoning religious community.

In 644, while praying, Umar was murdered by a Persian Christian slave girl. His successor was a controversial choice. Uthman ibn Affan was known to be weak, and was suspected of cowardice. He was, however, a representative of the old Meccan power structure, the only member of the Meccan clans among the early companions of the Prophet with enough prestige to even rate consideration.

For some time the powerful Meccan clans had been resentful of the usurpation of their position by Muhammad's followers, and by the dominance of Medina in early Islamic affairs. Some concessions had been made to them – such as the appointment of Mu'awiya, of the Umayya clan, as Governor of Syria by Umar – but these had not been enough. Muhammad's own clan of Hashim had been of minor importance in the pre-Islamic era, and the Umayya had from the beginning resented that their role in society had been usurped. They had agitated constantly for more power, and the appointment of Uthman as Caliph, himself one of the Umayya, finally opened the way for them. Soon every significant post of the empire was being granted to families of the Umayya.

In the summer of 656, Uthman himself was assassinated by Muslim rebels from Egypt and Iraq. Ali, passed over previously three times as leader, was immediately hailed as Caliph. He had to face the full brunt of the crisis of the changing face of the Islamic world. Opposition to his rule came immediately from A'isha and disgruntled Meccans, who began to actively organise armed opposition. Of them all, however, the most serious challenge to Ali's rule came from Mu'awiya in Damascus. Mu'awiya was in a very strong position. He was in control of practically the only centralised authority at the time, and commanded perhaps the most well-disciplined army in the empire. In a series of confrontations with Ali, questioning both his leadership and moral authority, he managed to reduce Ali's status to merely a pretender to the Caliphate, usurping his right to rule.

To those who could remember the time of the Prophet, the Islamic vision had been sadly misplaced. New wealth, visions of power and the ancient rivalries of pre-Islamic times were threatening to tear the society apart. A group known as the Kharijites decided it was time for a fresh start. For the first time in history, Muslims would attempt to use violence to return to the age of the Prophet. It would not be the last. Their plan was to assassinate the three most important men in Islam: Ali, Mu'awiya and 'Amr, one of Mu'awiya's supporters. Of these, only one was successful: Ali was killed while praying in the mosque. His son Hassan relinquished the struggle, ceding his rights to Mu'awiya, who was quickly hailed as Caliph throughout the Islamic empire. From him would spring the first Arab dynasty, the Umayyads, ruling from Damascus. Theirs would be a rule far more worldly than spiritual, but it was under the Umayyad Caliphs that the mainstream Sunni doctrine would develop. Its name came from the Arabic word *sunna*, traditions, denoting those who followed the traditions of the Prophet. The group we know today as Shi'a or Shi'ites, by contrast, are the descendants of those who remained faithful to Ali after his death: the *Shi'atu 'Ali*, the partisans of Ali.

Of course, none of this explains why such a group would necessarily develop anything that could be called a "martyr mentality", despite an unfortunate and bloody early history. It does, however, lay the groundwork for an understanding of Shi'ism's origins, and it was from these origins that such a mentality would arise. The development of an obsession with martyrdom would come later, in the years following Ali's death. It was history, as much as religion, that shaped the theology of Shi'ism. And it is this history we plan to mine as much as we can during our stay in Esfahan.

A Sixteenth-century saying held that "Esfahan is half the world." A blue jewel in the desert, pride of the Saffavid Persian empire, Esfahan was home to Iran's most famous Shi'a dynasty. Today, it is home to an architecture as eternal as the sky, powdered blue mosques, and inflexible Shi'a orthodoxy.

Iran has grown on us in the past few days, despite the fact that the border towns have been sad, disagreeable places. We have been bewitched by the most endearing of Iranian customs, that of refusing payment for anything we purchase, simply because we are guests. It is impossible not to feel welcome in such a country. At stores, food stalls, restaurants, we have to argue hard to get Iranians to accept money for items we have just purchased, food we have just consumed. Now that we have arrived in Esfahan, however, we can expect things to be different. Esfahanis have a sour reputation with their fellow Iranians; it is said that the city would be perfect if their were no Esfahanis in it. And the town lies on Iran's main tourist trail, what little there is of it, a crooked line between Turkey and Pakistan. If anywhere will refuse to treat our existence as a novelty, it will be Esfahan.

We arrive too late to be able to gauge such things. Too late to judge the town's reaction to us, to visit the burning blue glaze of its buildings, or to search for a glimpse of the Shi'a past. This all waits for tomorrow. The crisp desert darkness tugs at us as we wander through the city's bazaar, long since closed. Our light comes from shafts of moonlight, slanting through circular holes in the vaulted ceiling. We are in another time, surrounded by sand-coloured stone. All stores are closed, all shop fronts shuttered, and there are no relics of the modern age to haunt us. Our footsteps echo back along centuries.

Tuesday 30th May – Thursday 1st June
Esfahan

The Shi'a school of thought, which is the prevalent one in Iran, has had certain distinguishing characteristics from the very beginning. While other schools have preached submission to rulers even if they are corrupt and oppressive, Shi'ism has preached resistance against them and denounced them as illegitimate. From the outset, Shi'ites have opposed oppressive governments...

Ayatollah Khomeini, Islam and Revolution

It is late by the time I write this; it has been a long day. From the streets outside come the empty sounds of night, and from the corridor comes the soft sound of sandals echoing over tiled floors. An Eastern sound, the sound of a people forever ready to remove their shoes to pray or enter a room.

Today has been a battle against orthodox obstructionism at Esfahan University, a place more of politics than learning, more concerned with power and the political rule of Islam. It lies in north Esfahan, away from the ancient buildings, the bazaars, the religious schools, the crowded mass of humanity that is the old city. It lies in a different Esfahan, more spacious, more residential, where our barometer of Iranian conformity – the clothes worn by women – swung from Stormy to Fair.

In the northern areas of Esfahan there are fewer chadors; they are replaced instead by the more defined shape of the *manteau*. A manteau is simply a dark trench coat, worn in tandem with a scarf to cover the hair. It is no less oppressive than a chador, no cooler and only slightly easier to handle, but it is a limited expression of opposition to the orthodoxy, a statement more of style than tradition, more of independence than religion. It is the style of the wealthier areas of Iran, of young women who are more driven by fashion than their peers, or more opposed to government restrictions. The daring fashion among Iran's trendy female youth is to display as much of a puffed-up bouffant as they can – a towering mass of hair on which their scarves rest; the Iranian Islamic equivalent of the miniskirt.

At the University itself, however, things were different. A seething mass of black chadors flowed through its surrounding streets. Black and white portraits of Khomeini fluttered over the iron bars which circle the campus. Its gates were draped in black, the colour of Shi'ism. And at these gates, as we attempted to contact Dr Razmara, a name we were given by a friend in Australia, we were refused entrance.

Our captors, female security guards in flowing black themselves, refused to explain their reasons. The few students who helped us denied that anything was wrong. But through it all, one word whispered between them was clear. *Hijab.* Veil. Kirst's own self-constructed manteau did not pass the test of Islamic propriety. After five hours of trying, of argument, pleading with the women and waiting as helpful students went to search for Dr Razmara, we had to return the way we had come. Now, back in our hotel room, the fact that we accomplished so little seems depressing. I feel weary and beaten.

Clip. Slap. Scrape. The sounds outside continue. They tug at the corners of my mind; they whisper to the room.

A sound

        a knowledge

                of time and place and atmosphere. The sounds are echoes of where we are, of the feeling of timelessness and history that belongs to Iran. It is a history too old for a Caucasian Australian mind, one that accuses me of being born of a race without a past. And it is history I return to now, the origins of Shi'ism, not our failure to gain admittance to the grounds of the University.

In the years immediately following Ali's death, Mu'awiya consolidated his power substantially, centralising power in Damascus in order to continue the Arab conquests. Fuelled by the desire for further expansion, he and his successors in the Umayyad dynasty increased the military and governmental might of the empire. Successes on the battlefield continued, but it was clear that religion was fading in its importance to the Caliphate, a post that was meant to embody the tradition of the Prophet. Many in the empire were dissatisfied. Indeed, later Islamic historians would refuse to grant the title "Caliph" to the Umayyad rulers, only re-introducing its use for later dynasties.

The Shi'a were, at the beginning, a political group, not a new sect. Capitalising on the popular discontent, they claimed that power rightfully belonged to the line of Ali, gathering support behind his sons Hussein and Hassan. They claimed to be fighting against unjust and tyrannous rule, and established both Shi'a traditions and the Shi'a perception of itself as a movement which still remain today.

The transformation of the Shi'a movement began at Karbala, in southern Iraq, in the bloodiest massacre of early Islamic history. Hussein and the families of seventy of his followers met an Umayyad army of thousands intent on snuffing out any opposition to Umayyad rule. It was a terrible scene. All were brutally killed, including Hussein's infant son. Yet it galvanised the Shi'a cause, hardened its opposition to Umayyad rule, and shaped the future of the religion itself. For it was immediately after the massacre, which was condemned even by Sunnis as deplorable, that Shi'ism began its transformation to a religious movement. Failed as an Arab political party, it met far greater success when it emphasised its religious aspects, as the true path of Islam in its hereditary descent from Ali and the Prophet himself.

The martyrdom of Hussein and Hassan forged the mentality of the movement, shaped the way it viewed itself. So too did its subsequent persecution as a religious minority, as an aberration in the way of Islam. The imagery of Shi'ism was of death, of martyrdom, of suffering, of mourning. Tears and sacrifice became central to this breakaway sect, a sect rooted in its opposition to unjust rule. The concept of defying tyranny, even at the price of death, became a holy one.

Islam was sweeping into Persia at around this time, and this fact heavily influenced the growth of the fledgling sect. The Persians capitulated to the new religion, but the separateness of the Persian identity asserted itself through support of the minority Shi'a. From the very early days Shi'ism was more popular with the non-Arabs within the growing Arab Empire than the Arabs themselves.

As the sect developed a complete theology, differences between it and that being developed by the orthodoxy under the Umayyads became clearer. Sunnism had sprung from the consensus of the community as to how to elect a leader, and the first four Caliphs – Abu Bakr, Umar, Uthman and Ali, the four "righteous Caliphs" – were their guiding lights, their ideal to which they would forever seek to return. The Sunni clergy, the *ulema*, kept an extremely decentralised structure, and communication with God was perceived as completely direct, a personal communication between the believing Muslim and Allah.

The Shi'a were different. They saw Ali as the rightful successor to Muhammad, which meant the first three Caliphs were scheming impostors. Their line of Imams, in direct descent from Ali, were more than spiritual leaders: they were a direct channel through which the normal Shi'a could communicate to Allah. For Shi'ite Muslims to find their path to God, symbolised by the holy figure of the Shi'a Imam, they required the mediation of a highly trained clergy. The Shi'a came to view all communication with God in this way, and even after the line of Imams had been extinguished they would look to their religious clergy for leadership and guidance. In time, a complete set of different customs, rituals and prayer evolved. The differing views of Shi'ism would even inspire a brand of eschatology – the approach to death, the afterlife, the second coming and the kingdom of God – and mythology that was uniquely Shi'ite. In fact, it was the eschatology of Shi'ism which came to define it. One of the most important of all the beliefs that would differentiate the two sects was the notion of the *Mahdi*, or "rightly guided one".

The concept of the Mahdi was not limited to Shi'ism alone; indeed, Mahdi movements were quite popular in Sunni Egypt and Sudan a century ago. But it was in Shi'ism, where it was linked to a belief in the hidden Imam, the divine redeemer who would return to usher in an era of truth and justice, that the idea found its strongest following.

The idea of the Mahdi drew its inspiration from the influences of other religions, notably the Messianic expectations of Jews, and Christians waiting for the return of Christ. Indeed, such a concept has been common in all monotheistic religions from very early on, and it seems that the concept of an imminently returning Messiah strikes a deep religious chord in the yearnings of human nature. In the case of Shi'ism, the Messianic expectations came to be focused on the twelfth Shi'a Imam, who – according to the Shi'a – did not die but simply vanished. This idea took hold of the Shi'a faith, which came to expect his return in much the same way Christians came to expect the return of Christ. The Shi'a held that their line of Imams ended after the twelfth, and the sect's adherents are frequently today referred to as "Twelvers".

It is an attachment to this history that sets the Shi'a apart. Even today they mourn for their martyrs; even today they weep for Ali and his sons. For this quality, certainly, Shi'ism is worthy of the cry "martyr complex". But it is a mistake to use such a term to describe an innate desire for martyrdom in the Shi'a themselves. The two are by no means linked. And it can hardly justify the appellation "fundamentalist". Martyrdom was a component of Shi'a belief for a thousand years, yet for most of this time Shi'ism remained a moderate faith. It certainly rarely deserved the descriptions being applied to it today. We must, therefore, ask the question: why is Shi'ism perceived as a fanatical sect, one devoted to holy war and uncontrolled aggression?

The answer lies far more with the leaders of today than with the religion itself. The Sunni Iraqis may not have used human mine-sweepers during the war against Iran, but none of their religious leaders were claiming the war as a holy one. The Iranian government, on the other hand, was doing exactly that. And in Iran, the religious leaders and government were one. To stress the religious nature of their struggle in the Iran-Iraq war, Khomeini's men named each major Iranian offensive *Karbala* – the plain where Ali's sons were slaughtered – each numbered sequentially. Faith in Iran is tremendously strong, and in a religion structured around a powerful *ulema*, it was little wonder that each call for potential martyrs would be met with thousands of volunteers. The choice of the war as holy, however, did not belong to the Shi'a people: it belonged solely to the *ulema*, men who had only just managed to seize power in an unstable country. It did not mean that the Shi'a were innately more fond of holy war than any other Islamic sects: a glance at Sunni Muslims fighting in Algeria, Afghanistan, Egypt and even Indonesia, all in the name of Allah, is enough to testify to that. The Iranian people are no different from their Sunni cousins. To their leaders, however, a holy war was an effective tool, bound to generate by far the most support. In a country where religion is the single biggest passion, declaring just about anything holy is a sure way to guarantee its popularity. But the villain is not religion; Shi'ism as a sect can be blamed for very little. The blame can instead be placed on those who use religion as a weapon, as a tool to keep and strengthen their might.

In Iran, the *ulema* still rule. Religion is the greatest power they command, one that enables them to propagate their views, perpetuate their rule, better than any other. Religion justifies restrictions in almost every sphere of life, restrictions that are the hallmark of an oppressive regime.

But this religion, the religion of the government, is sometimes very different from much that could be called Shi'ism.

Blue Woven Stone

Friday 2nd June
Esfahan

I sit in air so heavy it could be water. Sounds reach me as though I float, sounds stretched and smoothed. Light filters down to us, in strands of blue, from an uninterested God above: we are at the bottom of the ocean. Boom. A clap, a wet sound, echoes seven times around this chamber of watery light, racing around the world.

This is the Lotfollah mosque, tiny and perfect. Above us is a dome of delicate eggshell, a twisting mosaic pattern on an off-cream. On the walls, blue tiles mesh, merge, with white and yellow and gold and grey; the ninety-nine names of Allah strike off in dancing calligraphy around the *mihrab*, the cavity that faces Mecca. Latticed windows filter shadowed light from outside; around them the walls are laced and traced with floral creations, geometric patterns, glorious spiderwebs of blue. If I stand close I can see them as mosaics of thousands of inlaid tiles, but from anywhere else this building is of unnameable unity. It is too perfect to be a creation of man; it seems to me more believable that the mosque was born of itself, a product of its own creation.

We have sat here on the hard tiles all morning, soaking up the cool beauty of the domes as though it were milk. The heat outside is a memory, an illness whose symptoms are impossible to recall. We know the world must still exist, but we do not care.

Lotfollah mosque sits on Esfahan's main square, in the heart of the old town. It is one of the architectural marvels of the Saffavid empire, and is the most beautiful building I have ever seen. And yet we have been the only ones inside it all morning. Iran's isolation means that such a creation can stand untouched, untainted, ignored. In the narrow corridors of the nearby bazaar, we have been mistaken as tourists from either Bosnia or Lebanon. Even in the most visited city in Iran, Western tourists are rare.

Most visitors venture into the old city not for Lotfollah but for the majestic Imam mosque, also on the square. The Imam mosque – until the Revolution known as the Mosque of the Shah – is indeed one of the wonders of the world. Vast and imposing, to drift through its columned halls is to swim through coral. An old woman, alone at the pool beneath a wide sky, washes before prayer: the scene oozes romance. Yet even so it cannot compare with the ringing wonder of Lotfollah. Together, the two mosques are as beautiful as anything in the Islamic world.

I gaze upwards. Lotfollah was built by the Saffavids as a family mosque for purely personal use. It has no minarets, no need to call anyone to prayer. It was built neither to inspire the faithful nor as a symbol of the empire's pride. Its beauty was designed to answer to itself alone, God set in stone. It is a reminder of Iran's most famous dynasty, a reminder that the country's religion and government have always been intertwined.

It strikes me that history, on this journey, will be a process of confrontation and inspiration. The difficulty will be that the questions each of our encounters raise will rarely find immediate answers, and that the answers we learn will never echo the order of history itself. I am in Iran, so it is of Shi'ism that we have learned, even though Sunnism, the more dominant of the two sects, still awaits. In Tehran I know we will be visiting Khomeini's tomb, meeting Khomeini's history, long before we get a chance to look at the earlier histories of Islam. What we meet is dictated by geography instead of the order of history, a problem inherent in any physical journey. The understanding of Islamic history we gain is not a sequenced narrative but instead a layered mosaic, one that I can only hope will come fully together by the time the journey is complete. We confront, we learn. Here, in Lotfollah, we confront a legacy of frozen beauty, an attempt at eternity from one of the great empires of history. We confront the Saffavids, whose history has echoes in the Iran of today.

The Saffavid dynasty, with origins in a Sufi mystical order, began as a revolutionary movement opposed to the Turks who occupied Iran at the time. Like Khomeini's revolution centuries later, the revolution was supported by religious and secular alike, fired by opposition to tyrannous rule. And like Khomeini's revolution it heralded an era of religious fervour, one unanticipated by many supporters of the movement. It saw an end to the mutual toleration between Sunni and Shi'a that had existed for centuries, as the Shi'a *ulema* set about creating a state where religion was inseparable from government, where Persian identity was asserted over Arab, where Shi'ism and Shi'ism alone was the state religion.

Odd sounds drift in to the mosque, reminding me of the modern Iran outside. Beyond these walls is a society that was forged by revolution similar to the one that gave birth to the Saffavids. The similarities between the two suggest that we may not be poised at an irrevocable point in history, of Islamic rebirth, of a new fundamentalism destroying old customs and tolerances and beliefs, but rather at a familiar point in a cycle of revival and decay that has occurred throughout the life of Islam. I find the thought oddly reassuring.

The gate opens in a high wall; we enter. We are high above Esfahan, behind the university, and all the houses here are like this: they hide from the world behind grim walls and iron fences, their exteriors bright and scrubbed and windowless. Secrets, the hidden, the precious: these are Iranian passions, reflections of the Iranian mind.

We pass through a shy garden, brief and enclosed, the kind of garden the ancient Persians called a *pairidaeza*, from which the English word 'paradise' comes. Beyond is the house itself. We remove our shoes and enter a scene from the Arabian Nights, infused with a sense of its own romanticism. There is little furniture, just Persian carpets crowded on top of one another, filling the space from wall to wall. Carpets rich in colour, hand-knotted and ancient. The house is old and white and crumbling; it might have been designed as a stage set to capture the exoticism of the East. Columns and arches and windows and doorways. A bowl of fruit sits on the floor; we are motioned to sit beside it.

Mahsoud and Farzaneh Razmara are both lecturers at the University of Esfahan; both hold doctorates, both have been educated in the West. They responded to our telephone call yesterday evening, and their answer was simple: wear dark, conservative clothes, and meet them inside the university gates. And they were right. This time, hidden inside her cloak of hot black polyester, Kirst invoked no hisses of "*hijab*", no swarms of worried women. Just friendly smiles and laughing welcomes from the same women on the gate who had earlier barred our entry.

Farzaneh sits beside us, her black chador collapsing beneath her, while Mahsoud vanishes to make tea. And then a waterfall of darkness, an Iranian striptease, as the chador slips off. Farzaneh shakes free a flowing black mane, long and full. Her eyes glint mischief as she encourages Kirst to do the same.

Kirst hesitates, troubled, and glances at me. No Iranian has seen her hair, and the barriers imposed by the government have affected us already. I can no longer tell what my own standards are, am no longer confident of how I should feel. I just know, like Kirst, that after only ten days in Iran, removing her veil seems *wrong*.

Later this evening we will encounter two young women in Esfahan's main square, intent on practising their English and netting themselves Australian husbands. Alone with them in a car I will feel guilty of some unnameable sin, my throat clogged with the breath of sexuality that comes from their company. If I, with my Western background, can feel this way, I cannot imagine the erotic impulse it arouses in an average Iranian male. Shabbir Akhtar, an Islamic commentator, writes that the aim of the veil is "to create a truly erotic culture in which one dispenses with the need for the artificial excitement that pornography provides." I feel he is right. The strict segregation of the sexes, the all-encompassing veil: these have not dulled sexuality but have instead enhanced it, and for us now even the innocent act of freeing Kirst's hair seems erotic and sinful.

The hesitation is brief. Kirst struggles with her Çar□af, then her own mane shakes free. The relief is immediate. Freedom! Gone are any thoughts of impropriety. For the first time in Iran, we can feel natural, we can feel real. The happy feeling of sitting and talking with friends, unrestricted by society or government, is something we have not felt for a long time.

Over the darkened features of Iran, Farzaneh's skin is washed with a golden hue. She is a large woman, and attractive in a large way; the bones of her face are broad but well-defined. Even her laugh is large. It is a laugh that has echoed ever since she met us at the university, heard our story.

"You see? This is what it is like for us in Iran. We have no freedom." She says it as if it were a joke, something to make us smile, with only the faintest hint of self-pity. "And it is the worst here, in Esfahan. Worse than Tehran, than Shiraz, than Mashhad."

I am surprised. Mashhad, rammed up against Afghanistan and Turkmenistan, is home to Iran's most holy shrine, and has a reputation as the most religious city in the country.

"Yes, even more than Mashhad," continues Farzaneh in response to my raised eyebrows. "Mashhad has the shrines and the religion, but Esfahan has the Hezbollah and the attitudes. When I go to work, I cannot wear makeup; I must wear the chador. After the Revolution it was like this all over Iran, but now – you will have seen – women everywhere are wearing makeup. And from the top of their scarf, you will see their hair. But not at Esfahan University. No makeup. No hair. And it must be the chador."

Mahsoud appears, bearing the strong tea, the rock-hard lumps of sugar. His eyes bear none of the mischief of Farzaneh's, no sense of being able to laugh at the state of his country. They are brown and dull, the colour of mud, and beneath this there is the even darker glint of despair. Around the edges his beard is tinged with grey; Mahsoud is a worried man.

"Those women who stopped you," he begins, his tone bitter, "they only show you what hypocrites we Iranians are. They're not strict and religious for any reason other than money. Before the Revolution, they would never have worn the chador; now they get paid to be religious. I know them, and I know people like them. Everyone is doing religion, just to get ahead."

It is a refrain we have heard many times. Nobody should be trusted; no Iranian emotion is real. We have met no one able to fathom the religious fervour of their countrymen, other than to attribute it to greed; none believe that fervent support for the government is anything but a sham. And yet such support still exists.

Farzaneh agrees. "You can ask anyone. The only way to get ahead in our country now is through religion. Everybody wants to be a mullah, because they are the ones with the money and the power. If you are a mullah, you are corrupt. All the merchants have to bribe the mullahs just so they can stay in business." She sighs. "You have to believe it. Religion is the best way to make money."

We have yet to encounter anyone who can verify this story one way or the other. To us, Iran remains inscrutable; the sham will remain real. We can have no way of knowing if the supporters of the regime view religion in the same cynical way, but the accuracy of Farzaneh's words is immaterial in any case. It is what Iranians believe that counts, the atmosphere of distrust and suspicion that is important. In Iran, no one trusts the motives of anyone else.

"How do you know what motivates the religious people?" I ask. "Couldn't you be mistaken? Couldn't it be faith rather than greed?" Harsh laughter escapes Farzaneh's lips in response; Mahsoud looks disgusted.

"How can we not know?" he replies. "When Iranians spend their lives bribing mullahs, it is impossible not to know. You tell me where ninety billion dollars in oil revenues has gone. Everybody knows: it has been stolen by the mullahs. You tell me if that is an honest society."

Mahsoud's eyes clear slightly when the conversation changes to less political topics. They have a son; they are worried for his future; the family is happy. He likes sport, watches basketball. A mundane conversation, but one empty of religion or politics. In Iran such conversations are rare.

Lunch is prepared. I follow Farzaneh to the kitchen, trying to help. I am a fool. Inside is a coiled, frail woman, incredibly old. She is shrunken, tiny, gasping, with skin like boiled cabbage. She wears a chador, pale white for household use, but even with this protection of her honour she is still wounded by my appearance. Her mouth works absently as she moves, trembling, to hide behind the stove, clutching weakly at her veil. There is nowhere to hide. The remorseless eyes stare at me as she burns in fragile shame.

I stumble backwards, ashamed of my stupidity. Ashamed of my sex.

Farzaneh laughs. "Don't worry. It is only my mother. She is old, and not used to other people."

Reza Shah banned the veil in 1936, but to people like Farzaneh's mother this was like declaring that they had to walk the streets naked. Most stayed indoors to avoid the shame, meaning the decree only restricted women further. "I don't understand," I say. "You can't really mean that all women in Iran wear the veil because of the government, that they are all hypocrites. Just look at your mother."

"No, of course not. The chador is an Iranian tradition, particularly in the villages and with older people. Many people cannot live without it. But people my age, and younger, know that the chador and the veil are really two different things. The chador is Iranian, not part of Islam at all. It is no more religious than anything else." A phantom of a smile is all she can manage. "It is just that the government declares that the chador is good *hijab* that we get the hypocrites. And now, more and more people are taught that this is how it should be, that this is the essence of Islam. These people, this government, are changing the religion, changing it for the worse."

We eat, sitting cross-legged on ancient carpets, food laid on a cloth before us. We eat meat kebabs and rice tainted with saffron; we drink sweet soft drinks from confiscated American factories. And we talk. As the afternoon slowly crumples into evening, we talk of anything but Iran. Here, in this open room with its bright carpets and ancient memories, amidst the smell of roasted meat, we sit with friends. These people, who have no link to us other than that we know their names, laugh with us completely at ease, and thread their way into our lives. The people of this country meet each other with guarded lives and suspicion and doubt, but foreigners, non-participants in the game of revolution and oppression, exempt from such things, meet only welcome.

Mahsoud's voice hardens when the conversation returns, as we knew it would, to life in Iran. His response to Kirst's question about the courses he lectures is pure bitterness.

"All my students are dumb. Dumb!" He spits the word, gives it a weight that is not its own. "They know nothing, they want to know nothing. They fight, they chant, they support the government. They think that the Qur'an will tell them everything they need, that it contains all the knowledge in the world. What kind of education is that?"

Farzaneh explains. "The students don't need to be intelligent to come to university any more. They only need to be religious. You know the Sepah Pasdaran?" I nod. Sepah is Iran's religious force, the might behind the mullahs. Distinct from the regular army, its soldiers are answerable directly to the President, and thus to the mullahs. It is the guardian of the Revolution, insurance that the Islamic Republic will never end.

Farzaneh's voice is strident as she continues. "Seventy-five percent of all university places are awarded to Sepah Pasdaran. Either to them, or to the brothers and sons of martyrs, or to the families of mullahs. Only twenty-five percent is on merit." She is becoming frantic, and looks as if she might weep.

We have tapped into their passion. The conversation continues in a flood of anger and frustration, of bitterness hurled at the government, the students, the mullahs, Iran. We learn that they are prohibited from failing these religious students, these sons and daughters of the Revolution. Those to whom the Qur'an is the only book of any worth, who, having given their souls to their God and country, see no reason to study, are unable to fail; the quota of failures is filled instead by those who deserve to pass. To Farzaneh and Mahsoud this is pure crime, a travesty that torments them every day. Again we hear that this is why the students become religious, again we hear that to gain any other position one must be willing to bribe. The couple are Western-styled academics and value education above all else; life under such rules is intolerable.

It occurs to me that the real issue of the afternoon, despite Farzaneh and Mahsoud's passion, is not the Iranian education system. Like much of what we encounter in Iran, the specifics of what they describe are not likely to remain the same for long; if there is one constant in Iran's history, it is frequent – and often violent – change. In the end, the students are a symptom, not a cause. The future may bring different symptoms to Iran, but the causes – the opportunism, the near-obsessive suspicion of others – will remain.

Eventually the conversation stumbles to a halt, all outrage spent. Our hosts, sitting slightly slumped, are quiet for a moment, as though their batteries have gone dead. Then Farzaneh sighs, lifting her head to gaze off into the middle distance.

"Things were so much better with the Shah," she says. It has surprised me how often we have heard this comment. "Twenty years ago we were a rich country; now we are poor."

Finally, we come to the crux of the matter. This, in many ways, is the real lament of Iran. In a country of oppressive rule, abrogation of freedom and corrupt government, it is economic failure that is the biggest crime. This morning, the owner of our hotel explained that, under the Shah, he could afford to buy a car; now he cannot. To him this was the only meaningful yardstick, this grievance cause enough for opposing the regime. The oppression and corruption did not concern him – it was no worse than under the Shah.

"Everybody knows we had problems under the Shah, terrible problems," Farzaneh continues. "You cannot understand how cruel life was. Even I supported Khomeini at first; everybody I know supported the Revolution. We all wanted a change, wanted some freedom. But what have we now? At least then we were rich. Now we still have no freedom, and we are poor."

Saturday 3rd June
Esfahan

We stumble into the tea house from one of the narrow streets near the *maidan*, the main square in the old city. It has been a morning battling customs at the post office, trying to post ancient Persian trinkets, both authentic and fake. We are tired; the tea house answers our exhaustion.

The sense of the maleness of the place is as strong as the odour of smoke and sweat. Old men, dried and quiet, smoke and drink tea on the meagre stools that line the walls. They sit mainly near the door, near the window, where a bodyless light streams in from outside. The air is thick with the smell of the ancient excitements of these old men: of smoke and sweat, certainly, but also of aged skin, blurred dreams, disappointment, stale soap, half-mumbled prayers. Hanging on the walls are the relics of ancient religious campaigns: a black flag; an iron trident; several flails.

A moment of uncertainty, unsure if a woman is welcome in such a place of faded masculinity, where custom and tradition and Islam somehow mingle together. She is. The proprietor, a lean man with a nose that cuts his face in half like a wound, waves us casually inside. We sit, like the old men, with our backs to the wall, while dust motes play weightlessly across our vision.

Tea comes.

By the river is another tea house, shown to us yesterday evening by Farzaneh and Mahsoud. It is designed for tourists and Iranian families, an acceptable version of Eastern romanticism, strung with portraits and carpets and silver, a place where Iranian women can visit. This place is nothing like it. It is authentic, no plaything for tourists; we feel as superfluous as we would at a religious ceremony. Romantic without a trace of sentimentality; functional and holy at the same time; bare and real.

I gaze once more around the room. The walls are tiled and grimy, the floor is raw cement. Metal rods, lanterns and cups dangle from the walls, balance on a few bare shelves. A picture of Mecca, a photograph of a religious parade, the name of God scrawled in black on a tile. At the end of the room, in dimness far from where the old men sit, hang two portraits of Khomeini over an ancient octagonal pool. Above them a tired fan slowly turns.

The greatest object of mystery and desire sits at this far end of the room, hiding in the shadows. It is an unreal creation, a work of iron and imagination that floats like a forgotten, half-mythic creature in its own world. It is a tree of writhing iron, constructed around a central pole and single crossbar. Pillars of iron tablets, sculpted and finely engraved in Arabic, support snarling heads of dragons in every direction. It has the air of something aware of its own existence, of a creature so dangerous it could only be evil. Its name, when we ask, sounds like 'fabagh'.

A grey-haired man, his face veined and shaded, beckons us across to where he sits, in a corner near the door. He is part of a group of three, each staring with unfocused eyes into the room while the smoke courses through their lungs. They do not talk to each other; they are content simply to be. With the chairs arranged against the wall, only one of us can sit beside him. It is of course I who do so: for Kirst to sit beside an Iranian man would be a grave indiscretion. Too polite to address an unknown woman, the man speaks only to me.

In a voice of gravel, he explains the role of the iron creation at the end of the room, tells us it belongs to the ceremony of Ashura, the religious festival that commemorates the martyrdom of the third Imam, Hussein. Ashura is the holiest date of the Shi'a calendar, a ten-day period of grief and mourning. The important ceremonies begin, the old man tells us, in a few days' time.

"You know about our holy Imam, don't you?" his voice grates softly. "You know what happened, you know how he was killed, how his family was killed?"

His voice is calm, quiet. I could almost believe he holds only passing interest in the subject. Yet as I watch, a slow tear begins its course down his face.

"We must all be very sad when we remember this tragedy. We feel *hurt*," – he clutches his chest as though trying to reach his heart – "hurt for our Imam's death. Our hurt is real."

The tears are dripping off his chin onto his collar. He turns his tragic eyes to me, a mournful petition for something I do not have.

Such intensity both frightens and captivates me. I have never known religious passion in my own life, and I find such devotion enthralling. My interest is tinged faintly with horror, placing its attraction somewhere between a child's fascination with spiders and the preoccupation a blind man might have with sight. I can only hope that Ashura will be this emotionally charged.

Then, suddenly, the tears are gone, the flow of emotion severed. The man orders us more tea, pays for us with the generosity we now expect of complete strangers no matter how strenuous our protests. His eyes are dry, his movements active. I cannot believe that this man was weeping moments ago, that his tears can have been real: such sudden emotion is difficult to trust. Is this what Farzaneh means when she claims Iranians are false?

The man nods briefly to one of his companions. "My friend is a mullah. He will be leading the parades."

I glance across at the man he indicates. He looks surprisingly unclerical, lacking both turban and gown. His face is still, barely acknowledging that we speak about him. That vacant stare, the slow bubble of the pipe. My attempts to question him meet with failure. I learn only that "Islam likes Christians" as a description of his attitudes to the West, nothing else.

We drain the last of our tea through our teeth and prepare to leave. Our companion merely nods, returning to his pipe. The performance is over, a brief exposure to inscrutable passions.

Outside, the sky is a screaming blue. We return to the *maidan*, lie on the grass, watch the sky fill with white as a storm gathers in the distance. Neurotic gusts of wind pluck at the trees; the afternoon passes peacefully. We have chosen a small patch of grass, hidden from the main square. All morning we have been harangued by Iranian hospitality, beleaguered by kindness. A family invites us to their village a hundred kilometres away; youths invite us to their homes; a child wants our photograph; strangers want to sit and talk and buy us food. To tire of such attention, to crave indifference in the Iranian people, would have seemed ludicrous to me two weeks ago. Is it ungrateful to complain of kindness? In Iran attentions are so extreme that privacy becomes a precious commodity, rarely found outside our hotel room. Even here, hidden from the world by ancient brick walls, we are a target for friendship: we are approached by a pair of doctors, eager to show us the sights of Esfahan. It is with them we spend the rest of our day, the rest of our time in Esfahan. It is a fitting conclusion to a town supposed to be the least hospitable in Iran: these men buy us pizza, take us to the zoo, stroll with us by the river eating ice-creams. Our stay has been characterised by the kindness of strangers, by a welcome I would expect from few cities in the world. If Esfahan is the least friendly city in Iran, we have an interesting time ahead of us.

It is late by the time our new friends drive us back to our hotel, some time after midnight. We have remained in their care far too long, eager recipients of hospitality in yet another Iranian household. Yet the memory is dimmed on our way home, swamped by the alien atmosphere that confronts us. The streets are filled with bizarre scenes: Ashura has begun. Mud caked on our windows renders the outside world as faint and indistinct as an extremely old film, washed in sepia. We peer through it into a black night, the scene outside vaguely threatening. Every few hundred metres, harsh halide lamps scale back the darkness, sear the world with a vicious light. Beneath them are gathered crowds of stern-faced men, dressed completely in black.

Boom, crash. Drums beat, crowds chant.

It is an eerie scene, foreign and malevolent. In long lines, in rhythmic unison, the men flail themselves with chains.

Ancient Stone, Holy Silver

Sunday 4th June – Tuesday 6th June
Shiraz

The surface is grey, smooth, cracked in places. A lion tears into the flesh of a horse; servants bring gifts to the king. The stone relief is carved with shadow, sculpted by the same desert sun that strips the strength from our shoulders. It is just after noon, and we are the only ones stupid enough to brave the midday sun, the only living shadows who move amongst the ruins of Persepolis, capital of ancient Persia.

We travelled here yesterday in heat like a kiln, entering the Iranian province of Fars. Fars is a place of easy antiquity, home of the great Persian Achaemenian and Sassanian Empires, of warrior kings and Zoroastrianism, of the Farsi tongue I struggle to speak. A day of dust whipping our windows, riding on the hot insanity of the wind, as our bus sliced the empty space of the desert into easy divisions: left and right; ahead and behind. An arrival late at night, to sleep on the carpeted floor of one of our fellow passengers. And then this morning, when our host offered to bring us here, to his country's most famous ruins.

I am awed by the antiquity of Iran. Rival of the Greeks, challenger to both Rome and Constantinople, Persia remains a place of legend in my imagination, and a part of me can only gape. The quality of some sections of the ruins are a disappointment – I can gain none of the sense of a living city, of the feeling of brushing the shoulders of men long dead, that I found in Byzantine ruins in Turkey – but it does not matter. We are not here to seek well-preserved ruins, not here to judge the architecture. We are here to taste age, to grasp the timelessness that belongs to Iran.

Our host is Mehdi, and he is eager to smother us with hospitality. He has a sick face: thin and blotchy, untrustworthy yet sincere. His kindness is second-rate, forced: he has tried all morning to convince us to organise him an Australian visa. To Mehdi, the easiest way to persuade is to flatter and fawn, drowning us in obsequiousness. His manner has begun to grate. At times, however, he can be blunt, punchy, proud. It is only in these flashes of his real self that I find it possible to like him.

"You want to go now? It is hot."

We have only been here a few minutes; with an entry fee for foreigners thirty times that of their Iranian counterparts, we have no intention of surrendering to the heat so soon. And after a morning of oblique arguments about visa restrictions, of claims of how kind he has been to us, our sympathy for Mehdi is limited. We wander across the hot stones to a forest of broken columns instead.

"You like it? You like that I bring you here?"

This is the third time Mehdi has asked the question. I shade my eyes, stare upwards through shards of sunlight at a stone arch, wishing he would leave us in peace.

"Iran has a strong history." The wheeze of servility is momentarily gone from his voice. "We were a great country."

"And you are not any more?"

Mehdi looks at me as though I am a creature that should long have been extinct. "We are not any more."

This is the bitter Mehdi, the only Mehdi I can bear. I ask him if he thinks there is a difference between Iranian culture and the culture of Islam.

"Of course they are different things," is the sullen response. "Iran has a wonderful history. We are a proud country, long before Islam. And anyway," he says, shrugging his shoulders, dismissing the power of the religion, "Islam only became great when it came to Iran."

He could mean anything with such a comment; when I ask him to explain, he groans in exasperation.

"Before Islam, Iran was great. Islam has nothing, no art, no learning, no poetry. It was Iran who gives these things to Islam." He stops, kicks a stone. The tone of supplication returns to his voice. "But now, we are a terrible country. I cannot live here, you must help me, I have been so kind…"

Persepolis stands on a bare hill, baking above the world around. We wander to the edge through spaces of breathless heat, look down. Below us is a threadbare forest of struggling trees; from their midst rise the brightly-coloured tents of a circus. These are the remains of the Shah's sumptuous celebration, in 1971, of what he claimed was 2500 years of Persian civilisation. These days the tent city is used for military training.

Mehdi catches his breath when he spots a green-and-white police car at the entrance to the ruins, and steps back into the shadows.

"You go now. You go out to the car. I follow soon." He sees our expressions, guesses, perhaps, that he must explain. "You know Gestapo? These men are the same. Savak under old regime, no different now. If they see me with you, they give me problem."

Savak, the Shah's secret police, had a terrifying reputation. An institution of brutality and torture, they were a symbol of the kind of repression that inspired revolutionary fervour in the Iranian people. And, as in Bolshevik Russia, as in so many revolutions throughout history, the machinery of the state survived to become a tool of those who were once its victims. Mehdi does not return to the car until they have gone.

We drive in silence through grey villages, back towards Shiraz. Fars has the largest number of nomads of any province in Iran, and it is immediately obvious. In a land of genetic uniformity, the pale desert eyes are impossible to miss. Blue eyes, grey, embedded in veils of black, these gypsy women capture my gaze as we pass. Framed by black lashes, black hair and dark skin, their eyes are even more striking than Kirst's blue.

41

Their multicoloured dresses billow from beneath their chadors like the exotic fins of slow-drifting sea snails.

Against bitter protestations from Mehdi, we install ourselves in a hotel. Mehdi feels that it is not right, that we do not appreciate his hospitality; after attempting to negotiate a higher-than-usual price, he sulks in the corner. We are his prize: he does not want us to slip from his grasp.

An Arab man, white-robed with fingers of gold, climbs the stairs past us, trailing an entourage of three women. Beneath their chadors, two of the women wear coloured masks, peaked over their noses; their faces smothered by permanent masquerades, an image of fluttering birds. Yet it is the third woman who disturbs me the most. Her mask is of black leather, a tight monstrosity that imprisons two doleful eyes. A mere slit twists in the leather in place of her mouth. In this knifelike heat, the sight does not need the sadomasochistic connotations of the mask to shock. It cools my blood, causes something inside me to harden. Before us walks cruelty.

Mehdi walks across to us, watching the group vanish upstairs. He shakes his head. "Arabs. From Bandar-é Abbas. Not like Iranians."

Mehdi is right. Outside, women – Persian, not Arab – crowd the streets, haggle with shopkeepers, cling to the back of motorcycles, their chadors flying. The faces of all are open to the world. For the first time, I see the freedom in their lives instead of the repression. They may be tied to their chadors, but to the Arab women of the Gulf, faces hidden beneath leather masks, they must shine as symbols of Muslim freedom. There are, it seems, things worse than being a woman in Iran.

Mehdi senses our disquiet. "This is what I tell you. Only Iran has the true culture of Islam. The Arabs do not treat their women well; they do not know true Islam."

Later, when I ask Mehdi how many Iranians follow true Islam, the question is only half-understood. His answer surprises me.

"Ah. Well, you know I am like many people in Iran today," he says, his face tight and hopeless. "They force these things upon us. People still pray, but they are no longer feeling. We are all losing our religion."

Wednesday 7th June
Shiraz

I cannot, after today, believe Mehdi's words.

This morning we visit the *Bogh'é-yé Shah-é Cheragh*, the "Tomb of the King of the Lamp". It is the tomb of Mir Ahmad, the brother of Imam Reza, the eighth Shi'a Imam. Imam Reza's shrine lies in Mashhad, and is the holiest place in Iran, a pilgrimage place for all Muslims, Shi'a and Sunni alike. As merely the brother of one of the Imams, Mir Ahmad occupies a far less important rung in the Shi'a hierarchy, but shrine veneration is a fundamental part of the Shi'a faith, and his shrine has been a place of pilgrimage ever since the Fourteenth century.

The tomb lies south of Shiraz's main bazaar, and we twist through narrow alleys of carpet merchants and tinsmiths, tea stores and spice sellers. The goods of Iran fill the dark corridors: hookahs, flails for Ashura, metal pots, carpets both manufactured and authentic, soap, cloth, chadors. The air is hot and rushed and crowded, filled with the sound of thousands of different voices, with dust scuffed by a thousand shoes. We are washed south with the crowd, flushed out into the unflinching heat and light of day.

The entrance to the tomb is an echo of Esfahan, a porcelain image in turquoise and cobalt and white. A huge portal, covered in the cool blue tiles of Iranian Islam, dwarfs a pair of open wooden doors; through this the faithful file. The arched portal supports a mass of stalactite moulding, an intricate hanging construction sculpted in coloured tiles. Flowers and swirls and shapes of turquoise. My gaze shifts upwards, to the line of blue tiles seared in white with the names of God, to the black flags of Shi'ism which flap in the scraping breeze.

The entrance is empty of any form of figurative art. This is the tradition of Islam. Islam's fierce iconoclastic ideal has meant that representational art is viewed with suspicion, seen as the first step towards idolatry. The calligraphy of the Arabic script, a tangled tracing difficult to follow with the eye, takes the place of such iconography. Yet while the calligraphic art before me is beautiful, this shrine has been worshipped for centuries in a way that could only be called idolatrous. That the white flutter of such lettering should adorn its entrance strikes me as incongruous.

We follow the faithful through the heavy wooden doors, inlaid with solid brass. Almost every pilgrim stops to kiss them, or to wipe their hands repeatedly over the brass and then over their faces, smearing themselves with an invisible holiness. Those leaving do the same, hoping to squeeze one last breath of God from the shrine, to coat themselves in the dust of Allah. They then back their way into the street outside, too respectful to turn their backs on such a holy place.

The gates lead to a huge stone courtyard, scorched colourless by the sun. The light is so bright I must squint.

The shrine lies at the near end of the courtyard, a squat construction supporting a single, egg-shaped dome of dreamy blue. Black flags, inscribed with Farsi and Arabic, hang over the arches that ring this blinding stone area, hang over the entrance to the shrine itself. Women drift across the square like black spectres; men, fierce and wild-eyed, stride purposefully past them. Only the children, playing or drinking water provided by metal fountains, are free of the grim air of religious intensity. Family groups, large enough to be whole clans, huddle in patches of shade. All eyes are turned towards the shrine.

We deliver our shoes like the hundreds of other pilgrims, treading on ancient carpets worn thin by the bare feet of the faithful. Unlike at many other Islamic holy sites, our presence is tolerated here; the Shi'a are less concerned by the presence of infidels. Our price is that Kirst must wear a chador, her coat and scarf being deemed insufficiently religious. We do not argue. Here is not the place to dispute the fundamentals of Islam. Kirst shuffles behind me, cloaking herself in the huge piece of fabric as well as she can. Most Iranian women grip the cloth between their teeth to keep the hooded cloak over their hair. The skill is a difficult one, gained with a lifetime of effort. It is beyond Kirst, and the trauma of having her veil slip and reveal her hair in such a holy place has turned her crimson.

We walk as slowly as those around us, people whose very movements are infused with reverence, as we climb the front steps of the shrine. On a carpeted veranda, shaded from the sun, proud fathers take photographs of their sons, shrouded women sit and wail, pilgrims cross the threshold to the shrine itself. I am filled with a tangled feeling of guilt, a sense of transgression, of *wrongness* at being here. I feel we do not belong. I sit on the carpet for a time, wrestling with this feeling of trespass, watching the slow steps of the pilgrims as they enter, trying to force myself to feel at ease.

The doors to the shrine, framed in marble, are a shining gold, carved with the delicate beauty I have come to expect from Islamic art. Patterns in turquoise and sapphire weave through the metal. The stylised names of Muhammad, Ali and Allah all intertwine with the engraved patterns on the door with verses from the Qur'an. These doors are more holy than the main gates: pilgrims press their foreheads to them in reverence, pause as their mouths shape silent prayers. A man with a shaved head, knobbed and angular, dressed in combat fatigues, rubs his hands on the door, on his face, on the door, on his face. On the threshold, the devoted reach a state almost of religious trance.

Gradually the disquiet inside me shifts, softens, settles. We stand and walk with heads bowed into the shrine. The dazzling light of day outside means it is impossible to see in until we enter; and then we are dazzled further still.

Inside, the light is bright and hurtful. The modest dome, every available surface, is covered in tiny mirror tiles too numerous to guess at. From both a single lamp and lattice portals that admit fragments of sun, light is amplified, scattered, bounced. White and savage, splintered and bright. Each tiny tile is its own shard of light, its own angle, its own universe, and each sets free light that hurts the eyes.

The few surfaces not of glass, are of silver. Silver threads lace the walls, and the silver form of the tomb fills the room. It is a huge and heavy lattice, a cage of solid silver, all shiny knobs and rods of metal. Inside it, imprisoned, is a single slab of marble. Each rod of silver is as thick as a man's arm, and where they join the metal is knobbed and rounded and thicker still.

We stand, motionless, watching the pilgrims approach their saint. The cage is fastened with a heavy silver lock, as large as a child's face, inscribed in black with the names of God. It is an object of immutable beauty. The men and women before us grasp this lock, kiss it, smear their faces across its surface. They cling to the tomb, touching and reaching in, yearning to merge their bodies with the cold metal, searching for union with their saint.

And everyone weeps.

They cry, not in the sad, subdued manner of the man in the tea shop in Esfahan, but with an unrestrained wail, with the savage jagged emotion of those whose children have just died. Tears smear the silver, run down every face; gobbling sobs compete with any speech. They weep, and my mind trembles.

Slowly, we approach the shrine, hang back, hover to the left. The urge to touch it is intense, but I cannot commit such violation.

With a start, I realise that all the women in the shrine are on the other side of the tomb. A small partition, no more than a few feet long and unnoticed until now, divides the approach to the lock and the tomb. This experience is meant to be segregated, and Kirst is in the male section. She flushes with fright, rushes to the other side; the last thing either of us needed was to feel even more uncomfortable.

Behind me, crouched in a corner, sits an old mullah, shrivelled almost to futility. From his mouth escapes an uninterrupted wailing. It is not mournful, possessing instead the timeless sound of the muezzin call to prayer. Before him lies a huge, ancient Qur'an. The man is reciting surah from it, filling the air with an awareness of God, as if such an awareness wasn't already here. The presence of God fills the room.

I sit down across the carpet from the mullah, and shift my gaze to those around me. The men's side is far less populated than where Kirst now sits. Perhaps, in the middle of the day, more men are at work. Those near me do as I do: sit cross-legged, dine on the intense religious fervour, the spectacle, the atmosphere. Only our reasons differ. A few touch their foreheads to the ground in supplication towards Mecca; none show any signs of noticing my presence.

Since we entered I have gathered a tightness inside once more, as a result of Kirst's error and the hard stares that followed it. Only gradually this begins to fade. I allow myself to feel washed by the intensity of the experience. The pain of these people is vivid, palpable. Is it grief for Mir Ahmad? Or themselves?

Such emotion for a figure of history, not even a major religious figure but merely the brother of one, is entirely foreign to me. But it is not to the Shi'a. The focus on martyrdom and death and mourning in Shi'ism, a focus that sprang from its origins as a religion, means that the Shi'a are well versed in grief. Every year they mourn the death of their Imams, men long dead, in their Ashura commemorations. They flail themselves to share the pain of their martyrs. In some places they cut themselves with swords. Every year they train themselves in grief, train themselves to conjure this intensity of emotion. I watch the tears roll down a woman's face, down a soldier's chin, from the eyes of a youth I would otherwise have classed as thoroughly Westernised, and I feel hollow inside, inadequate. I have never felt more foreign. I cannot imagine what the *hajj* must be like. Sir Richard Burton, disguised as a Pukhtun doctor in the last century, managed to visit Mecca. He wrote that seeing the Ka'ba for the first time created ecstasy in non-believers. I do not doubt it.

Yet I cannot avoid wondering how Muhammad would have found such a scene. His opposition to the religion of the Meccans was driven by an abhorrence of the idolatrous practices in the shrine of the Ka'ba. He forbade anything that could reduce the worship of God to the worship of an image, of an object. The veneration of shrines devoted to individuals would horrify him.

It was for the same reasons that Muhammad forbade representative art, just as the Jews had done before him. It could detract from the worship of God, could encourage idolatry, could reduce to an image that which was beyond the human capacity to comprehend. Yet today, outside this shrine, buses are adorned with pictures of Ali, of Muhammad, dressed in the familiar clothes of Biblical shepherds.

Throughout the ages there have been periodic Muslim backlashes against such practices, but they have never fully succeeded. The human spirit yearns for something solid, something possible to grasp. A God impossible to describe, to visualise, is a God too distant for worship and comfort. And the yearnings of the human spirit will always create failures in creed, manifested in different ways: the worship of the figure of Christ in Christianity, the worship of shrines in Shi'ism.

I am alone with these thoughts. I glance over to where Kirst sits, sampling an experience completely different from my own. The men around me are entirely within themselves, intense, focused on their inner worship of God. Around Kirst is a group of women, smiling, eager to talk. Once their devotions are complete, these women feel no need to retain their religious intensity, and focus instead on making Kirst feel welcome. Kirst smiles while I turn my gaze, liquid and sombre, to the fragmented light of the ceiling. When we leave, we each carry entirely different feelings in our chests.

At the golden doors, as though of the same religion as the pilgrims around us, we turn and walk out backwards.

Thursday 8th June – Saturday 10th June
Shiraz

We drift through these days, which are full of heat and ice-cream but little else, for the city has all but closed down for Ashura. We wander the streets in the day, try to escape the muffling heat, but there is little to see. The luxurious Homa Hotel is one of the few places not shuttered and barred. It is air-conditioned, blissful, its open foyer full of exquisite carpets, sculptured fountains and studied opulence. It is like any other luxury hotel in the world, except that above the entrance, in huge gold lettering, is the sign: "DOWN WITH USA".

The sign strikes us as comical, incongruous. The claim is too simple, too ideological, too racist; to be simplified in this way is patently absurd. The same is so often true, however, of how we portray Islam in the West. We no longer tolerate the characterisation of blacks and Jews in such simplistic ways. Yet we do so often reduce Islam, and Iran in particular, to a mass of screaming fundamentalists bent on the destruction of all things Western, flaming with zeal at the prospect of an Islamic holy jihad. The sign is a reminder that to do so is just as absurd.

The day passes, slow and lazy. From time to time the sounds of chanting drift over the city, the sounds of clashing cymbals, banging drums. Ashura, invisible, calls to us; a sense of anticipation settles over the empty streets.

Men in our hotel tell us that tonight is an important one in the Ashura commemorations. Ashura means "tenth night" in Arabic; tonight, *tasua*, is the ninth night of the festival. In Farsi the night is known as *sharm-é gharibiam*, "the strange night". A feeling of strangeness and dislocation certainly fills the air as the day settles into evening. We walk the poor streets near our hotel in the dying light. They have a pre-festival atmosphere. Youths with shaved heads, dressed in black shirts and army fatigues, erect stages and loudspeakers, looking as mad and as dangerous as neo-Nazis. They stare as we pass, lance us with unease. The air tastes of threat.

Javad, a fellow resident at our hotel, has told us that most people who participate in the Ashura parades are paid to do so by the government. It is a claim we have heard many times. It smacks of the Iranian preoccupation with conspiracy, of the unforgiving suspicion Iranians hold for each other. It may be true; it may not.

The parades begin once darkness descends, moonless and complete. We return, after a meal, to the streets near the shrine, where the crowds are at their thickest. The men wear black shirts, black pants; most are darkly bearded. Charcoal chadors cloak the women with black invisibility. We are drowning in a sea of darkness, broken only occasionally by a cool pool of light. The air is taut. Chadors line the sidewalks, the pale moons of their faces only just discernible in the dim light. Men spill on to the road, chanting in unison, clashing cymbals, beating drums. The scene is as grim as a funeral, as crowded as a fair. Yet unlike this afternoon, we do not feel threatened. We pick through the crowd, watch the parade, feeling neither part of the proceedings nor fully excluded.

The flailing begins. In time to the chants, the men beat themselves over their neck and shoulders with heavy chains. A step to the right. Thrash. A step to the left. Thrash. Those without flails beat themselves with open palms over the head or across the chest. Thump. Pause. Thump. Pause. The chanting does not cease; it has a quality of incantation. And neither does the gruesome ritual of self-inflicted punishment.

The faces are not those of fanatics. Old men near the front of the parade could have been buying us ice-creams this afternoon. Fathers gaze proudly at their sons towards the rear of the parade, youths flailing away at their bodies. Everyone looks utterly, excruciatingly, depressingly normal. And still the flailing continues.

We have no such night-time religious celebration in our culture; the re-enactment of the death of Christ cannot compare. I cannot orient myself emotionally, cannot form a base from which to judge my surroundings, and I am left grasping for inadequate comparisons. It is not really a parade: the participants are going nowhere. The crowd is not here to be entertained, for such bleary repetitiveness is not entertaining. Yet it feels like a parade, feels like a fair. The grim intensity on the faces of many of the participants, while we stand alongside eating ice-creams, only adds to my confusion.

Are these people willing participants, or are they coerced by the government? I cannot say. Before we leave Iran I will need to speak to these men, to hear the story behind their passion, in order to tell if the stories of conspiracy, stories we hear from bystanders even tonight, are true.

We watch for an hour, for two, before the macabre ceremony becomes too much to bear. We walk through empty streets back to our hotel. The sounds of the night continue, echoing up at us from all over the city. They do not invade my dreams.

Jahiliyya

Sunday 11th June
Shiraz to Bushehr

From Shiraz we descend steeply for two hours. Mountains rise around us as we descend, veined and bulging muscles of rock. Our road is a thin ribbon of tar poured down the hill. The surrounding vegetation struggles; the impression conveyed by the ragged trees, right down to their lowest branches, is one of utter wretchedness. Brown heat thumps at me through the windows and I can feel my eyelids drooping. I do not like to imagine how Kirst feels under her coat, her black scarf.

Time passes, the heat increasing as it does. We reach the desolate plain, grey-brown and uninteresting. A lone shepherd tends a flock of mud-coloured sheep, scuttling beneath low bushes in search of shade. The air at this level is as brittle and dry as bone, the hot breath of tormented souls, searing my eyeballs.

We stop for prayer at a small village, join the believers as they wash to purify themselves, rejoicing in this dictate of their religion. The moisture is sucked from our skin. I cannot remember ever being this hot, despite a lifetime of Australian summers. An Arab beggar climbs aboard as we leave, mumbling passages from the Qur'an about the giving of alms. A man across the aisle, tall and lean and tanned, turns to me with mischief in his eyes. "He's doing the same job as the mullahs, except they use better technology to rob the people," he says wryly. He hands the beggar a few coins.

Our friend is Ahmad, an engineer on one of the many oil platforms in the region. He has spent the journey feeding us roasted watermelon seeds; I palmed most of them out of the window. He would like to invite us home to stay, he explains, but his wife would kill him if he brought strangers home without asking. "She is very much the boss in my house," he smiles. Instead, he arranges to meet us tomorrow. The image of the oppressed wife of Islam has, in the people we meet, proved less common than I expected.

We take three hours to find a hotel willing to accept foreigners. Bushehr forms the focus of international confrontation over Iran's nuclear program, and it seems the authorities are suspicious of outsiders. The heat completely saps both energy and will; we have little strength with which to fight. By the time we find a modest place by the water, it is dark, and we feel completely crippled. We have seen very little of the city in our mad, pack-laden scramble between hotels, but we have seen enough to know we despise it thoroughly.

The signs of our proximity to Arabia have been easy to spot. Most of the inhabitants of Bushehr are Arabs, and the hotel's television picks up Saudi television just as easily as the local product. The differences between the two countries are not as marked as I might expect. The television output of both stick to Islamically conservative topics, though the Saudi channels are noticeably more professional. Iranian channels depict normal family life – the women suitably veiled, of course – while those from across the Gulf inform us, often in English, of the evils of alcohol, the beauty of prayer, the unity of God. Religious programming takes up almost seventy percent of Saudi air time. This is no less extreme than Iran, and I cannot really account for my own impressions of the two countries: Iran, a country of fanatical Islam; Saudi Arabia, more acceptable to Western palates, its Islam a more moderated kind.

A common misconception in the West is that Iran is the biggest backer of Islamic fundamentalism throughout the world. Iran is an inspiration to Islamic revolutionaries everywhere, and certainly plays a major role in supporting them, but the Iranian economy is in ruins: it simply cannot afford the cost. The real main players in terms of backing fundamentalism are, as one might expect, those countries with the most to give: Saudi Arabia, Kuwait, the UAE. All openly support the Middle East peace 'process', and all, unlike Iran, are staunch allies of the United States. Yet all fund fundamentalist organisations such as Hamas, both abroad and on their own soil. In a single year, one Saudi Arabian payment to Hamas was $72 million; payments to the PLO have been even larger, long before the organisation ceased its avowedly terrorist stance. The governments of each country – which are hardly more representative than that of Iran – attempt to walk the fine line between Western support and the appeasement of terrorist organisations for their own benefit. Compared to the fabulous wealth they command, Iran is far too much of an economic basket case to single-handedly fund the entire Islamic revival.

For Iran *is* suffering. There are severe housing shortages in all major cities: a simple rental deposit costs the equivalent of five or six years' average annual salary. Most of Iran's industries have seen savage slumps in production, partly because Western embargoes have caused major shortages, particularly of spare parts. Farmers are drifting to the cities, unable to produce. Irrigation systems are tumbling into disrepair. The regime's own statistics, most likely to be as optimistic as possible, show that heavy industry is functioning at only a quarter of its pre-Revolutionary capacity. Most important of all, the oil industry has crashed. It now only produces about sixty percent of pre-Revolutionary levels. The oil that it does sell fetches reduced prices due to a slump in the world oil market. And, incredibly, Iran has increased its population by almost eighty percent in the same period. After the war, the mullahs insisted that births were essential to replace the Iranian lives that had been lost. The birth rate soared: the population leaped from thirty-seven million in only 1978 to sixty-seven million today. With its economy in tatters, its population bulging, it is little wonder Iran cannot match Saudi Arabian cash for terrorism.

My impressions of the two countries make even less sense in the face of Saudi orthodox doctrine. I have always associated Iran with fierce and backward religious convictions, yet Saudi Arabia is dominated by the Wahabi sect, one of the strictest and most puritanical forms of Islam that exists. The Wahabis embrace an attitude to life so strict that it bans whistling as impious. Their interpretation of the Qur'an is so fundamentalist, so inflexible, that its followers have frequently attempted to destroy all the holy sites of Arabia – even the tomb of Muhammad – because the worship of place can only detract from the worship of God. Today, Wahabism imposes incredibly strict religious and social conservatism on all Saudis. It forbids luxury, dancing, gambling, music and tobacco. Among Wahabi pronouncements there have been claims that the earth is flat, that teachings at Riyadh University were heretical because they discussed the existence of the solar system. To claim that the Saudi version of Islam is a tolerant, moderate one, acceptable to Western sensibilities, only betrays a poor understanding of the religion and its history.

What raises cause for concern is that the Wahabi sect dictates the behaviour not just of a nation, but of much of the Islamic world. For few could deny that Saudi influence, backed by vast sums of money, extends far and wide. In the Afghan war, for example, the Wahabis wielded immense power, funding only those rebel groups aligned with itself, exporting its own ideology to the fighters of the desert. The moderate groups could not hope to compete, and the transition of Afghanistan to a place of extremist Islam is the work, in many respects, of the Wahabis. The Wahabis continue to jockey for influence in fundamentalist groups throughout the world; one country, Algeria, had an organisation called "The Committee for Protection Against Saudi Ignorance" in an attempt to oppose its influence.

In no way could Saudi Arabia be classed as a moderate Islamic society; in no way does it deserve any image of tolerance. And yet it remains a close ally of the West and retains a perfectly acceptable international image, while I sit in a country breaking under international sanctions, a pariah among the nations of the world. Iran may deserve the image, but it does not deserve it alone.

In my hotel room, I finger the lump of orange clay placed discreetly by my bed. It has most likely come from Mecca, a lump of sacred earth. The television tells me that it is time for prayer.

Monday 12th June
Bushehr

We walk with Ahmad along Bushehr's promenade. Cracked, crumbling buildings lie to our right, expressions of decay in brick and concrete. It is only early morning and already the asphalt is soft; a crazy steam rises from the pavement. On our left, over twisted iron railings, lies the Persian Gulf, a great brown plateful of polluted water, the same colour as a sky tainted by burning fuel and the aftermath of the Gulf War. A few children play in the remains of light industry on the shore, soft waves shredding themselves again and again on rusting metal, but otherwise the beach is as empty as the water. In this heat the sea will be the temperature of blood.

Bushehr sits on a promontory, and we follow its curving horn of land around into the old part of town. It is even more decrepit here than elsewhere. The world has left Bushehr behind, and it feels as if both the town and its inhabitants know it. We lean against the rails, cast our minds adrift, gaze out to sea. We are as near as we will come, on this trip, to the birthplace of Islam. Only two hundred kilometres across the water is the Arabian peninsula.

I have always known that following Islam through the Asian continent would bring with it its own inherent problems, not the least of which being that we will be unable to travel to the land that is home to this perplexing religion. Any investigation into Islam, no matter where, needs to look for some understanding of the land where Muhammad lived and died. I can, of course, say little of modern Saudi Arabia without travelling there myself. But in many ways modern Arabia is not important to this journey. Far more fundamental to an understanding of Islam, to the structure of Islam itself, is the life of pre-Islamic Arabia. The society that gave birth to Muhammad shaped both him and his religion, and many of its attitudes remain virtually unchanged in Muslim society today. This was the time Muslims now refer to as the *jahiliyya*, the dark age, the age of ignorance. An age waiting for a revolution.

Meccan Arab society, at the time of Muhammad's birth, was fiercely insular and tribal. To the Arabs of the time, the Arab nation was the noblest on earth, and fundamental to the pride of a tribe was its ancestry. Their political structure was rudimentary. *Sunna*, or custom, governed the day-to-day life of the tribe, the principle of following the practice and tradition set down by the tribal ancestors. The rules formed in the *sunna* were extremely arbitrary; the authority they held owed itself entirely to the overwhelming Arab respect for tradition. Their major function was as a replacement for any kind of central law. The world was of prevailing anarchy and warfare, with no central authority; the only restriction on complete chaos was the concept of blood-vengeance, the principle of avenging a murdered man in the slaughter of a member of his killer's tribe. Punishments of individuals did not exist. Justice was too easy to escape, and strong tribal bonds meant such measures were far more effective. The tradition of the blood feud and a general indifference to property encouraged a deep egalitarianism and an indifference to material goods among the early Arabs. Attitudes of generosity and largesse, with little thought for the consequences for the future, were a strong part of tribal culture.

The religion of the nomads was a type of paganism, focusing worship on beings who lived in single places; trees water and sacred stones, combined with a handful of gods whose powers were recognised beyond simple tribal boundaries. In many ways the gods of each tribe were less a religion than a badge of tribal loyalty. Loyalty to God was loyalty to tribe, and religion was a very political statement. In this atmosphere, apostasy meant a rejection of the tribal society, and was viewed in a way one might view treason. The grounding for some of Islam's traditions is already clear: today, apostasy can mean death.

This type of cultural relic appears often in Islam, with traditions of pre-Islamic Arabia surfacing in the religion itself. This is hardly unexpected. Throughout the early period of Islam's evolution, the beliefs and customs of the *jahiliyya*, the age of ignorance, remained vitally important. They were the rules of contemporary society; and would shape Islam as it grew. Muhammad's early community, known as the *ummah* – a name still applied to the global community of Islam today – supplemented rather than supplanted the social structures of pre-Islamic Arabia. Most of Muhammad's ideas remained within the structure of tribalism: his laws on property; on marriage; relations within the same tribe; apostasy; the principle of arbitration. Muhammad made many changes, but he was a shrewd politician, aware that the success of his ideas relied on their acceptance by a tribal society. Indeed, many of his changes would vanish after his death. Muhammad had attempted to use faith, rather than blood, as the bond that held society together, yet clan loyalties would be responsible for much of the power struggle between the early Caliphs and the eventually victorious Umayyads.

I think of the limits of the change one man can impose on an entire society. Muhammad shaped a social revolution, but his power was not complete, his influence not eternal. Many aspects of Islam today, both good and bad, owe themselves not to Muhammad, but to the society that was his audience, to the jahiliyya. Now, standing against a thin wind from across the Gulf, I remind myself that this awareness will have to guide my interpretations of all that I encounter of Islam.

We turn back towards the hotel. It is too hot for such musings, too hot for such meanderings.

Ahmad's wife has agreed to have us to stay; Ahmad organises a taxi to take us to his home. Our driver is an ex-policeman, a lumpy-faced man constructed from spoiled slabs of meat. He complains, the entire journey, that the Revolution has strayed far from its original ideals, that the new society of Khomeini has failed the people of Iran. It could be the story of any revolution, the story of Islam itself. No ideals are pure enough to remain forever; no revolution is permanent. Yet to hear such things from a stranger, in the politically crushing climate of Iran, in the company of a fellow Iranian, strikes us as strange. Kirst asks Ahmad how anyone can say such things, when Ahmad himself could easily be a government informer.

He shows us a smile without humour. "Everyone is unhappy in Iran. The government cannot arrest us all." He shrugs. "But even if everyone hates them, it cannot do us any good; we cannot hope for change. The mullahs have the guns in their hands and the money in their pockets. Why should they worry?"

The taxi driver says something, a grunt I cannot translate. I ask Ahmad what the man has said, and his reply carries a sound as dead as metal. "The best mullah is a dead mullah."

Khomeini Sighs

Tuesday 13th June – Wednesday 14th June
to Tehran

Tehran, "hot locality" in Farsi, less a city
than a sprawling slice of urban Iran. No centre, no focus,
endless. A place
(a place where the airport tourist office offers us money as a welcome)
of clamouring crowds, bullying buses, gossiping noise, metalwork,
"Hijab for Islam"
        "Bad hijab is prostitution"
                beneath silhouettes of covered female heads.
Khomeini stares, blue
        towering
        grim
        from murals large as buildings. Lodged in traffic,
        smeared sooty black, the pollution

> cough
> > the third worst
> wheeze
> > of any city in the world. Lodged in traffic,
> > angry hot bewildered, the bus driver leaves us
> for a cup of tea. Iran. Cannot catch Kirst's eye, she
> hidden behind a wall shadowy grey, the bus
> like all in Tehran,
> segregated.

Thursday 15th June
Tehran

> The nearer a man is to government, the further he is from God; the
> more followers he has, the more devils; the greater his wealth, the
> more exacting his reckoning.

> > > The Prophet Muhammad

Our ride to Imam Khomeini's tomb is organised for us for free by a stranger in the South Tehran bus terminal. "I am a Marxist," is his eager whisper, his words squeezed out sideways. "The government allows me to work nowhere other than here."

The tomb, lonely and isolated, sits in the desert just south of Tehran on the highway to Qom. Our bus slows to a halt in the sunburnt dust, intent on its journey ahead. A quick scrape of gravel as the bus pulls out, stretches away from us, leaves us standing in the dust. Nobody has stepped off with us. We have been deposited in a landscape as ugly as an open cut mine. Sand deserts at least lay claim to a lyric emptiness, but this world, of hard dirt and torn stone, free of vegetation, is grotesque.

We cross the road towards the indomitable shrine. It is more a construction site than anything holy. Its dome and minarets are clad in bronze, and small parts of the courtyard have been tiled a Persian blue, but the rest is cement rendering, rusted scaffolding and unfinished walls. The echoes of our footsteps are lost into a courtyard designed to hold thousands, now filled with the sense of their absence. We are completely alone. Can this be the final monument to the man whose Islamic Revolution gave birth to the Iran of today? Blind loudspeakers, oblivious to their lack of audience, issue an incessant tirade into the air, a speech so monotonic it could be an incantation. Khomeini's voice, calling the faithful to the Revolution? Or a minor functionary, exhorting the public not to litter? The voice drones on, lost in a desert deaf to sound, emptied into the world with not a soul to hear. The scene cannot possibly be real. The seeds of the Islamic Revolution were planted long before Khomeini started preaching his revolutionary message. It was clear to most Iranians, in the years before the Revolution, that their country was being sucked dry by foreign powers, with a corrupt and brutal government propped up by the West. All attempts at an equitable deal for oil had been crushed by Britain and the US. The Iranian Prime Minister who fought hardest for the rights of his people, Muhammad Mossadegh, was ousted with the covert aid of the CIA. And the Shah was removed from reality, living a life of luxury and extravagance while his secret police tortured his subjects. Iran was crying for a revolutionary figure, someone strong enough to defy the regime. Strict, uncompromising, strong: Khomeini fitted the bill.

Yet the yearning in Iranian society was more complicated than simple rebellion against the regime. Somehow, Khomeini persuaded Iran that Islam itself was a revolutionary act, that only Islam could save the country. Something in his message touched an emotion far deeper than a dissatisfaction with the Shah. Something persuaded thousands of Iranians to risk their lives to call for a return to ancient laws that would restrict their freedom, remove the rights of their women, return them to a world of chadors, child marriage and wife beating, a world of war, violence and martyrdom.

The search for someone like Khomeini has not been restricted to Iran. In the last century Islamic nations all across the world have witnessed the cultural rupture of rapid modernisation, of societies fuelled by oil and driven by greed. Every country has had to suffer intimidation by foreign powers, to feel the sense of helplessness and shame at being unable, despite independence, to determine their own future. Almost every Muslim country has known the pain of living under headstrong regimes whose policies have only brought poverty and tyranny, whose armies have brought repression. As a result, the entire Islamic world has witnessed a frantic search, amongst some for culprits, amongst others for saviours.

There is, of course, a difference between what these feelings have generated in most Islamic countries and what they produced in Iran; the difference may lie in the Shi'a mythology more peculiar to Iran than anywhere else. Throughout history, the Messianic concept of the Mahdi, the righteous one who will appear to usher in an era of truth and justice, has inspired Shi'ites far more than any other branch of Islam. The idea found a resonance in their yearning for the return of the Twelfth Imam, and has become part of the backbone of their religion.

The notion of the Mahdi has provided a promise of hope, but also uncertainty, to Muslim society. Unlike Christianity, the hoped-for return would not be the return of the divine, but of an ordinary mortal, divinely appointed to avenge wrong, correct injustice and restore the Islamic ideal. The obscurity of his origins and necessary vagueness surrounding his identity enhanced his mystique, and ensured the recurrent success of the idea. Any person, no matter who they were, could assume the role if the situation demanded it. The Mahdi was thus a destabilising force in Islamic history, a figure not content to suffer the rule of corrupt or improper government.

It was to a society with these beliefs that the call for opposition to the Shah came from Imam Khomeini. To a people waiting eleven hundred years for the return of the Twelfth Imam, *Imam* was a loaded word, Khomeini an almost holy figure. To Khomeini's most devout followers, it was clear: he was the Mahdi, chosen by God to right the wrongs of their age. Khomeini's word was the word of God.

Not all, however, felt that Khomeini was their saviour. Like Farzaneh in Esfahan, many Iranians felt only that he was an acceptable figurehead, and would retire as a ceremonial figure once the Revolution was over. Even the Communist movement, archly atheist, worked hand in hand with the Islamists, understanding that the only way to oppose the Shah was in unity. Now, with people like the Communists hunted down, imprisoned, and expelled from their jobs like our Marxist friend in the bus station, many who supported Khomeini are questioning their wisdom.

I raise my face to the sky, to the four lustrous minarets reaching towards it. Clouds are driven on the wind above us, soft creatures of disquiet trying to flee this eerie place. We cross the courtyard, creep through the only open archway, and find a different world waiting for us in the shrine's northern courtyard. Here the building is just as raw and unfinished, but it is almost a relief to discover that we are not the only people present, to find couples playing with their children on manicured lawns, sitting around large pools of still water, removing their shoes to enter the shrine itself. We follow the meagre crowd through our separate entrances, deposit our shoes, suffer our searches in silence, and are waved through into the final domain of Iran's most famous *Ayatollah*, or "reflection of God."

I stand at the threshold of a vast country, trying to absorb the vision before my eyes. I am stunned, lost. After the fragile blue wonder of Esfahan, the heady smell of God in the tomb in Shiraz, Khomeini's tomb is a savage disappointment. It holds the atmosphere of a huge suburban shopping centre, modern and vacant and tasteless. Its floor, wide and flat, is of a shiny fake marble; children kick footballs across it, sliding and screaming. The ceiling is a tangled mass of scaffolding, air conditioner ducting and glass, and the walls are embedded with clouded plastic that admits a gaudy, pinkish light. I have expected a place of reverence, prepared myself for an air thick with religious awe. Nothing has hinted at anything so banal.

Even more difficult to wrap my mind around is the emptiness of the place: the vast floor is only sparsely spotted with bodies. There is probably a modest crowd, one made thin by the enormity of this steel and cement cavern, but I cannot reconcile what I see with the unforgettable scenes of mourning at the Imam's death, of the largest funeral the world has ever seen, of continual remembrances in his honour every year. The few groups which are here, camped on rugs dotted around the area, seem to me less in mourning than here for pleasure, visiting the site as part of a pleasant day's outing.

In the middle of the open floor, beneath black hanging drapes and a vast and garish chandelier, is the tomb itself. We walk towards it. It is a lattice cage, like the tomb in Shiraz, but made from cast aluminium, hard-edged and simple, not sculpted silver. Perspex shielding lines the cage, and we gaze through grubby plastic to the tomb. This, at least, is real marble. Money litters the floor around it, with gaps in the perspex provided for the faithful to make their donations.

A small group is huddled around the tomb; we stand near to watch. They are all women, wrapped in black, wailing with torn Iranian grief as they push money through the perspex. They carry none of the emotional power, none of the intensity, of the scene in Shiraz: these are quiet tears, this is controlled passion. But it is passion nonetheless, a snippet of the grief I had expected to find. Some, it seems, still care for their Imam.

The subdued, uncrowded scene is far removed from my imaginings. The comparison with Shiraz is the most telling. Mir Ahmad was merely the brother of an ancient religious leader, a minor figure in the Shi'a faith, while the scene here belongs to Iran's great and glorious leader. A few fathers lift their sons to the window to glimpse a piece of their country's history; some youths try to brush their faces with the Imam's still lingering holiness, and a few weeping women purchase favours from their saint. The Iranian remembrance of Khomeini is muted and shallow, and is very disappointing.

I know what my Iranian friends would tell me. They would say that the people around us are only here in their own interest, for political reasons, to get ahead in government, to push for promotions in their jobs. Who can say? The emotion here has a different texture from what we have seen elsewhere, certainly, but the tears seem real to me, the passion genuine if restrained. Is it an act? In this land of mutual suspicion and fake emotion, I no longer feel I can tell. Iranians would claim that the women weeping before us are part of a peculiarly Iranian performance. But is it an act when the entire world is in the play? When the whole world is false, is there any difference between appearance and reality?

Friday 16th June
Tehran

Today we received the news that Kirst has been dreading. Post-graduate admissions have just been announced at home, and she must return to Australia from Pakistan, to complete the final qualifications of her law degree. She will finish some time in December, and will be able to meet me in Jakarta, but her journey has effectively been cut short by four months, sliced almost in half.

The news, when it came, precipitated a flood of tears and anguish, and I have spent the remainder of the day comforting her. She had hoped to be admitted four months later, enabling her to complete the journey with me, and she is heart-broken. Even now, after discussing it for hours, she is liable to begin crying at any time. What can I say about my own feelings? That I am terrified of being alone, that I will miss her desperately, that the absence of the laughter and joy of travelling with her will leave me empty for four months? I know all these things are true, but I cannot truly imagine them, feel unable to picture the suddenness of being on my own. And I know that they are only half the truth. I know, and I think Kirst suspects, that part of me is thrilled by the thought of travelling on my own once more. This kind of emotional blindness has happened to me before: I cannot visualise sadness until it is upon me, yet I find it easy to imagine the romance of travelling alone, to wait eagerly for the empty independence of thought and deed that comes with solitude. I know that the time will have its pain, but for the moment all I can fully imagine is its pleasure. Lone travel is a strange beast. One is sentenced, in countries without fellow travellers, to a humourless existence, lacking a companion to share the endless joke of a travelling life. Yet the world is so much more open and penetrable, strangers so much more eager to share their secrets, that the balance between the advantages and disadvantages of travelling alone is difficult to judge.

I can, of course, say none of this to Kirst. The admission that I see a positive side to her departure would seem like a betrayal. I instead keep my thoughts to myself, and we try to focus our attention on our remaining time together.

Saturday 17th June
Tehran

The women dance with arms held at length, clicking their fingers; their faces, painted and bright, are flushed with alcohol. The eyes of the men shine with smuggled whiskey as they join in. All are clad in Western clothes; we have never seen this much female Iranian hair. The music is as loud as the laughter, and the conversation becomes more and more animated as the night wears on. Smiles widen, mouths whisper close into ears, the alcohol takes its toll. A voice chokes with distress over the noise, with fear of the Komité, the dreaded Revolutionary Guards, guardians of all things Islamically proper in post-Revolutionary Iran. It is ignored; the party continues.

The scene shifts, jumps; the shot changes to a close-up of a swaying rump, viewed from near the ground. Mahmud waits for this final provocative dance to finish, then switches off the video. "It only gets boring from here. You know what parties are like."

Mahmud owns a spare parts store not far from our hotel. We have passed his office every morning, also passing his perpetual insistence that we come back to his house for dinner, in Tehran's luxurious northern suburbs. Even in downtown Tehran we cannot escape Iranian hospitality. I glance at his face now, registering how it betrays his background of wealth. His eyes are baubles of contentment set in bunches of well-fed flesh; he smiles the smile of a man to whom the world holds no threat. No older than we are, Mahmud is round, not in a flabby sort of way, just firmly round. If he were an insect, I would be tempted to classify him as an entirely different species from the Iranians who live and work in our hotel, gap-toothed and thin. His apartment, within the Iranian constraints of embargoes, sanctions and poverty, expresses opulence and ease. Wide and open and Western, it is more full of furniture than carpets, spotted with the spoils of the modern era: stereo and television, video recorder and microwave, arranged with the tables, chairs, couches and bookshelves that are found in very few Iranian households. Antique mirrors and silver candelabra, simple and tasteful. Our journey here was a long one, through tree-lined streets, past comfortable apartment blocks. These were buildings which we gazed at in envy yesterday, when we were in the north to visit the museum of the Shah's palace. We hoped vainly for someone to invite us inside, to offer us a vision of life in that other Iran, the Iran of Tehran's North; we even hoped for a glimpse of one of the illicit parties still held, as every Iranian knows, in these neighbourhoods. So when Mahmud offered us a video of his last birthday party, we eagerly agreed.

Mahmud walks to the kitchen, calls out, "Would you like a beer? Or a gin?" The punishment for drinking alcohol, even for us, is a flogging, but the temptation of flouting the laws of the Islamic Republic is too strong to resist. I request a beer; Mahmud will later tell me that its bulk and difficulty in smuggling means that beer is far more expensive than straight spirits. Kirst refuses, aware that the pink smell of alcohol on our breaths, in a country empty of it, will be impossible to miss.

"Come on!" urges Mahmud. "You can't come to a barbecue without having a beer! Nobody is going to find out – we drink it all the time." She agrees to a sip, no more.

Almost unnoticed, the afternoon vanishes, and offers its place to evening. Mahmud's friend Reza arrives to complete our strange little troupe. Reza is a huge man, hewn of stone and sharpened at the edges, with bulging eyes and a wide mouth that belong on some kind of amphibian. He is lost in the company of English-speakers, and heralds a mute conversation of senseless smiles and nods and maddening politeness. Downstairs, in the apartment car park, the two men drink beers with us over roasting kebabs. Iron gates hide us from the street outside, but not from the dark sky, the stars, or from the apartments of those around us. Yet the easy abandon of the two men gradually loosens the tension inside me, and my unease about committing a crime in full view slowly fades. Over the sizzle of meat and the smell of smoke, the conversation returns to the realities of social life in Tehran.

"We have these parties all the time," says Mahmud, to a dumb nod from Reza, the golem, the figure of stone magically brought to life. "What do you think, that we don't have fun in Iran?"

To have thought such a thing would not have been completely ridiculous:

six months after the Revolution, Khomeini declared on national radio, "There is no fun in Islam." And his administration, his Komité, his army of mullahs and government officials, have always been there to ensure that it stayed that way.

"Yes, yes, sometimes we get in trouble, sure. The noise is the big worry; we must rely on everybody in the building not to telephone the police," Mahmud explains, his voice casual. He shrugs. "Most of the time it is no problem. Everybody understands; besides, they want to have their own parties too."

"But sometimes it is a problem? "

Mahmud's eyes roll. He crosses to the barbecue, pokes at one of the kebabs. The barbecue is merely a narrow box of thin metal, set on two bricks and filled with glowing coals; smoke leaks into the night as he fans their warmth. For a moment I think he is not going to answer; when he speaks, his voice is a blend of fear and mischief.

"Yes, it sometimes happens. The party just after the one I show you." He pauses, seems to roll a memory around in his mind until it gathers the smoothness and momentum he requires. Something about it gives him pleasure: he grins roguishly. "It was not here, it was at my friend's place. We were lucky, because the party had finished mostly, and just four of us were staying there. We were complete drunk. Rolling around drunk, you know?" And then the note of bitterness. "The man downstairs is a bastard. Complete bastard. He calls the police... wham! Four of us in jail."

Mahmud turns to me. I cannot tell if it is anger or laughter in his eyes. "Do you know what the punishment is for this sort of thing? We get whipped." His shudder is intended to be melodramatic, but I can see the fear beneath it.

"And did you get whipped?"

"No, this is what I am telling you. We get some money, we bribe the mullah." The carefree voice has returned. "No problem."

"Is it so easy to bribe mullahs?" For weeks we have been hearing of their corruption, but this is the first encounter to verify it by direct experience. Mahmud's reply fits with everything we have heard.

"This is Iran! Mullahs are the most corrupt of anyone. So it makes it easy for us; if you have the money, you never have to worry about your party. You can always bribe these bastards." He grins with an exquisite malevolence. "But the man who report us, he is not so lucky. He should know how things work; these people are the lowest under this regime, everybody hates them. My friend, he is rich, he paid the bribe, but he also paid someone else. This man, soon he will have his bones broken."

The regime has spent enormous time and effort trying to eliminate the hedonistic pleasures of its subjects; as with most things in Iran, its ire has fallen most heavily on women rather than men. Young unmarried women found at parties are automatically given virginity tests. If they do not pass, they are given a choice between a hundred lashes and forcibly marrying the man they are found with at the party. Unless, of course, they can afford a bribe. Earlier, just after we arrived, Mahmud was visited briefly by his girlfriend, Mernush. Bold, rebellious, standing unveiled before us, she struck me as precisely the kind of woman to suffer the most under the restrictions of the Iranian government. I ask Mahmud about the difficulties involved with trying to get a relationship like his to work.

He shrugs casually. "It is no problem. Or perhaps I should say it is not too difficult. I know it was bad just after the Revolution, but I was only a small boy then: the whole thing was just a game, a reason I didn't have to go to school. But nowadays we can have our parties, or a girlfriend, much easier than ten years ago. For the last five years, we are hardly ever stopped when we are with a woman. But you know," he says, his smile declaring that the game has not finished, "we still have to be a little careful. You know – not wearing Western clothes, not laughing in public, that sort of thing. If you can do that, then you've got these bastards fooled. Mernush comes here all the time, we walk out together, it is no problem. At least, not in North Tehran."

From what we have seen of Tehran's northern suburbs, Mahmud is right. North Tehran is a place wrenched from the heart of Europe and crudely inserted into an Eastern world. Constructed with oil money by men and women more at ease with the West than with Islam, it is a place of wide avenues, gardens and trees, fast-food restaurants and Western tastes. Here, fashion stores line the streets; the rich and trendy youth of Tehran meet and gossip together freely; boy and girl sit together in restaurants, sharing pizzas and cokes. Chadors are rare, and beneath well-cut manteau are likely to be the latest fashions from Europe. The southern city, in dazzling contrast, is an Eastern city, of open drains, narrow alleys, chaos and noise and crime, bare and muddy and treeless. It is where our hotel lies, amidst the insane traffic and noise around Imam Khomeini Square; it belongs to the rest of Iran. It is a terrible, screaming place, a place of poverty and religion, and yet it is a place which, burning with faith, has toppled this northern world. It is the city of the south, with the mentality of the East and the mind of Islam, that rules Iran today.

Separating us from the southern city, the region we would recognise as Iran, is the massive sprawling corpse of Tehran itself, spread along the longest avenue in the world. By the time we prepare to make the long drive it is almost midnight, and our two companions stagger, giggling with mischief, to the car. They have not drunk enough for such an intoxicated performance; their enjoyment is in the act, not the alcohol. We climb inside the car, sharply conscious of the smell of beer.

Mahmud turns to face us, his eyes lazy, his voice slurred. "Let's hope we don't get stopped by the police."

The journey is filled as much with the fear of Reza's driving as of the authorities: our tyres screech as we loop across the street and hurtle down the wrong side of a four-lane highway. Kirst grips my arm, her nails biting. We peer through darkened and empty streets for any sign of the police, shout as we lurch down narrow alleys to escape road blocks. Just as eerie are the crowds in black, the remnants from the Ashura celebrations, wandering the streets mournfully beneath black banners and bright lights. We hide from these bands too, and by the time we reach our ghostly street my heart thumps at me through my veins. We smuggle ourselves past the hotel reception, holding our breath tight in our lungs.

Word of God

Sunday 18th June – Monday 19th June
to Tabriz

We have spent the morning discovering that our journey back to Tabriz has been a complete waste of time. We came in the hope of participating in an annual pilgrimage of Armenian Christians to a church in the mountains around Tabriz, but after a morning of blank looks and shrugged shoulders we have discovered that the pilgrimage is not for another month. In fact, the only thing the last two days have accomplished is allowing me to make a start on my attempt to read the Qur'an. Until now it has been sending me to sleep every time I have opened it.

We will leave for the Caspian Sea tomorrow. With little to do until then, we amble back to the bazaar, in search of Nasser, our first enthusiastic welcome to Iran.

We find him in his shop, surrounded by the old watches, the broken clocks, which listened to our conversations with him almost a month ago. Then, he seemed an answer to our prayers, a confirmation that Iran wasn't going to be as frightening as we had feared, a broad face filled with kindness and geniality. Now, though he is amiable as ever, we are better able to judge. We have seen Iranian hospitality at work, have grown to expect it in those we meet. Beneath Nasser's welcome lies the saddening feeling that he views his geniality more as a duty than a pleasure.

"So, my friends! How have you enjoyed Iran so far? The boy will bring us tea."

Nasser's main concern is that his fellow countrymen have treated us well, in a way befitting an Islamic country. Yet throughout the conversation he is uneasy, distracted, speaking with an odd formality, as though someone more important has just entered the room. He discharged his religious duty to us a month ago; he retains only a residual interest in us now.

"And Ashura? Did you see?"

"We couldn't miss it. We were stuck in Shiraz for a week while the city closed down."

"And you enjoy? I tell you would find it fascinating."

"It was fascinating."

Nasser sips his tea through a hard rock of sugar. After four weeks I have only just mastered the skill myself. "Every year I am in this marching," he says. "It is very important to the Shi'a people."

Nasser is the first participant in the marches we have met whom I feel I can trust. I am therefore quick to phrase the question that has been nagging me ever since Shiraz. I want to know if what we have been told about the marches is true, whether the participants really are induced by the government, whether the suspicion and distrust is justified. He looks blank, stunned. "No. This is not true." He shrugs his shoulders, mystified. An exasperated expression has taken hold of his face. "Why would it be true? This is our religion! Why would the government need to do this? We get barbecue, but…" He opens his palms, as if to show how little the government has given him. His eyes lose their focus as he gazes out the window, seeming to contemplate the proposal. When he returns to us, his expression is filled with the kind of mistrust we have come to expect from Iran. "What was their profession, these people?" he asks archly, eyebrows raised. The truth doesn't really matter in Iran; it is what other people suspect that counts.

Tuesday 20th June – Thursday 22nd June
to Sari

A rat has just run along the wall by my bed. Our hotel room is sordid and musty, littered with cockroaches, and the smell of mould and damp is of clothes shut in a cellar for fifty years. My skin creeps away from the bed as I write.

The last few days have been a monotonous blur. A purposeless journey through the green rice paddies of Iran's Caspian coast, stunned by the contrast with the desert dryness but struggling to find anywhere to stay. Arrival in Sari, the wet heat of the sea still weighing on the air. Tedious to experience, even more tedious to relive and describe. At least the journey allowed me to complete my appraisal of the Qur'an, the only thing of substance to have filled these last few days. I reached the final chapters this afternoon.

My first reaction to the Muslim holy book has been one that is shared by many Western readers. Its arguments seem crude and simplistic, the narrative overly repetitive. Montgomery Watt, an Orientalist, attacked the Qur'an for a lack of logic and method in its arguments; Carlyle saw it as "a wearisome, confused jumble; crude, recondite."

Chapter after chapter describe Paradise as a place of "gardens watered by running streams", where the faithful will be tended by "dark-eyed houris", where fruit and water will be in plenty. A Paradise aimed at people of the desert, presented again and again. Tales drawn from biblical stories grow familiar through constant repetition. Muhammad's arguments for the existence of God seem inordinately simplistic: he does little other than point to the 'signs' of God's existence on page after page:

By another sign of His you sleep at night and seek by day his bounty.
Surely there are signs in this for those who hear.

The Qur'an, 30:23

Among His signs is the creation of the heavens and the earth, and the
living things which He has dispersed over them.

The Qur'an, 42:30

Lightning is yet another of his signs, inspiring you with fear and hope.
He sends down water from the sky, and with it He quickens the earth
after its death. Surely in this there are signs for men of understanding.

The Qur'an, 30:24

Yet it is not the lack of convincing logic in its arguments that grates, but
its stultifying repetitiveness: each statement is repeated dozens of times,
each claim to God's power on earth re-phrased again and again. The
legislative rulings are of interest, detailing God's will on many subjects –
sexual intercourse, adultery, women, alcohol, inheritance, prayer, justice -
but these discussions are embedded so deeply in the text that I must
wade through endless chapters of sameness to find them.

I know, of course, that I have done the Qur'an an injustice; that I, like
thousands before me, have failed in my approach. The Qur'an was never
meant to be read in translation. It was never intended as a logical
argument meant to convince unbelievers of the existence of God. And,
most important of all, it was never meant to be simply read.

The Qur'an did not exist in the form of a book during Muhammad's
lifetime. His revelations followed each other at various intervals, and did
not come to him in the order I read today but in a random manner, as
contemporary events inspired him to listen to the voice of God.
Muhammad could neither read nor write, and the revelations were at first
committed to memory by the early Muslims; even today the ability to
learn the Qur'an by heart is a point of pride. In Muhammad's time, verses
began to be written on palm-leaves, stones, broken bits of pottery,
shoulder bones of sheep: any available material. Their collection was only
completed after Muhammad's death, during the Caliphate of Umar, and a
fully authorised version was only established under Uthman, some twenty
years after Muhammad's death. No chronological order is followed in its
chapters, or surah, which are instead arranged arbitrarily in order of
length, the longest chapters first and shortest ones last, some of which
are no longer than a couple of lines. This fact alone removes any
emphasis on a strict linear narrative, on any structure designed for
coherent argument.

To a Muslim this is not a problem, for the Qur'an is neither narrative nor
argument. Muhammad did not have to prove the existence of God to the
Quraysh; the existence of al-Lah as the prime force behind the world was

already accepted. Muhammad's arguments are intended only as reminders of how worthy God is of worship, reminders that those who do not pay God his due have surely strayed from the true path. The existence of God is never in question.

My inability to appreciate the Qur'an, however, comes from a far more fundamental source than simply a limited understanding of Muhammad's aims. I understand these aims. My failure comes from the form of the Qur'an itself.

The early biographers of Muhammad often describe the amazement, bordering on shock, experienced by the early Arabs upon hearing the Qur'an for the first time. Many were converted immediately because to them, only God could account for the beauty of the language. The Qur'an repeatedly makes reference to this phenomenon, claiming its own existence as the surest sign from God, a wonder that is akin to magic. To someone who cannot feel the glowing beauty of the Arabic, the Qur'an offers nothing of this experience, offers no taste of the divine sweeping through their soul, and is little more than a jumble of arguments and ancient tales. This is why Muslims are not meant to read it in translation, the way I am doing. There is too much opportunity for inconsistency, too little opportunity to be awed by the language. Yet even this does not fully account for the power of the book. Even in Arabic the Qur'an was not meant for private perusal but for liturgical recitation of the most public kind. The chanting of a *surah* in the mosque can remind Muslims of the entirety of their faith, can strike to their core and touch the part of their soul in constant wonder and awareness of God. Muslims are taught *how* to read the Qur'an; many chant it out loud, swaying back and forth, trance-like, in rapture. The experience is more powerful than a mere book; it is an experience of God himself. Not all Muslims speak Arabic fluently enough to appreciate its language, to hear it as a transcription of God's very being, but the discipline of their approach to the book focuses their mind on God just the same, carries them into a realm of transcendence in a manner more akin to meditation than reading.

Reading the Qur'an is a spiritual discipline as much as anything else. Westerners, with a history rooted in Christianity, find this a difficult concept to grasp, not least because we have nothing that approaches a holy language, no text that is holy in and of itself. We have nothing to echo the power that Hebrew, Sanskrit and Arabic hold for Jews, Hindus and Muslims. For Christians, there is nothing sacred about the Greek of the New Testament: it is Jesus who is the Word of God, and the concept of language as holy is foreign. As I struggle through these final *surah* I am aware of a sense I do not possess, a gaping hole inside my soul which renders me unable to fully appreciate what I read. I have reached the limits that constrain all outside observers of Islam, crept to a boundary beyond which I cannot, or dare not, step. I know already that this boundary will remain, no matter how long I make this journey, no matter how much I learn. It is impossible to fully understand Islam without *being* a Muslim, impossible to fully comprehend al-Lah without believing in him. I can hope to come close, but full conquest is beyond me.

Friday 23rd June – Monday 26th June
to Yazd

The desert howls around us. Sand whips across our vision; everything outside is the colour of dust. Cars, bricks, roads, people: all are dimmed, diminished, washed with a pale brush. And the white heat of the desert is frightening. Our two-day journey to the south-east wastes has only just begun.

A micro-community has formed around us already; it happens on every journey in Iran. A family across the aisle, a young couple behind us, their parents, the bus conductor, us. We are fed at every juncture: salted cucumbers, pistachios, Iranian sweets, cherries. They have all brought far more than they could have possibly consumed themselves, simply in order to be able to share. We have been in Iran long enough to have learnt to do the same, and supply the others with food of our own. An utterly unnecessary exercise – I don't want to eat so much food – but strangely comforting. More and more, we feel we belong.

Morning. We stop for prayer. On such a long journey, the rhythm of such interruptions is both noticeable and welcome. I disembark with the faithful, wash my feet as they do, wash my hands, the back of my neck. It is a nice time, full of a sense of community and togetherness. And for an infidel it is a time to stop, stretch, refresh.

"*Shoma mussulman ast?*"

The voice is dry and distant, empty of emotion. It asks if I am a Muslim.

I turn slowly. Before me is a mullah, one we have only recently realised occupies a seat in the back of our bus. This is the first time I have truly seen him. He is tall, his features more northern Mongol than classically Aryan. Between camel-coloured cape and doughy white turban is a round face, set with a beard of whisper thinness. He has eyes the colour of smoked glass, and the overwhelming effect is of some kind of reptile.

No, I say.

He nods, offering a tiny, Oriental smile. A small crowd gathers while we talk, while we attempt, in fumbling Farsi, to communicate. His accent is even stranger than the rasping lisp we found on the Caspian coast, and I am unable to progress further than basic politeness, a handful of useless questions about religion. I leave him to his prayers, and return to the bus. Our seat is directly behind the driver, and I sit watching for the mullah to return. I want to offer him a symbol, to witness his response; I want to show him our copy of the Qur'an.

I know that Muslims have to purify themselves before reading or even touching the Qur'an. The book itself, in any incarnation, is regarded as so holy that formal rules of conduct define how to handle it, how to behave in its presence. It is unclear how these rules apply to translations. I have read that a Muslim would be "shocked rather than flattered" by a non-Muslim pulling out a Qur'an for a quick read while not in wudu, the state of Quranic grace, but the temptation is too strong. When that reptilian face returns, I offer it my English copy of the book, battered and torn and quite clearly mistreated.

He gazes at me sternly, eyes impenetrable. He takes the book in both hands, his movements slow and thick with ritual. The grubby cover moves to his lips, touches his forehead, returns to me. And that gaze, those eyes absorbing light like those of a cat.

"Shoma mussulman," he says, the Oriental smile on his face once more. You are a Muslim. He stalks to the back of the bus.

He is mistaken. I am not a Muslim. Yet only one thing lies between me and membership of the ummah, the world-wide community of Islam of which this man is part. It is the Shahadah, the first pillar of Islam, the Muslim profession of faith. It is the honest pronouncement of the words: "I bear witness that there is no god but al-Lah and that Muhammad is his messenger."

No god but God. The eternal Muslim pun.

Yazd, its yellow alleys timeless and eternal. Yazd has a modern façade, with main streets of petrol fumes and the bustle of modern Iran, but it is only a façade, nothing more. Behind it lies the soft silence of mud alleys, as calming as a drug, as addictive as love or heroin. The blue of the sky is seamless, just like the mud walls of our camel-coloured world. Further south, in the town of Bam, we visit an impossibly preserved citadel, lonely ramparts the colour of straw, scorched motionless by heat and time and a waterless sky. There, ghosts of people long dead surrounded us, but in Yazd the ghosts drifting through the streets, clad in black, are real. We trail the narrow and winding paths, beneath arches of caked mud, past ancient carved doors studded with brass. Apparitions in black float through alleys ahead of us, vanish suddenly around hidden corners, appear behind. Always just out of reach, unattainable. A glimpse through a doorway, a sliver of a private Iranian world. As the day cools, women gossip on the steps of these hidden houses; young girls vanish at the sound of our approach.

At some stage in our wanderings, I do not know when, we stumble upon a middle-aged woman, bent over a pile of boxes and rusted metal. She wears a faded blue floral dress, the kind that belongs on a farm in Australia; she is not veiled. A rush, not of surprise but of guilt. We have not seen female hair in public for over a month; the sight shocks us as much as it would an Iranian, it is as shocking as seeing a naked woman on a city street. Despite lifetimes in Australia, the sight of a woman's hair now fills us with fear and awe: such is the power of cultural conditioning. The woman is not real; she has slipped through a crack in space. And like everything else in these alleys, she vanishes.

Cruelty And Sadness

Tuesday 27th June
Yazd

Today, after a month in the country, we confront the dark side of Iran. We have been lulled into a sense of complacency by our welcome here; today was a reminder that there is another side to the country.

A lone woman in a billowing chador confronts us in the morning outside Yazd's subterranean bazaar. She has the sharp movements of a bird; in her hazel eyes is the sort of look of apprehension which can make complete strangers apprehensive too. Her fist gathers the cloth of her veil beneath her chin as she speaks, twisting it, knotting it, tirelessly fidgeting. It is rare for a lone woman to have the boldness to approach us in the streets, yet this woman, Nasreen, does not appear bold, and she seems unlikely to defy social mores. And then she reveals that her husband used to beat her, that he was addicted to LSD. In the uncomfortable silence which follows, Nasreen invites us to her house for dinner.

Darkness, like a silence, has settled over Yazd by the time we begin the search for Nasreen's house. It lies in the old city, on the edge of the earthen labyrinth yet close enough to the modern world to be on a street wide enough for a vehicle. The lights of a stationary car play on dusty air to produce a golden haze, making vision difficult; boys materialise to play a sudden game of football in its glare. The sounds of their feet scrabbling on ancient caked mud echo behind us as we wait at the heavy iron gates of Nasreen's house.

They open an inch, spilling a private light out into the night. Beneath the low fringe of a pale chador, I can make out a single eye, framed by metal. Nasreen pauses, glaring anxiously at something over our shoulders, then opens the door wide enough for us to slip through. We cross the bare Iranian garden, remove our shoes, enter the house. I think once more that Nasreen has a touch of bird about her – darting, blue-black, vivacious in a nervous way – as she leads us in. She attaches herself to Kirst's arm. "Did you see how people looked at you as you entered? Was it bad? I worry that they chatter behind the back of me."

Nasreen's house is like any Iranian's: open, with hand-knotted carpets covering the floor, almost without furniture, its simplicity an embarrassing reminder of the profligacy of our own lives are in the West. I often contemplate how easy it would be to shock these people with our lives, how superfluous all our belongings seem. The difference is somehow even more acute than if we were surrounded by true poverty. I am accustomed to making allowances for poverty, but not for the middle class. Nasreen's house is more crowded than most: a sofa, a small table, a faded photograph of a bearded mullah on the wall. Nasreen insists we sit on the sofa, while her family crowd around us on the floor like awed children. Nasreen introduces us: her uncle, a tight effigy of a man, straight and erect; Nasreen's mother, the woman with the agile eyebrows and a ready chortle; her younger brother, the serious youth. And, briefly, three generations stand before us when Nasreen's grandmother appears, the matriarch of this family, the mould from which these women were taken, thick-legged and thick-faced. The three are so similar they could be images of a single woman taken from different stages of life. The matriarch is the least concerned about Islamic propriety of the three, only occasionally imitating the others as they clutch at their pale cream chadors, constantly pulling them forwards over their heads as they slip. She reveals pigtail plaids of a straw-coloured blonde, dark grey at the roots, the schoolgirl style utterly incongruous on a seventy year-old woman. And she laughs and giggles in the role, this ancient Iranian version of Heidi, as does the mother, even the uncle. Only the younger generation, Nasreen and her brother, seem to have absorbed the seriousness of modern Iran.

Nasreen clings to an English-Farsi dictionary, her guide through the labyrinth of conversation; she finds the word 'depressed', points us to it. "My husband, he was too cruel to me," she says. He beat me, beat me, all the time. He take drugs, and he beat me. Now what can I do? I am sad, every time. But now you are here, you make me happy."

Her face beams at our presence yet trembles perpetually close to tears. It is a face I can imagine weeping through a radiant smile; a face which, like those of certain dogs, relaxes most comfortably to an expression of mournfulness. "I can only be happy with my Australian friends. Kirsty, who looks like Mary. Yes! So beautiful, you are Mary, mother of Jesus. I must make more tea." She stands, leaves the room, and commands her relatives into a frantic bustle. They will be present only occasionally for the rest of the evening, remaining on the move as they cater to their impressions of our needs. I look at Kirst. Small, pale, blue-eyed, her brown hair light by Iranian standards; through my biased eyes she is beautiful. But to Nasreen and all the Iranian women we meet, she is something more. To them, she cradles the dangerous essence of the exotic. She is as foreign and unreachable to them as those gypsy shadows outside in black, with their hidden dark eyes, are to me.

I look around the room, find my eyes drawn back to the faded mullah's face glaring portentously down at us, bruised eyes wedged above a white beard. I wonder who he was, what he would think of Nasreen emptying her secrets to us. I have forever bemoaned the impossibility of being able to truly thrust myself under the skin of a country, to have true access to the thoughts of its people. I have yearned for the insight of a native instead of the cold role of the outsider. Yet on rare occasions it works the other way around. In countries like Iran, land of distrust and suspicion and wary backward glances, some people feel able to expose themselves to outsiders more than they ever would to each other. We stand outside the structure of Iranian society, sometimes learning things forbidden. And so it is with Nasreen.

She returns, bearing tea and delicate plates of poached fruit, and gestures that we should sit on the carpet to eat. There, on carpets of indigo and crimson, beneath the watchful gaze of the mullah, the garden outside filled with the unidentifiable sounds of night, Nasreen tells us her story. Her husband worked in America for ten years, she tells us; when he returned, he was addicted to LSD. He had changed in other ways too, had become cruel. She tells us her stories of beatings, of torture, of years of entrapment and helplessness, of the escape of divorce. Her piercing sorrow now is that he still has their children, that she had not known the Iranian laws specifying that children can live with their mother after a divorce if the father is a drug addict. As she tells her story, velvet tears, Iranian tears, silent, trace their way down her face. These are the tears of Shi'a mourning, only here they are not religious. "My husband," Nasreen cries, her breath caught somewhere in her chest, "he puts out cigarette in my daughters arms." She pauses, rifling through her dictionary for a word. "My husband, he is a *sadist*."

I am always at a loss for a response when confronted by another's suffering. It may come from a lack of tragedy in my own life, an inability to imagine true pain whether it is mine or somebody else's. Any comfort seems superfluous, trivial in the face of pain I cannot hope to alleviate. As a result, I end up silent where words are needed. Kirst is not so emotionally inhibited: she gives this soft, helpless woman a tiny embrace, asks if there is anything that can be done to get the children back.

Nasreen tosses a gesture of despair from her shoulders. "His family too rich. We cannot bring justice to him, they have too much money." In a country of corrupted power, such a story is only too believable. "Or he just take the children away. Here, I can sometimes see them. The head of their school lets me see them now and again. I don't want to lose even this."

"So what will you do now?" asks Kirst.

"Ha." A laugh without a smile. "I try for other husband. I need to take care of me. But now, all the men who are interested... they are too old, or they are too poor. Or they work in the West before, or study there."

"Is that bad?" I ask. "That they work in the West?"

Nasreen, a school teacher, looks at me as though I am one of her poorer students. "Yes! My husband a drug addict because he spend time in the West. And he so cruel. Cruel because of drugs, because of the West. I don't want a man who is drug addict, who is cruel. I don't want another man who has been to the West."

To Nasreen, the West represents a place of drugs and cruelty, and I briefly wonder how we seem to her. Yet her hospitality cannot be faulted; she takes genuine joy in our presence. I long to alter her views, to remove the blame from our culture, but she will not hear of it. "No, no. I don't want to take the chance. You say not all Iranians come back like this, but how do you know? Maybe, maybe not all bad, but how do I take the chance? My husband, he was not a bad man until he went to the West."

Nasreen's story, of course, is not about the West. It is about the dark side of Iran, a story of female helplessness, of male power, of injustice and cruelty. This is the side of Iran in Betty Mahmoody's horror of *Not Without My Daughter*. Suddenly, the negative images of Iran, the images that have been washed away over these last five weeks, scramble back into my mind; images of a frightening place, cruel and insane. For the first time, they are possible to believe. I suddenly fear that we have allowed ourselves to be misled by simple kindness.

I realise, as I write this, that this fear, this reaction to Nasreen, is unwarranted. It is a reaction that accords far greater weight to the frightening than to the kind, to the negative than to the positive, to the bad than to the good. It is the reaction we experience every time we witness the horrifying or sensational when we watch the news, a reaction that guarantees that this is precisely the type of news we continue to see. Graphic, alarming stories not only entertain us more, they lodge themselves more firmly in the front of our minds, drowning out everything else. It is a reaction that makes it easy to limit Iran to the spectacle of screaming crowds of fanatics. And it is wrong. I have only to listen to Nasreen as she continues to tell Kirst of her fear of the West. She is judging Western culture, my culture, on a single horrific incident. From where I stand, her error is obvious, yet I have allowed myself to do the same with Iran. If I were to judge the country on this single incident, I would be no different from the Iranian government, from Nasreen herself, pointing to all the crime and drugs and cruelty and sadness in Western society and judging it on them alone. I would be no different from the millions who judge Iran, who judge Iranians, solely on the story of Betty Mahmoody. I would be ignoring the weight of kindness, the memory of friendship and gentleness, bequeathed us in our time here.

Nevertheless, Nasreen's story demands consideration. It demands a wariness, a scepticism, to be applied to my interpretation of the rest of Iran. If I am careful, if I ensure that her story does not dwarf all it surrounds, I may even approach a view that is balanced. Iranians are not monsters, but they are rarely angels either. They are human.

Nasreen falls silent, seems to grow suddenly older. She clutches her chador around her head, poking at her stray hairs: her Islamic propriety is complete. She is a *hajjah*, this woman before us, a woman who has completed the fifth pillar of her religion, the *hajj* pilgrimage to Mecca. Slowly, drawn by Kirst, she begins to tell us of the experience, describes her hope that union with God would cleanse her of misery, would offer her rebirth into a happy life. She is deeply religious, and tells us with pride how she was enriched by the experience. No amount of religious exaltation, however, can hide the fact that it left her life no less depressed than it was before.

"And when I am there, I meet an Indonesia man and wife. They are staying in my hotel, and we become friends. They are so nice people. They look for me, help me in the *hajj*. I think they will be my friends for always." We sit cross-legged on the carpets; Nasreen looks at us, a pale red ruin around her eyes. "But there are Iranian spies in Mecca. Watching, they are always watching Iranians, always watching me. So they see me when I shake my Indonesian friend's hand. It was a mistake! I did not mean to shake his hand. But he offered... what can I do?"

"So when I return, the spies, they tell the police, and tell the mullahs. They drag me to the police station, and the mullahs, they... *interview* me. Questions, questions, shouting at me. They tell me I am *pogon*, a bad woman. They tell police I am a bad woman. And now..." – pain and distress gouge themselves into her collapsing features – "...now letters, they do not reach me. People, they are watching me. I am too afraid to write to my friends – even though I say nothing bad! I am religious, more religious than other people. It was a mistake... Islam says you should forgive mistakes. Now I have no chance. How can I get my children back? How can I get a better job? How can they do this to me?" Those tears, the silent Iranian tears that come free of weeping, begin.

The image of Iranian people in the West may be unwarranted, but the image of the Iranian government as repressive and cruel is not. In Esfahan, a friend accepted Kirst's hand when she offered it, then recoiled in horror when he realised what he had done. The problem, he said just before he turned to flee, was not that he might have offended us, but that he might have offended one of his countrymen. In Iran, the fear of being watched, the fear of a government cruel and inflexible.

The evening progresses slowly, awkwardly. The family returns. We dine, our bodies still laid out over the floor. If I had expected them to show sympathy to Nasreen's plight, outrage at government persecution, I am disappointed. Government repression has generated no discontent here. I cannot tell if their acceptance of oppression is an Iranian or Islamic disease, but here, like so many places in Iran, the complaint is more about economics than injustice. Nasreen's uncle, a mannequin arranged to sit bolt upright, despises the mullahs only for their corruption, for the poverty they have brought to Iran. He waves to the haunting picture on the wall, of the mullah with the judgmental stare. "That man was Nasreen's grandfather," he says. "He was a very religious man. Very religious. That was many years ago, before this government, even before the Shah. Then, the mullahs weren't political. Now, they aren't religious. They are political; they are administrators. And they are bad administrators."

Only Nasreen's mother is affected by her daughter's story. The delighted giggle of earlier in the evening is now gone; her tears mirror those of Nasreen as she tells us of her plight. She begs us to pray for Nasreen when we visit Iran's holiest shrine, that of the eighth Shi'a Imam, Imam Reza, in Mashhad. She fears, she says, that her daughter will never be happy.

Nasreen offers us a tremulous smile. "She will go to Mashhad in a week herself. To pray for me. She wants Imam Reza to speak to God for me, to

help my problems. I know. God is my only hope." She touches her mother on the arm. "But she worries too much."
Dinner finishes; the family leave us with Nasreen. The evening sinks its roots further into the earth. Nasreen takes us through her photo album: Nasreen at university with friends; Nasreen at work; Nasreen sitting demurely in a park with her sister; Nasreen alone at a desk. No photographs are of her husband; none are of her children. Most date from the time of the Shah and show Nasreen completely unveiled, or wearing only a simple scarf above jeans and a short shirt. This is the same woman who sits before us now, in the security offered by privacy, clutching her chador tightly to her head, terrified of crossing the boundaries of Islamic decency. This is a woman persecuted by a cruel and unjust government, yet who has fully embraced that same government's religious dictates, swallowing completely its Islamic propaganda, coming to cling desperately to the chador, the symbol of the Revolution. I find it terribly sad.
Soon we must leave. Nasreen attempts to force us to accept a pair of ceramic candelabra, brightly coloured and heavy, as a gift. It is her parting offering, a present from a woman who lives with little hope of meeting us again. "No, no, don't write. It is suspicious to get letter, and they do not get to me. The police will open and read. But one day, maybe one day we can write. I treasure you in my heart always." Nasreen wrings her hands tightly together, worrying aloud what her neighbours, the eyes outside constantly spying, will think of two foreigners leaving her home so late. She embraces Kirst repeatedly, then leads us out into the night, conjuring up a thin gap in the iron gates wide enough for us to squeeze through.
A metal clang, loud, behind us, an emphatic punctuation mark that rings out into the gloom.
Do eyes watch us from the darkness as we trace our way out through the narrow streets? Nasreen's paranoia is infectious. The earthen lanes are no longer quite as welcoming as they were yesterday evening, as we drifted through them at dusk, and the embrace of the darkness is no longer warm.

Infidel Crimes

Wednesday 28th June
to Mashhad

The province of Khurasan, its name plucked from antiquity, has an identity beyond the borders given to it by modern Iran. It was once a far larger region, encompassing Afghanistan's Herat and Turkmenistan's Merv. Khurasan, long the eastern extremity of the early Islamic empire, where Shi'ism found its strongest following, from where the Abbasids would rise to succeed the Arab empire of the Umayyads. Jammed up against both the Afghan and Turkmen borders is its greatest jewel, Mashhad, the holiest city in Iran and our final Iranian destination before Central Asia. The overland journey there from Yazd, through Khurasan's endless salt wastes, could take two days; it could take four. We cannot spare such uncertainty, so we instead fly to Tehran and take the train.

It is a shame, so late in the journey, to discover the luxury of Iranian train travel, the injustice of air-conditioned pleasure and a sleeping berth after five weeks of overnight bus journeys full of sweat and dust and sleeplessness. I stand in the corridor, gazing at the golden sight of low afternoon sunlight on fields of wheat. Afternoon sun in the desert, so much richer than any other kind; here, now, it is breathtaking. Above the trembling gold is a sky dark and purple, a darkness not of storms but of something else, like a shadow cast upwards from the land. I stand, lean against the window, examine how I feel. My spirits always soar with a sense of freedom and happiness when I am on the move, and the beauty of the scene touches my soul, yet I cannot escape the knowledge that Mashhad is our final destination in Iran. Our time here will soon be over, and I feel a sinking of the spirit.

"It is beautiful is it not?"

The voice is croaked and old, its accent impeccable. I do not need to turn my head very far to find its owner. Beside me, leaning on the window's edge, is a white-headed, white-bearded Pakistani male, in a Pakistani *shalwar kameez* of pale cream. These clothes, of staggeringly baggy pants and over-long shirt, reminiscent faintly of pyjamas, give Pakistanis an air that lies somewhere between easygoing and shabby. I shift my gaze back to the scene rushing past, and can only agree.

My companion introduces himself as Abdul. He has a blunted head, old in a strong way. I judge him to be over seventy. "We are in these next two cabins," he says. "Men in one, the women in the other." He smiles, opens his palms. "We are Muslims, after all."

Abdul explains that he and his entourage are on the final leg of a pilgrimage that has taken them to almost all the Islamic holy sites in the Middle East. "Some of us come from Pakistan, some from India," he explains. "We started in Mecca, with the *hajj*, then wanted to continue, to see it all. Saudi Arabia, Jordan. We couldn't get visas for Israel, so we went to Iraq." He shakes his head. "A terrible place. Worse poverty than India. No, I mean it. If you could see what the sanctions were doing to the people... It was depressing. But we did see the shrines in the south, the Shi'ite shrines, Imam Ali and the rest. And now Iran. Mashhad will be our final stop for the whole pilgrimage."

Abdul has the finest English we have encountered on our journey. It is the English of a man born long before independence, an approximation of Oxford mingled with an India long past. Importantly, it is a voice shared by many of the women of his group. All are of Abdul's age, trying to cherish this final part of their life, to make this final, all-encompassing pilgrimage, while they are still able. Until now, most of our English conversations in Iran have been with men; the women have had to suffer my clumsy Farsi. Kirst has often been left out altogether, so it is pure joy for her now, as the women fuss over her, drag her into their cabin, discuss their lives, their thoughts, discuss Islam. Speaking Farsi has opened Iran to us, but it is no match for the flawless English of these men and women. I stand outside, only half aware of their chatter, watching the world clatter past our carriage.

Later, a young couple enters our cabin. The man is grim and bearded, the woman cloaked in a heavy chador. Until now we have been alone, and have been hoping for the privacy of a cabin to ourselves. We are unsure what Islamic propriety dictates for the behaviour of couples in a sleeping cabin, how the rules of sexual segregation apply, so we stare stubbornly out the window until the darkness outside is complete, waiting for a sign from our companions. And then it begins.

> The man – standing, stretching –
> darkens the cabin,
> closes the blinds,
> abandons the world outside:
> the agony and sand of the desert.
> > A giggle.

> First the chador
> slips
> > a purple blouse, a shimmer
> *long*
> *dark*
> *hair*
> > pornography before our eyes.

> > A gentle caress
> nothing serious just a rub of the neck a stroke of the leg a touch
> of the arm
> > But

> this is Iran.
> > > In Iran
> this is outrageous.
> > > In Iran
> this is criminal.

> One couple, one bunk   one cuddle,
> nothing more than that.
> Her raven
> hair

hangs
down
    over the bunk.
Meanwhile
the corrupt evil tainted debauched depraved immoral impure
Westerners
lie
embarrassed
in separate bunks,
trying not to look.
All night I wonder how they would have behaved if we had been Iranian.

Thursday 29th June
Mashhad

"I know it makes no sense. But this is Iran. This is a crazy country." These are the words of the Turkmen consul in Mashhad, and serve as his explanation why we are not permitted to cross to Turkmenistan by land. "It is not an *international* border. For Turkmen people, for Iranian people, it is no problem. But for you..." Ashgabat, a quarter as far as Tehran, and we have to fly.

Central Asia certainly feels tantalisingly close in Mashhad. Faces that call to mind Mongol raiders mix with the thick beards and square Aryan jaws we have become accustomed to this last month. Round heads, almond-shaped eyes lidded by epicanthic folds, thin and scruffy growths. Their clothes, soft and baggy and high-booted, suggest mounted horsemen, tribes on the margins of civilisation, wild nomads ready to fight and die.

The Turkmen faces we see on the streets of Mashhad cast our minds to the journey ahead, and thus, in a sense, back in time: all we know of Central Asia is history. Yet theirs are not the only strange faces to drift through these deserts: Persians, or Farsis, only make up just over half the population of Iran. The rest are Azeris and Gilaki, Mazandarani and Kurds, Arabs and Lur, Bakhtaris and countless smaller tribes. Though they inhabit other parts of Iran, most have gravitated to this most holy of cities, and the ethnic medley here is more eclectic than anywhere else we have seen. And these faces, these chattering demonstrations of human genetic variety, are not limited to the faces of Iran. On the crowded streets stalk the turbans of Afghanistan, the *shalwar kameez* of Pakistan, the skull-caps of Uzbekistan; we see thick-moustached Turks, flowing Egyptian robes, a pastiche of clothes and bodies from all over the Islamic world. All are here for one reason, the one reason that has drawn countless pilgrims throughout history, the same reason that has brought us, these last few days, across the wastes of Iran. All are here to visit the shrine of Imam Reza.

Mashhad was once known for three things: religion, commerce, and tourism. Now, heavily shuttered borders with Afghanistan and the old

Soviet Union surround the city, stifling trade, and tourism has crumbled as much as it has in the rest of Iran. All that is left to Mashhad is religion. But as our guidebook says, Iran is Iran, and this is more than enough.

In other cities we have been a novelty to the local Iranians, a pair of foreigners who need to be coddled and cared for. Here, an easy indifference meets us: we are pilgrims, no different from anyone else. Waiters in the restaurant beneath our hotel ask us to pray for them at the shrine. Black-clad strangers, eyes set above fierce black beards, welcome us in Arabic. All in our hotel are foreigners, pilgrims themselves. Profiteers try to sell us Islamic memorabilia, tokens of our holy visit; photographers compete to take our photograph before cardboard replicas of the shrine. In the last five weeks I have cultivated the shaved head and thick beard of the most fervent Hezbollahi Shi'a; a comment heard from those we meet is that I could easily pass as one of the Komité. With such an image, accompanied by a wife in demure Islamic black, it is little wonder we are seen as pious Muslims, here for the same reasons as everyone else, here on pilgrimage to the shrine.

The air of Mashhad is stretched thin, brittle with anticipation. We feel as though we must tread softly, must move quietly and respectfully, as if a word or a sound misplaced could open a crack to religious hysteria. Mashhad is a town focused, intense, concentrating on one thing only: Imam Reza, martyr of the Shi'a faith.

A morning of organisation, an unavoidable delay before our pilgrimage to the shrine begins. Our Iranian visas expire on Saturday, and with the Muslim holy day tomorrow, today is our only opportunity to extend. A taxi ride to the edge of town, a polite struggle with friendly authorities clad in olive combat fatigues, armed with reams of paperwork. Poorly-transcribed quotations from Khomeini line the bare walls: *Be sure neither East nor West will avail you trusting in God and relying on Islam combat against Israel.*

Kirst submits her passport-sized photograph, receives a grim shake of the head. *If the universal arrogant forces stand against our religion, we will stand against their world.* "This is a very bad photo," says the officer with the narrow face. He waves it up and down before us. "Very bad." He places it on the desk in front of him, paints her hair with correction fluid, a smile creeping over his face. "There. Now this... this is a very good photo." All the hair is now gone; Kirst's pale face is framed in white. For our original visas, we were conscious of offending Iranian mores, but these photographs were taken with other countries in mind. A rose blossoms in Kirst's face with the realisation she has just submitted an obscene photograph of herself to the police.

Standing by the door, unnoticed until we leave, is a round man, young; his face is soft, made of dough, with a permanently set grin, as if he never stopped pouring tea for guests. This is Mehrdod, a man irrepressible and impossible to dislike, who fastens himself to us as soon as we strike the sunlight outside. Smothering enthusiasm, eyes wide and innocent; he has us in his spell in minutes. "Oh my friends! You do not know how *happy* I am to have two foreign friends, two friends from Australia! All my friends at work will be so jealous!" Mehrdod is a teacher; he tells us that it is a point of pride among Iranians of his age to have foreign friends. Yet I sense no insincerity in his manner; Mehrdod's delight in our presence is pure.

"Now," he says, his tone parental, "you must not go to the shrine yet. You must wait until later today. It is *too* hot, and the best time to see it is at sunset. And today is Thursday. So *everyone* goes to the shrine to pray, the evening before Friday." He extends his hands to the imaginary shrine, like a connoisseur beholding a work of art. "We go when they go, in the evening."

In many ways Mehrdod is extreme for an Iranian; his kindness is familiar, but his manner is not. When he speaks, a sense of superlative follows; his gestures are wide and excited and dramatic. He would be affected if he were not so open, irritating if we did not think his delight was real. It is a relief, for once, to find the subdued Iranian version of Islamic rectitude so utterly absent. "We will go to my house," Mehrdod decrees. "I will have you for lunch. My mother will be so proud to have you as guests. Then, later, I will take you to the shrine myself. I can tell you *all* about Imam Reza." And return to Mehrdod's house we do.

Lunch, then an afternoon waiting out the dreamy heat on soft Persian carpets. Mehrdod cannot sit still; he is too excited by our presence. In his animated voice he tells us what we have heard so many times before: religion being forced on people by the government is not pure religion, is not real Islam, and was a cause for many to stray; most people are against the government, it's unpopularity blamed on "the bad economic situation in our country." I comment that this is all we ever hear, that nobody mentions the lack of personal freedoms, the violations of human rights.

Mehrdod considers this for a moment. "Yes, I think you are right. People resent the lack of freedom, but... you know, life goes on. Much more important is... prosperity? Is that the word? Much more important to them is prosperity. Iranians are a very greedy people. Terrible people. Make us poor, and we get very unhappy." What had Farzaneh said, in Esfahan? *Now we still have no freedom, and we are poor.*

The laugh he lets loose at his people, at himself, is one of mad, barbaric mirth. Laughter, for Mehrdod, is the only way to shrug away the problems of his world.

"Our country has so many problems," he says. "Me, I am studying English and economics. But it will not do me any good. In our country, educated people don't get ahead."

"Then who does? Religious people?"

Mehrdod shrieks with pleasure. "Aha! Of course! You *must* have been in Iran a long time. You understand."

As the afternoon wears on, I realise Mehrdod is no different from his countrymen, despite his effusive exterior. His cheeriness only covers a deeper sadness; bright paint over rotting wood. Behind every laugh at Iran's predicament is a sigh; behind every smile a sadness. Missing, in Mehrdod's cheery view of life, is hope for the future. He can laugh at the past, laugh at his people, laugh at the present, but when he speaks of the future, the smile has gone from his voice. "You look at me, and you think I am a young man. I am young outside, yes, but inside I am old. You can't understand. Nobody can understand what it is like to be Iranian. Not unless you live through these things. People from your country... you can't understand what it is like to live through torture. Through your friends being killed. Or parents vanishing. Or being frightened. *Frightened.* Of the government, of the Komité, of the mullahs." He offers us a smile, but it is one of sadness and regret. "This is why," he says in a slow voice, "this is why young Iranians, we are becoming less religious."

I think of Nasreen, of her new acceptance of the Islam of the regime, despite the destruction it has wrought in her own life; I think of the millions of youths mindlessly accepting government propaganda, giving their lives as martyrs to what they are now told is Islam. And then there are the people like Mehrdod. In Iran, the dichotomy is extreme.

The threads of the afternoon begin to slowly unravel. Mehrdod orders a taxi for us to the shrine, and spends most of the journey berating the driver for not leaping out to open the door for Kirst. I gaze out the window, watching Mashhad pass by to the sounds of Mehrdod's chatter. Traffic is thin; the streets are far emptier than usual. Only gradually, as we move closer to the centre of the city, does the usual jolting traffic of Iran appear once more.

I keep watching: a fruit store, its façade a collage of bright colours and Arabic numerals; a park lined with pink roses; a family of five jammed onto a single scooter with comic desperation, the sight such a part of the Iranian urban landscape.

Mehrdod grabs my arm. "You see this square? It is called *Istiqlal* Square. You know what *Istiqlal* means? It means 'independence'. The three pillars of Iran are 'freedom, independence and Islamic Republic'. But we have *no* freedom, *no* independence!" He laughs loudly. The state of his nation, the killing joke.

Suddenly, Mehrdod adopts the role of guide, and an element of gravity taints his voice. "I tell you about the shrine. You know Imam Reza, the eighth Imam? You know our Imams? Good. So I tell you. Imam Reza, he died – I think maybe a thousand years ago – by being poisoned. By the Caliph Ma'mun. The people became very angry, so Ma'mun buried him in Mashhad, beside Ma'mun's father, Harun ar-Rashid. You know ar-Rashid? A *very* famous man. A famous Caliph of the Abbasids. It was his court in the story *The Thousand and One Nights*."

These are the collection of tales known as *Arabian Nights* in the West, the stories of Sindbad, Aladdin, Ali Baba and the forty thieves. Mehrdod shifts his weight slightly, changes his voice. "Under him, he makes knowledge the *number one* importance for Islam. Religion, philosophy, science... everything. He should tell the mullahs today, I think. Now the only knowledge they want is the Qur'an and guns."

The shrine of Imam Reza lies in the middle of a vast island of holy precinct, imprisoned by a ring road in the heart of Mashhad. Postcards depict the area as large, peaceful and grassy, but there is no green in the scene that confronts us. A hundred metres from the ring road the streets degenerate into an excavation site the colour of dust. The buildings closest to the shrine have been reduced to rubble, and we angle over a vacant lot of broken bricks.

Mehrdod explains. "The government is making the road go underground. Listen. You can hear some traffic from down there already. The government buy up all the shops around here, and knock them down. All this," he waves to the rubble, to the empty brick walls, "was part of the bazaar." The construction has formed a vast moat around the shrine precinct, a chasm protected by high wire fences and rods of scaffolding. The only way across, into the holy realm, is on one of the bridges that lie at the four corners of the compass, under heavy guard. "We had a bomb here three years ago," explains Mehrdod. "A terrible thing, you must have heard. No? They were monsters. They took a bomb into the shrine; they killed hundreds of people. Women, children, all pilgrims. So now we have a lot of security, especially now, in the main pilgrimage time of the year. You cannot take your camera."

At the northern gate, the press of bodies has the froth and surge of surf in a storm. Men fight for position at a tiny window in the wall, trying to deposit their belongings before they file through the body search at the gates, silent and intense. Beside them, a sea of billowing darkness pushes at the 'sister's entrance'. As we watch, Kirst realises with a start that she is the only woman without a chador. Before meeting Mehrdod, our intention had been to wait a day before visiting the shrine, and to obtain a chador for Kirst if one was necessary. Mehrdod, however, assured us several times that a manteau and scarf would be sufficient. His vehement denials that her clothes could possibly cause any offence calmed our fears completely. Now, however, we are not so sure.

We back away to wait. Kirst watches the crowd, hoping for some indication that the presence of a female infidel Westerner, without a chador, will not be viewed as an insult. She searches for some sign that what she wears is acceptable clothing for the shrine.

I gaze over the heads of those around us. Across the chasm, the shrine looks no different from the building site of the ring road and the demolished buildings around us: raw brick glares dully back at me. Only above it is the promise of glory. The domes and minarets of the shrine precinct float above the dusty ruin, some eggshell creations of blue and cream, others a gold that roars in the dying sunlight. Only they declare that this is the shrine of Imam Reza.

In many ways the shrine's popularity is a result of the political manipulation of Islam which has echoes in the Iran of today. The tomb was always a minor pilgrimage site, though Imam Reza was not a figure who deserved intense devotion. Its status came only during the Saffavid era, when rivalry with the Ottoman Empire meant that visiting shrines under Ottoman control were discouraged, and the Saffavids promoted the shrines in their own territory. Official doctrine deemed that one pilgrimage to Mashhad was worth any number of pilgrimages to Mecca. Judging from the crowds before us now, the air clouded with religious intensity, the propaganda worked.

Finally, Kirst spots a pair of Turkmen women without chadors, their hair tied into brightly-coloured scarves. This is reassurance enough. The women frisking the 'sisters' tell her that her presence is fine as long as she keeps her hair completely covered. She is waved through; we follow across the bridge.

Mehrdod explains, in English which jars conspicuously against the silence of those around us, that the construction work inside the holy precinct has nothing to do with the ring road outside. It is, instead, part of the Islamic government's expansion of the shrine, a project of lavish expense that continues the tradition of the Saffavids. He waves to a small corridor, covered with the exquisite blue tiles of Esfahan, applied over the bleak cement and brick only recently. The work is so perfect that I cannot distinguish it from any of the ancient sites we have visited, and I am impressed: the architectural legacy of Persian Islam lives on. Yet this is the same government that housed its most beloved leader in a shopping-centre travesty of Muslim architecture, a place of plastic and scaffolding and painted air-conditioner ducts. I cannot fathom such taste.

"Oh no," replies Mehrdod when I describe my amazement. "Imam Khomeini's tomb is not the same thing as here. This is *real* religion. This isn't politics."

We are walking around the edge of the moat, back towards the main entrance to the *haram-é motahhar*, the sacred precincts. A few women pass us on their way out, their faces modestly downcast, but most of the flow is inward, towards the shrine.

"These people come to pray to Imam Reza to help them, to ask God to help them," explains Mehrdod. "Every Thursday night they come, and many stay here all night. They tie themselves to the tomb, and sleep here... some try not to leave until they have had their prayers granted. I have a friend who was crippled in the war. He came here on a Thursday, and crawled through the shrine again and again, and slept here. And soon, he was cured."

"Really cured? You think he was cured because of the shrine?"

Mehrdod gives me a look, grave and slow, that contains a shard of his personality we have not seen before. Yes, he tells me. Yes, of course he was cured because of the shrine.

Mehrdod's talk had lulled me into thinking that he viewed himself as separate from the faithful all around us. All that talk of losing religion, of disdain for the mullahs. But this is Iran. The fundamental belief in the power of God is unshakeable, even among the educated élite. When Mehrdod speaks of losing his religion, he means only his faith in the mullahs, in the forms of Islam. He would be mortified to think that I had interpreted it as losing his faith in God.

We round a corner of dull brickwork, then stop, transfixed. The courtyard before us is only one face of the exterior of the shrine, yet it is powerful enough to drill us into silence.

We enter, slowly, this vast area, our footsteps against the tiled surface lost in the hidden murmur of thousands of voices. We pass a small domed building, tiled gold and blue, dispensing water to the faithful to purify themselves; we pass four giant octagonal pools, pieces of broken sunlight floating on their surface. All possess the chilling beauty of a foreign faith, but the main attraction lies beyond them, at the far end of the courtyard; it is to this that we walk.

Before us lies a vast *eivan*, an arched portal sculpted with stalactite moulding, shaped just like those of the mosques in Esfahan. A huge frame for an unseen door, it is a spectacle in gold. Every visible part of it shines with a fluid light, fragmented flashes of gold cast by angles of precious metal. Around its border are the names of Allah in blue and white tiles; a mosaic of faith, of floral patterns, of geometric designs. Arabic calligraphy forms the underlying motif: even the dome above is traced with delicate patterns in metallic blue.

And suddenly, explosion.

The sun pulses with a last desperate surge. The world is filled with an explosion of colour and energy. From the blue tiles now shine more words of Arabic, pouring down the surface like a molten liquid, seen only now because of this new light. The huge wall of gold and the dome above come alive. We stand motionless, captivated, for the brief time that the sun remains, before it settles itself in the skyline behind us.

The crush of bodies towards the *eivan* and the golden door set in it is even thicker than at the gate outside. The door leads in to the shrine, in to the tomb itself, and it is therefore forbidden to us. Instead, we move to its left, where the sea of bodies is just as thick.

Over a mass of shrouded heads, I can make out a metal grid, like the one around the tomb in Shiraz. This one is set into a wall, offering a view of the interior of the shrine. Clutching it, like bodies clinging to rock in rough seas, are dozens of women, all wailing, weeping, crying out for God. They pass their hands over the metal, caress it, bring their hands to their faces or their hearts; some appear to hug themselves. Their faces are tear-stained, red, grief-stricken, far more so than in Shiraz. Others try to clutch their way to this holy portal, this glimpse of Paradise, this offering of hope. Some have tied themselves to it with cloth, just as Mehrdod described, and all are lost to this world, immersed completely in a sorrow of religious ecstasy. They weep for Imam Reza, they weep for themselves.

Beside them sits a bearded mullah, cross-legged, releasing a wailing of his own that fills the square. All else is silence; we are not the only ones subdued by the air of blind faith. We stand and watch for maybe ten minutes. Women approach the grill, stroke it, drop money inside as their personal sacrifice to God, their personal appeal for a miracle. The sound of hysterical weeping mixes with the wail of the mullah, and as I listen I have a sense of them both being embroidered onto my mind. The scene is so unreal it feels almost like a dream.

The building of the shrine is, itself, a large square shape, bounded on all sides by two stories of arched Islamic portals, all covered in glorious blue tiles. This courtyard is joined by three others just like it, each with a giant gold *eivan*, each with its own entrance to the tomb. It is to the next of these we go now, in the dying light of dusk, as the faithful prepare for evening prayer.

As we approach, I catch a timid glimpse of the second square. The crowd is thick; all eyes are turned inwards, towards the shrine. If there is a word inscribed on every face, it is *Islam*.

We see no more. A guard, large and stern, wielding a ceremonial silver staff, barks at us, then draws us off to one side. Our worst fears are realised. Mehrdod at least does us the courtesy of not translating an increasingly heated argument, but it is clear what is at issue: Kirst, without a chador, is improperly dressed. The argument of the Turkmen women is useless; in this man's opinion, we should leave immediately.

We stand beside an archway, the entrance to the square, one that had been thick with the movement of the crowd. Now all these faces have stopped to listen to the argument, to contribute, and the crowd is instantly huge. Kirst, red-faced, shifts away like her own disease, a woman in quarantine; and children push me out of the way to catch a glimpse of this sacrilegious woman, this mocker of all things Islamically good and proper, this infidel daring to come here improperly clothed. I feel vaguely ill. Our greatest fear has been of insulting Muslim sensibility, and now a crowd of over a hundred presses around us, every face staring, many full of hostility, all contributing to the air of disapproval. In their eyes we are guilty of crime.

The discussion ends as abruptly as it began: Mehrdod explains that Kirst's clothing is not appropriate; that we should not enter this area even if it was, that the first square is all that is allowed to unbelievers. We escape the clutches of the crowd, our mouths thick with the taste of shame. A few onlookers follow, some to abuse Mehrdod, to claim that he cannot be a true Muslim; others to offer us support. Mehrdod waves them away. He is distraught. "I am so ashamed. How can I apologise to you enough? These people are ignorant. Ignorant! What is it to them anyway? I am ashamed of my countrymen!"

I try to calm him, to tell him that we understand; but it is no use. I suppose his reaction is reasonable. If he was refused entry, in my company, to a church, I would be equally outraged. But I cannot find it within myself to blame these people, when an overwhelming feeling of the sin of transgression permeates my being. My own sense of shame and embarrassment is far too strong to allow me to feel anger.

We stand for a while, attempting unsuccessfully to merge with the crowd, to lose the feeling of conspicuousness. Mehrdod, his face angry and tight, appears to sulk. And then, suddenly, an idea strikes him; he begins to lead us away, in the other direction, to show us another part of the shrine. We protest mildly; we have been expressly forbidden from leaving the main square.

"No, come on, don't worry!" is Mehrdod's response. "It is this way to the museums, and you are allowed to go to the museums. So how can it be a problem? But," and he lowers his voice to a whisper, "I think you should pretend to be Muslims." With no word as to how this might be done, he strides off towards the third courtyard; we have little choice but to follow. A brief courtyard, a darkened arch, a final swallow as I realise where we have come. Before us, vast and blue and dangerous, is the courtyard of the largest mosque attached to the shrine. It is a mosque in the holiest site in Iran, in the most popular time of the year, on the most popular night of the week. Awe constricts my breath as I step inside.

Before us is a crowd of over a thousand people, all kneeling on the hundreds of patterned rugs that carpet the square. Every shining face is turned to the *mihrab*, the massive arch of the mosque that directs the prayers of the faithful towards Mecca. I follow their eyes to it. The mosque is an open cavern, a dome cleaved in two, a blue of infinite detail. Inside it sit the most holy of the gathering, all men, many mullahs. A soft stirring fills the air, the noise of a crowd quieted by a powerful God. In the square outside the arch of the mosque, beneath the darkening sky, is the crowd. Closest to the front are the women of Islam, their eyes cast downwards to the well-thumbed copies of the Qur'an that lie in their laps, their lips moving in grave silence. We skirt the crowd, sliding towards the rear, past the arched wings of the courtyard crammed with even more souls preparing for the beginning of prayer.

At the back of the crowd lies a large octagonal pool, carved from smooth marble and filled with water from a score of running taps. We stand near it, amongst those yet to take their positions for prayer. The faithful wash themselves at the pool, purifying their bodies, scrubbing their arms, their feet, the backs of their necks.

I glance quickly around, trying to sear the scene irrevocably into my memory before it vanishes. I have rarely felt less comfortable, yet I do not want to lose this image that I was never meant to see. All manner of Islamic civilisation is presented before me: Pakistanis with shaved heads and thick beards; mullahs in black and white turbans; Turkmen in their wild tribal clothes; barefoot Arabs in white robes stretched tight over satisfied paunches; a tight phalanx of kneeling women in black, not one without a chador. Single sounds strike me: the scrape of a bare foot behind me, a cough, the splash of water. Time is congealed, crystallised;

the moment is endless. And then the world shrugs beneath us. The moment is over; the abuse has begun. A relief that it is once again directed more at Mehrdod than at us. This time, even mullahs arrive to deliver their stern disapproval, and once again we depart beneath a wave of shame. Yet this time I do not feel as stigmatised as before. No doubt in the eyes of those we pass we are disgraceful, but this time I have snatched something from the shrine that makes the guilt worthwhile. The memory of the settled peace of that large crowd, of the concrete being of God filling that huge blue world, comes with me as I leave.

Word precedes us to the gate. We are detained; Mehrdod again argues on our behalf. He is outraged, belligerent. We stand, embarrassed, while he convinces them that we should be allowed to return to visit the Islamic museums housed in the complex, as long as Kirst wears a chador, and we vow not to stray into the holy areas again. Earlier today I had imagined that, accompanied by a Muslim, I would get to see the interior of the shrine itself. I allow myself a thin disappointment, but I know the result could have been much worse. And it does not matter. Already, the experience of Imam Reza has been carved, clean and complete, into my memory; I can hardly wish for more.

A downpouring of immense darkness has now begun. We circle the shrine, cross the vacant lot, watch as the purple of the horizon fades with an exquisite subtlety to the darkness above. The call of the muezzin from inside the mosque floats absently over the world. A taunt? Or a farewell? Mehrdod wants to take us out for pizza and ice-cream, to apologise, but I am emotionally drained, physically exhausted, and quite dizzy. I feel the beginnings of some kind of illness, and want only to return to our hotel.

We walk away from the shrine, with every step able to breathe a little easier, able to feel less guilty. It has been easy to fool ourselves, after being surrounded by Islam so completely these last two months, that Islam has embraced us as much as we have embraced it. We have lulled ourselves into a feeling of ease with the religion, the kind of ease that comes with familiarity, and it has been a mistake. Islam, the religion of the pure, is a faith closed to outsiders. In the eyes of its fiercest followers, unbelievers are *najis*, unclean. It is this feeling we take with us now. The feeling of unwelcome, of the impermeable barrier between us and true believers, of the impurity of our souls, is a strong one. It will be a long time before it fades.

Full Circle

Monday 3rd July
Mashhad...

We sit with Mehrdod on the bare carpets of his home, in an empty lounge room that could only belong to Iran. We look through his photo albums; we try to forget that today is our last day in Iran.

The photos are all of Mehrdod: Mehrdod at the beach, Mehrdod at a hotel on the Gulf, Mehrdod in army fatigues with grim companions, faces of the Revolution. This last one takes me by surprise.

"Ha! You like? Yes, I was in the army for three years. Not quite the army, but Sepah Pasdaran. You know Sepah?"

Sepah Pasdaran, the religious army of Iran, feared and loathed by so much of the population. It stuns me that this rounded, putty-faced man, with his earnest and amiable nature, with his critical views of the regime, was once part of them. It was Sepah who aroused so much ire in Farzaneh while we were in Esfahan, as the group of students whose privileges made a mockery of education. It is Sepah who back the regime's ideology with military might. It is Sepah who ensure that the inheritors of Khomeini's Revolution remain in power.

"Mehrdod! I thought you had to be religious – a fanatic – to be in Sepah." Mehrdod waves his hand, dismisses the idea. "I know. I just pretended to be religious." He smiles conspiratorially. "Many people do it, you just have to be careful."

"But why?"

"Why? Because life is *much* easier than the regular army. We don't have to serve as long either: I would still be in the army if I had not joined Sepah. And we get special privileges. For many things. Being in Sepah meant I could go to university. I just have to pretend to be a fanatic."

We have come full circle; a final piece of the puzzle that is Iran has only just come together. Iran, land of unrelenting suspicion, has had us unbalanced from the very beginning, unsure whom to believe, whom to trust. According to Farzaneh, the religious passion of the supporters of the government was entirely self-interested, driven by what she saw as purely Iranian qualities of greed and self-preservation. Yet the religious fervour we have witnessed throughout these last six weeks made such a claim difficult to believe. Only when we chance on both sides of the story can we gauge some sense of its shape. It has happened to us already in Iran: for a long time I had felt that the constant denigration of the clergy as corrupt was simply an excuse for the failure of Islamic government, a way to divert the blame away from Islam itself, until we met Mahmud in Tehran and heard his stories of bribing the mullah.

Similarly, I was unsure what to make of the claims that Ashura marchers were government stooges until we spoke once more to Nasser in Tabriz, an Ashura enthusiast who could refute the accusations. Yet none of it – the suspicion, the unforgiving distrust, even the empty tomb of Khomeini – none of it makes sense until we can believe that people like Mehrdod exist, who are content to use the system. I cannot blame Mehrdod; from where he stands, it makes perfect sense, and is the natural reaction to an imperfect world. But for Farzaneh, or Mahmud, or the countless people who stand isolated and powerless on the outside, such opportunism is sinister and evil, a symptom of the Iranian disease, a cause of the country's woe.

In many ways they are right. Mehrdod, an amiable cog in the regime's machinery of repression, holds a vitally important key to understanding the logic of Iran. People like Mehrdod, normal people concerned for their own lives in worlds governed by oppression, are the true might behind revolutions and dictatorships. Mehrdod is a good person, harmless; yet without people like him, the Revolution would not have survived. In Mehrdod, I feel I am close to understanding something fundamental about Iran; he offers an answer to the nagging, half-formed suspicions that have been with me ever since Khomeini's empty shrine. Nothing in Iran, not even fanaticism, is ever what it seems.

He does not realise that my questions pertain to him personally. I search for his thoughts on the implications of Iranian opportunism, for what it means to have an entire country of people feigning their religious passion. To Mehrdod, this is nothing particularly special; it is the Iranian disease.

"Everybody does it," he says, "you have to believe me. For instance. You saw those women at the shrine the other day, all crying? They were just pretending. I mean it. Iranians are very good at pretending."

It is early evening by the time Mehrdod accompanies us to the airport in a taxi. "Just be happy you are flying to where there is no water," he says. "Iran Air has removed all the life jackets from their planes because people kept stealing them. I had a friend who did this. When he told me, I immediately thought: you will not be my friend any more. Such a thing disgusts me; it's *disgusting*."

We bid him farewell outside the boarding lounge. Around us is an angry chaos: the Iranian government decided this week to expel all its Afghani refugees, and it seems most have installed themselves, their families, and all their belongings in Mashhad's airport. I am happy that it is Mehrdod, of all those we have met in Iran, who says our final goodbye. With his effervescent character draped over a grey core, tiny and sad, he is impossible not to like; and he has shown us more of Iran than perhaps anyone else.

I find it difficult to manage my own feelings towards the country and its people. Iran is impossibly divided. Many countries are split bitterly into identifiable groups – Christian against Muslim in Lebanon, Catholic against Protestant in Northern Ireland – but in Iran the division is atomic, a division between individuals. Every person is cut off, isolated from everyone else, hermetically sealed by a brooding atmosphere of fear and suspicion. General divisions can be made: between those weeping at the shrines and those who dismiss them as frauds; between those who use the government for their own ends and those who find such people despicable; between those who are truly religious and those who view the faithful as pawns of the regime. But within these groups there is nothing that could be called unity. There is only the sense of frightened people coping in a frightening world.

At the same time, no matter how we feel about the divisions in Iranian society, our image of that society has changed forever. No longer can we imagine it a bleak place of mindless fanaticism, of terror and burning hate. It is instead a place of extreme kindness, of real people, proud of their history and their religion, whose view of themselves is formed by far more than just Islam. It remains a country under the control of a brutal regime, but for the first time we can see the difference between the government and its people.

If there is one thing we will take with us, it is religion. Religion in Iran is inescapable, both politicised and pure. In Iran, religion is politics, it is science, it is life. And six weeks of the cool air of Shi'a piety and religious intensity has left us with a feeling of familiarity with the religion I did not expect. Shi'ism, the faith of martyrdom and tears and darkness, burns bright in our minds. The images of the weeping faithful, of the self-punishment of Ashura, of religious grief kept alive for a thousand years, will remain with us forever as vivid reminders of the pillars of the Shi'a faith. Ali, Hussein, Hassan: still mourned as martyrs; all this we will take with us. And now, finally, we prepare to enter the world of Sunnism.

The chaos reigning inside the departure lounge is just as severe as in the airport outside. The crowd around us is a strange one: lost Afghani refugees, frightened and hoping that some country will accept them; gold-toothed Russian shoppers each with large, odd-shaped loads; smooth Iranian businessmen, travelling with only their briefcases. Our plane is delayed four hours, and it is not until well after midnight that we are subjected to our final Iranian body search and ushered on to the tarmac towards the waiting Turkmenistan Air jet.

I climb the stairs slowly, far too exhausted to mourn my final touch of Iranian ground. At the top of the stairs, I stop, gaze back at the dark shape of Mashhad, buried beneath a midnight sky. And then I enter the plane.

The shock is a double one. Before me is a stewardess, her head unveiled, displaying the first female hair I have seen in public since the alleyway in Yazd, only the second I have seen in six weeks. I am shocked as much by my own reaction as by the sight; I find I am gaping. The woman's skirt is hardly short by Western standards – a conservative cut, just below the knee – but here it is akin to sexual assault. Above it is a thin, diaphanous white blouse, but what shocks me the most is her shimmering mane of red hair. I glance at Kirst; she is just as spellbound. We take our seats at the front of the plane, then turn to watch her walk down the aisle, staring without shame. We are not alone: we look back at a planeload of turned heads, all doing the same. After six weeks the woman oozes sex, and not a soul can tear their eyes from her figure. She is a model walking through a rapturous crowd.

We are brought tea in old, cracked ceramic teapots. We wait, we doze; and then the journey begins. The engines fire, the lights dim, and we move slowly into the darkness.

Only when the wheels of the aircraft leave the ground am I struck by the full realisation of what is happening; only then do I see this voyage as a daunting, irrevocable choice. Confidence and security drop away from me like the darkened land beneath us. Travelling in Iran has become the known; Turkmenistan is now to be feared. Iran at least feels like an old, if somewhat bewildering, friend. We speak its language, we understand its culture, we have even had a guide book. About Turkmenistan, about all the Central Asian republics, we know nothing. We have no information, no understanding, no language, no conception of what awaits. And we will be arriving at three in the morning.

PART TWO
CENTRAL

TURKMENISTAN

(for map see page 14)

Fragments Of History

Tuesday 4th July
to Ashgabat

Heat thumps at us, wet and heavy, from the tarmac. Even at this hour the air presses against us like a hot sponge. We shuffle, as numb and tired as those around us, into Ashgabat's new airport, into white corridors that gleam with the clinical sterility of a nightmare.

A taste, sour, of what Iran must be like for those with no Farsi, only worse, for here there is no English at all. The Cyrillic script is more of an affront than Arabic; it taunts, nagging at me, its similarity to Latin suggesting I should understand at least something. We blunder through.

Outside, there is no glow from the city to paint the horizon blue, no light to fight back the darkness. An empty car park. We have no money, no information about the city, no language, and it is three in the morning. In the shadows, desperate taxi drivers wait with the only English they own, accented heavily in Russian: "Dollar, yes?"

> Fat Russian women,
> A fumbling without language.
> Adopted, we cling.

The van, filled with two of the women and a mountain of their baggage, stops at a nameless wooden gate beside a low, rural building embedded in the darkness. Trees cover us from the night; opposite are the deep rows of either a forest or a park. We have formed no concept of Ashgabat, no idea of where we are, not even if we have entered the city. The feeling of dislocation is complete. These women, part of a large group at the end of an Iranian shopping spree, accept our presence, but can tell us nothing.

Dogs bark in the darkness at our arrival; the torn cry of a rooster responds.

The gate opens; a man appears. We have conjured a collapsing creature into the light, half ghoul, a greying figure in striped pyjama pants and a grubby singlet. His face is square and sunken, misshapen and unshaven, a red-eyed thing of white flesh. A cigarette already hangs from his lips. He eyes us, looks angrily at the women, begins a game of shouts and gestures. It is far too late and we are far too tired to care what this man thinks; we grab our bags and push past, through the gate.

There is no light, and it takes several seconds until the shadowy outlines before us resolve themselves to a scene vaguely identifiable. We stand in the courtyard of a bedraggled farm house. Above us, quieted with vines, a wooden lattice blocks out the sky. To our left is a shack of peeling timber; to the right, similar buildings huddle around the yard. The angry shapes of a pile of rusted scrap metal; an ancient refrigerator, abandoned; a sheep standing in a pen in the bare dirt. Somewhere, hidden by the darkness, a pump tirelessly disgorges water into a drain, its sound an echo of the waste of Communism.

We sit at a table and watch as our mute companions enter, harassed by the gruesome spectre. I want only to sleep. We have assumed we were being taken to some kind of guest house. If this does not turn out to be the case we will sleep where we sit. We are too exhausted to try anywhere else, and even if we had the energy we would have nowhere else to go.

A cough, a harsh laugh, and a blonde emerges from one of the rooms. She sits near us and lights a cigarette. Her dress is a thin attempt at sensuality, and her face is thick with makeup. With her bottle-blonde hair, her chiselled features, her gold teeth and her deadened eyes, she is the perfect image of a Russian prostitute, flawlessly conveying an essence of sad criminal decadence. She ignores us, blowing smoke into the night. After a small pause an enormous shape appears behind her, a female apparition the size of two people, huge and fat-armed in a tent-like dress and scarf, both of which are pale and insubstantial in the dim light. A ghost, massive and weightless at the same time, it drifts past us, vanishing behind the pile of scrap metal.

Nothing we see seems real.

The man vanishes, reappears, begins to shout and wave, this time at us. I yawn and blink at him through tired eyes. I do not have the energy. Only gradually do I realise that the garbled tone of his Russian voice has changed, that he is instead trying a rough version of Farsi, one only vaguely recognisable. But it is enough; it is relief. As long as we pay, we are welcome.

Within minutes, we are nursing our bewildered thoughts to bed. We are lost and confused, reeling from the change from an Iran only a few hours old, but too tired to care. Our room is small, painted the bright primal colours of an African building, with the same glassless windows, the same shapeless door that refuses to close, the same single piece of cloth protecting us from the outside world. But it has beds; it is perfect. Outside, the man and the new arrivals open a bottle of vodka, beginning a long and loud journey to dawn. I struggle against their noise, against the feverish, sweat-drenched heat, and claw my way into oblivion.

Wednesday 5th July
Ashgabat

It would be wonderful to retain the unreal, dreamlike atmosphere of the night, but with sunlight Ashgabat is returned to the realm of the believable.

In daylight the courtyard outside our room feels far less threatening, far less dislocated from reality. It does, however, remain utterly foreign. Women constructed from slabs of tremulous, flabby white flesh sit around fires set in drums of metal, roasting bread. Their hair is thrust haphazardly behind their heads and into scarves, and the effect is more of convenience than religion. Iran is less than a day behind us, and the sight of bare arms, no matter how fatty and collapsed, strikes me at first as obscene. The culture shock of Turkmenistan is clearly going to be twofold: I must adjust to it with both newly acquired Iranian eyes as well as my own.

Outside, Ashgabat does not feel like the capital of a brand new country. It is small and close and empty, and I imagine that it might never lose the air of life under the Soviets, of a tiny outpost at the edge of a vast empire. The streets of large communal apartment blocks are Stalinesque visions of Soviet greatness, dating not from the era of socialist concrete sameness but earlier. They suggest some half-forgotten Russian film, dreary and ordered yet old enough to cling to an air of romance and character. All are painted in colours that were once cheery but have now faded to peeling pastels. The failed attempt at happiness seems very sad. Sandwiched amongst them are the trees and plots and animals of a country town; even the centre of the city manages to feel rustic. The overall impression is of a city far removed from anything important, run-down and remote, one looking somewhere else for instructions.

We spend the day exploring, searching for visas, for places to eat, for anything worth visiting, in air like melted resin. Ashgabat's heat is debilitating, and from the moment we rise a large damp patch of sweat stains my shirt. The air demands effort even to breathe, and the words of the Turkmen consul in Mashhad come back to me: "Oh no, you will not stay long in Ashgabat. It is a terrible city, far too hot. My advice is to leave as soon as possible."

By early afternoon we have been defeated by the heat. We have failed to obtain either Uzbek or Kyrgyz visas, failed to change money, failed to find anything of interest, failed even to find anywhere to drink, and are about to head back to our guest house when an American accent, fast and furious, snatches at us from behind.

"Excuse me, what are you doing here?"

The woman is small, with the toughened look of stretched leather. She wears a thin linen shirt and khaki shorts; hers are the first female legs we have seen. She glares at us, her hands on her hips, something slightly crazed in her eyes. We are too surprised to reply.

"You're not aid workers, are you?" the voice continues, snapping tightly out between her lips. "You're tourists, right?" We nod. "Well what the hell are you doing in Turkmenistan? I'm sorry, but I can't think of *any* reason *anyone* would want to come *here*."

The woman introduces herself as Suzie, a Peace Corps volunteer at the end of a three-year term in Turkmenistan. The look in her eyes reveals itself as a hunger for company, for a break from the crushing Turkmen tedium. Turkmenistan, she explains, is the most boring country in the world. It is a desert with four towns, with few links to the outside world, no natural sites worth visiting, no restaurants or shops, one of the last bastions of Communist dictatorship that remains. Choices for travel elsewhere do not exist – Iran is closed to the Americans, Tajikistan and Afghanistan are torn apart by war, and the Uzbek border guards demand exorbitant bribes – and after three years, Suzie yearns desperately for a journey to Turkey for a holiday. Turkmenistan is a place of nomads, flat and hot and empty, with hardly any relics of ancient civilisation, little identifiable culture; Suzie cannot understand its appeal to anyone.

In many ways her question is beyond me. Why are we here? What do we hope to find? I have half-formed hopes, vague ideas of what I might learn, but these mean nothing when I am ignorant of what awaits us. My images of these old Soviet republics are so ill-formed that only after we have experienced them will we know what they offer.

My only response is that we have come to taste the rare flavour of Central Asian Islam. For Islam still exists in all the Central Asian republics, despite the strictures of Communism: nine-tenths of Turkmenistan's population is nominally Muslim, with similar figures for Uzbekistan, and over half of Kyrgyzstan makes the same claim. But what does this mean? Being a Muslim in Ashgabat, even from the little we have already seen, means something far different from what it means to the Iranians to the south. It is this difference I have come here to sample, the shape and reality of Islam in Central Asia. Until we experience Central Asia I can only guess at what this means, but I suspect that it will be mixed inextricably with the grey stain of Communism. Eighty years of Soviet domination has to leave its mark.

Initially, most Muslims in Central Asia supported the overthrow of the Czarist regime. The Russian Empire had worked hard for control of the region, in a shadowy battle against British influence from the south, and its suppression of revolts in Turkestan during the First World War had been brutal. Like so many revolutionaries with unfounded hopes, the Muslims believed that the Bolshevik uprising would finally give them the chance for freedom, to rule themselves. It was not to be. It became rapidly apparent that self-rule for Turkestan was far from the Bolshevik agenda. They moved swiftly and ruthlessly to crush all opposition, and to establish their own form of control over the region, one far more insidious and pervasive than the Czarist regime had ever been.

The Russians knew that Islam alone provided the only viable and cohesive framework for opposition against them in what was otherwise an ethnically and linguistically mixed region. Indeed, all resistance to them was led in the name of Islam. Accordingly, the prime aim of the Bolsheviks was to attack the strength of religion. Beginning in the early 1920s, Stalin liquidated not only nationalist Muslim intellectuals, but nearly all of the pre-Revolutionary Muslim intelligentsia, regardless of whether they opposed the Soviet regime or not. In 1928, the attack widened to include the infrastructure of Islam itself, as thousands of mosques were closed and destroyed, and Muslim clerics were arrested and killed as saboteurs and spies. Islamic texts were burned, institutions of religious learning were closed, all public forms of Muslim worship were outlawed, and even Muslim names were forbidden. By 1941, only 1000 mosques remained of the 25,000 open in 1920; all of the 14,500 religious schools, or *madrasa*, were closed, and fewer than 2000 of 47,000 clerics had survived. The traditional religious establishment of Central Asia had been destroyed.

This typified the Soviet approach to the cultures of Central Asia. New artificial borders were drawn up. Arabic was banned, with modified forms of Cyrillic adopted instead. Local languages were forced to give way to Russian. Soviet social engineering meant that Central Asian Muslims became completely cut off from both each other as well as the outside world. The intellectual and cultural isolation of Central Asian Muslims from the rest of the world, from their place in history, and from each other, was almost total.

Even under such conditions, Islam survived. No doubt the religion was forced to change in many ways. Its essence – faith in God, belief in Muhammad as his prophet – could still remain the same, a simple formula, timeless and eternal. But a religion is, after all, as much the culture it spawns as its doctrine, and I cannot imagine Islam in Central Asia is the same Islam as a century ago, or anywhere near the same Islam as the rest of the world. Islam may have survived, but I expect it will be difficult to recognise.

Thursday 6th July
Ashgabat

We hope to leave Ashgabat tomorrow, beginning our journey through the desert towards Central Asia's most fabled desert cities: Samarkand and Bukhara. Both of these places have been legends for centuries. Both also serve as reminders of how important Central Asia has been to the history of Islam, and it is worth considering this history before we commence our journey.

Central Asia has been part of the world of Islam almost from the beginning. In the decades after the death of Ali, the Umayyad Caliphate expanded rapidly. Ruled from Damascus, it pushed its boundaries North and East and West, establishing Arab garrison towns in all its conquered territories, creating a realm based on Arab supremacy over vanquished peoples. Muslim forces established themselves firmly on the Indian continent, taking the territories of Sind by force and establishing the image of Islamic warriors converting at the point of the sword. There was the extremely important landing – from a Western perspective – in Spain in 710, followed quickly by the occupation of most of the Iberian peninsula. Islamic armies crossed the Oxus – the river which now forms the border between Turkmenistan and Uzbekistan – for the first time, taking the cities of Bukhara and Samarkand.

This Central Asian region would not play a major role in Islamic history for several centuries, however. In the early years, the empire had other things to worry about. Its focus was as much on Arab rule as the rule of Islam, and in an ethnically mixed environment this created a bitterly divided society. Eventually the frustrations of the non-Arab Muslim majority in the Empire boiled over into revolution, when the Abbasid movement emerged from Iran to overthrow the Umayyads and establish a new Caliphate in Baghdad. Their rule, which would last five centuries, was intended to be based purely on Islam. The empire they began was at the heart of a period of learning, civilisation and culture unlike any to have gone before it.

Interestingly enough, the rebellion against the Umayyad attitude of Arab superiority ensured, in the end, the Arabisation of the Islamic world. When the purity of Arab blood lost its importance, the very perception of what constituted an Arab changed. Language, not blood or tribe, became the badge of Arab identity. Under the Umayyads, one had to be a member of an Arab tribe by descent in order to be labelled an Arab. Beneath the Abbasids, the only requirement was that Arabic was your language. Soon Arabic became the main language from Persia to the Pyrenées. The cities of Islam changed from being garrison towns that ruled over conquered people to true cities, places of commerce and trade. The empire began to settle into itself.

The peoples of Central Asia would become vitally important to the history of Islam in the later years of the Abbasid Caliphate. As the centuries passed, the Islamic ideal envisaged by the early Abbasids began to vanish. The Abbasid court became a place of indulgence and extravagance, corruption and wealth. Marvellous palaces and lavish mansions were constructed, not only in the capital but in all the provincial cities, a litany of romantic names: Bukhara; Samarkand; Shiraz; Damascus; Aleppo; Jerusalem; Cairo; Tripoli; Fez; Cordoba. It was this structure, eventually, that led to the downfall of the empire in a long, spiralling decline into indolence and weakness. The caliphs increasingly began to delegate their authority to ministers of state and government officials, and found themselves losing control over their Baghdad guards. They concentrated on the religious guardianship of the position of the Caliphate, and before long their military commanders and guards were often able to appoint and depose them at will.

It was this empire, with Turks and Arabs and Persians all vying for influence at an emasculated Abbasid court, that would fall before three waves of conquest, each sweeping from the wastes of Central Asia. Three times – with first the Seljuqs followed by the Mongols and finally the conqueror Tamerlane – Central Asia would prove its importance to the destiny of Islam, its armies eradicating empires and establishing new ones.

The nomadic tribes of the Seljuq Turks entered Abbasid lands from Central Asia in the Tenth century, capturing northern Iran and accepting Islam for themselves. By the end of the Eleventh century, they had made themselves protectors of the Caliphate, and extended their control into

Syria, Palestine and Anatolia: it was Seljuq victories over the Byzantines in central Anatolia that would alarm the Christian world enough to provoke the First Crusade.

The Seljuq Grand Sultans will be remembered for their conflicts with the European Crusaders, and for the Turkish tribes that would remain in Anatolia after they had gone. Their importance, however, was minimal compared to the wave of conquest which followed in their wake. In 1258, the Mongols swept into Iran from Central Asia, capturing Baghdad and snuffing out the Caliphate. Theirs was a chronicle of devastation and conquest that ranks as one of the most remarkable in human history, an invasion that scorched Islamic civilisation to the ground, leaving it crippled and humbled for two centuries. The Arabs were destroyed by wild tribesmen who had, just as they had done themselves centuries earlier, ridden out of isolated deserts to destroy the established, sedentary systems.

The Mongols, under descendants of Genghis Khan, saw clearly the crumbling foundations and decadence of Muslim society. In the past, the Muslims had always believed that it was their faith that had led them to victory. The Mongol general Hülekü Khan warned them, using references from the Qur'an itself in his arguments, that they could rely on God no more. "Prayers against us will not be heard, for you have eaten forbidden things and your speech is foul, you betray oaths and promises, and disobedience and fractiousness prevail among you. Be informed that your lot will be shame and humiliation." His final verdict was prophetic: "You will suffer at our hands the most fearful calamity, and your land will be empty of you."

The Mongol armies withdrew to their Central Asian heartland, leaving the once mighty Islamic empire a shattered ruin, beginning an era of despair and poverty. Muslim life went on – indeed, one reaction to the Mongols was the rise of Islamic political radicalism, a fundamentalism in the face of defeat that characterises the religion even today – but the structure of government and civilisation had been broken.

This period of decay and desolation would remain for two centuries, until the final wave of conquest swept its way from Central Asia into the world of Islam. The Muslim warlord Tamerlane, an astonishing man characterised by both viciousness and artistic taste, would claim victories second only to those of Alexander the Great, and would conquer all the lands from India to the Mediterranean. Only after Tamerlane had come and gone could the glorious Ottoman, Saffavid and Mughal empires fully begin their rules.

Tamerlane – whose name is a European corruption of the name Timur-i-Leng, or "Timur the lame", given to him because of a slight limp – was a brutal man. He was not exaggerating when he warned Shah Shujah, Sultan of Iran and Persian Iraq: "Know that three things go before me: devastation, barrenness and pestilence." When cities fell to him, they burned; when populations fell to him, they were slaughtered. In many ways he was as merciless, bloodthirsty and destructive as the Mongols had been before him. Yet a savage Mongol he was not. Despite being illiterate, for example, he was a lover of the arts. He spoke two or three languages, played chess, and liked to have history read at mealtimes. His great love was for the aesthetic: for architecture, for gardens, for porcelain. Great foreign buildings, such as the Umayyad mosque in Damascus, were sketched by his official artists even as they burned. He brought back knowledge as well as riches from his conquests, making Samarkand a city of glittering beauty, of fantastic buildings and extraordinary wealth. His empire, its court based in Samarkand, became a true Renaissance society; one where learning, literature and art were valued more highly than ever before, as Timur stressed the aesthetic sensibilities of his empire, an empire founded on conquest and murder.

Timur marked the final period of Central Asian glory. The dynasty he left behind, the Timurids, were lords of a sophisticated culture, an empire of wealth and colour and cultivation, but theirs would be a short-lived rule, a rapid decline. They would flourish briefly, drawing intellectuals, artists and poets from all over the world, expanding their empire through trade rather than conquest, focusing their energies on science and learning, politics and trade. And this, of course, would be their downfall. In a pattern repeated throughout Islamic history, the Islamic ulema contrived to bring the Timurids down, bringing an end to the era of greatness for Central Asia, ushering in three centuries of petty khanates and tribal, nomadic rule.

However, while Timur's empire could not last without him, his cities remained. His greatest legacies are the cities of his Central Asian heartland, Bukhara and Samarkand, in present-day Uzbekistan. He ruled from them, and beneath him they became places of legend, cities without peer. To me they represent, as much as any single place, the history of Central Asia. Tomorrow, if all goes well, we plan to head off through the desert towards them.

Friday 7th July
Ashgabat…

The Turkmen landscape is grey and lifeless, without end. Our car spears through it like a troublesome dynamo, tossing dust and sand and distance casually backwards. I am filled with a heightened sense of being alive, a recognition so often found when travelling of the joy of a life there to be lived. Hardly profound thoughts, but it is in these strange odd moments, far removed from any cause I can name, that I sense the essential joy of childhood, the bubbling joy of life. If I were not constrained by this metal box I would stretch my arms out wide, point my face to the sky. So strange that outside is only the bored earth.

For the first few hours we follow the ridge of dark mountains that separates us from Mashhad, but before long the only landmarks are the black wires running beside the highway. The world is flat, dead, a shimmering image of tedium not even relieved by the drama of rolling desert sands. Even the sky is a blue almost without colour, as though it too has been drained of life by the Ashgabat heat, or perhaps sucked dry by the spectre of Communism.

"The Mafia come and rule these roads after dark. We try for the border, for Chardzhou, tonight. We not stop, especially when dark. We see Mafia, we go."

This is Meten, a Turk on his way to Kazakhstan, who has plucked us from the wet heat of Ashgabat to the bone dryness of this desert. Met at the Uzbek consulate, Meten was eager for companions for his journey across half the continent, and as I yawn at the lack of anything worthy of interest outside, I can see why. He is returning from a business trip back to Turkey; based in Kazakhstan, he manufactures shoes.

"Here, see my passport. I am Kazakh citizen."

The passport is in Cyrillic. "Can you read this?" I ask.

Meten shakes his head. "No. These people, they can speak Turkish, but we cannot read each other when we write. I live in Kazakhstan five years, still I cannot read."

In many ways Meten's journey is a kind of homecoming, a return to the steppes that gave birth to his people. Of course, the Turks of Anatolia – Meten's Turks – have travelled a long road from their nomadic beginnings in lands to the north of these sandy wastes. A thousand years has seen his people left in Anatolia like jetsam after the tide has receded, seen the mighty Ottoman Caliphate become a secular state, seen the tribal regions of Central Asia crushed by the Soviets. Yet through it all, the two peoples have retained the thread of their shared cultural identity. For Meten, with a Kazakh wife and a Kazakh home, the feeling must be a strong one.

The Twentieth century has been a time of as much wrenching social change for Turks as it has for the Turkic people of Central Asia. Attatürk's vision of a secular Turkey furiously rejected the past. At the same time that Central Asian Muslims were having Cyrillic thrust upon them, the Turks themselves were adopting a new, Latin script. The Hagia Sophia mosque was converted to a museum. The fez was banned. Sufi and dervish orders were suppressed; Islamic Shari'a law was replaced by European legal codes and the Caliphate itself, seat of Islamic power for centuries, was abolished. For Central Asia the changes were thrust upon them by a foreign power, while for Turkey they were the moves of a single country, imposed by its own immensely popular leader, but the results in both cases were remarkably effective and very similar. One hundred years ago Meten would have shared the Arabic script with the Turkmen guards he must bribe at each of the various checkpoints strung out along the desert. Now, with their own scripts, their own languages, the baggage of their own recent histories, it is a wonder that any sense of brotherhood between Central Asia and Turkey remains, yet remain it does. We cut through the desert in the hands of an Anatolian-born Kazakh Turk, with the strange feeling of being part of a far larger, pan-Turkic world. Night, when it comes, is hot and silent, the night of a desert in summer.

It is late when Meten pulls away from the road, shining his headlights at the first building we have seen for hours, yet the sand is still warm from the heat of the day. The building is open and without glass. Bare and cement, it sits alone amongst the dunes. I glance at the sky. Gone is the euphoria of before; now I feel only exhaustion, with the sting of dust in my eyes. At least I am not ill, like Kirst – for hours she has endured the cramping pains of dysentery. I scramble after her into the dunes, lit bright by the moon, to guard her as she succumbs to the trials of her sickness. The sand is smooth and blue under the moon; laughter behind me echoes out into the coloured night.

We return to find that Meten has organised a rough meal of kebabs and warm fruit juice. We eat on stools in the open, the heat far too unpleasant inside the building. The shapeless men who have prepared our meal hang back in the darkness, working noisily at a pile of hot coals, whilst flies nag at our faces.

Meten continues to worry. "We stop on these roads, the Mafia sure to get us. It happen to me before. Sometimes they wild men, sometimes they police." He shakes his head. "In these country, Mafia is police; police is Mafia."

Despite these fears, which he articulates to us constantly over the next four hours to Chardzhou, Meten decides he will drive on into the night. His fear of staying in the darkened border town seems even greater. Its nameless and confusing streets swallow us, and an increasingly frantic Meten becomes focused on one thing only: finding the border and continuing his sleepless journey across Uzbekistan. He has promised to deposit us in Bukhara. We do not look forward to arriving, yet again, in a Central Asian country well after midnight, confronting a world as impossible to decipher as Turkmenistan was. But we are too tired, too coated in sweat and grime and dust, to care.

We find the border, an array of pontoons stretched across the Amu Darya, and roll our way across black water under the dim light of the distant city. Russian guards wave us through after suspiciously questioning why we smile in our passport photos. And then, on our way across the final hurdle, the collision that ensures our entry to Uzbekistan will not be in darkness; a car of men in green uniforms trimmed with red, screaming and laughing and singing and drunk, whirls around a corner and slams into our car. A crunch of metal. Silence washed over the sound of spinning wheels. A moan from Meten.

Our purgatory of detention lasts four hours, until six in the morning. The beleaguered Meten is too exhausted to explain the situation to us as it unfolds; his only words, much repeated, are "big problem". It is apparent, however, that the officers blame Meten for the accident – naturally enough, too: this is a lawless country, corrupt, and by "Mafia" Meten has meant men such as these – and his fight is to avoid a serious charge. We are confined in a literal and metaphorical no-man's-land between two countries, beneath buzzing electric lights and alongside large army trucks. I stretch out in the sand by the road and try to sleep.

The glow of dawn is strong by the time Meten agrees to the bribe that sets us free.

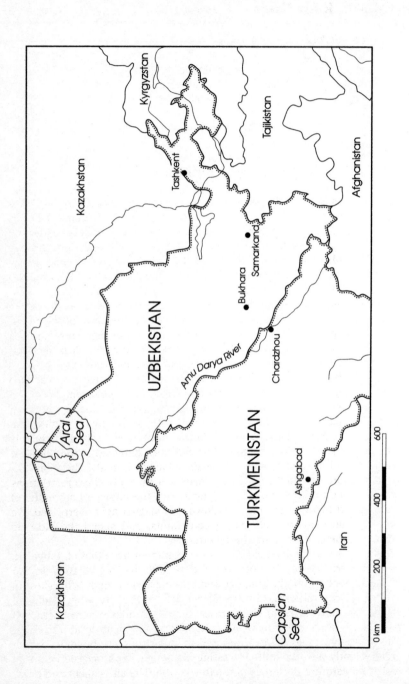

UZBEKISTAN

Faith In Knowledge

Saturday 8th July - Sunday 9th July

Bukhara
a name of stolen antiquity
barely imagined

smothered in silence

eternity, myth
the poetry of stone.

Bukhara has long been part of the Muslim world. First taken by the Arabs in the early Eighth century, it was a leading centre of Islamic learning under the Abbasids, and its reputation retained a quality of legend through successive waves of Muslim and Mongol conquest, right through to its establishment as the capital of the Uzbek emirate in 1555. It has foundered as a centre of religion and knowledge since the Russian and Soviet domination of Central Asia, but its air of mystery and inaccessibility has only increased over the last eighty years, as the Soviet Republics of Central Asia became the least accessible parts of the Soviet empire. Even now, obtaining visas as independent travellers, not part of a tour, has been almost impossible. After trying for six months, Turkmenistan was the only place they could be found with ease.

The city is a bizarre mix of Soviet concrete and ancient stone, and all of it is crumbling and decayed. It has two centres: one is what remains of the Socialist vision, while the other is the memory of a golden age of Islam long since past. We wander through them both, searching for somewhere to stay, once Meten leaves us early in the morning. Even in daylight this simple task is difficult enough; had we not been detained at the border it would have been impossible. Our main difficulty is that Uzbekistan has been far more reluctant than Turkmenistan to shed Soviet-era restrictions and embrace the free market: foreigners have the choice of a handful of state-owned hotels, each one run-down and staggeringly overpriced. We refuse to be held to such galling constraints, and spend the morning searching the city for somewhere better.

The heat, as we wander the town, is very different from that of Ashgabat. Here the cruelty comes not from the smothering hug of wet air, but instead directly from the sun, dry and burning and mean. It is harshest in the town's central square, in the Soviet part of the city, where Bukhara seems far more Russian than Uzbek. We skip quickly across cracked pavements, squeezed with weeds, radiating yellow heat up at our chins. The area is vast and empty, bordered by huge concrete buildings which groan silently into the still air, rusting neon signs, and occasional social realist iron statues of Heroes of the Revolution. The air is silent and dead, and so are most of the trees, scrabbling for existence in rows at the centre of the concrete field. Fetid green water lies still in thin channels; a pond once meant for a fountain exposes dry concrete to the sun. Not a person is seen, not a leaf stirs, not even birds can be bothered with this sky. The weekend, perhaps, is to blame, but the sense of decay is thick enough to have been here for years, and I cannot shake the feeling that this is a graveyard of Communism.

Our salvation, eventually, lies in Bukhara's ancient stone heart, surrounded by the remnants of Bukhara's Muslim past, in an area of narrow lanes and hidden doors. The Kukeldash *madrasa*, an ancient school of religious learning, lies at the centre of the old part of town, one of the many buildings gathered around an ancient pool. Here, at least, there is life. Dozens of men, most old, sit on hard wooden beds, drinking green tea and eating pilau, a dish of rice cooked with meat, beside the pool. These are the Uzbeks, this is what remains. Each face is topped with a delicately patterned skull-cap in black and white; flat-topped, square-domed. Each face, lined with years of serious talk, is intent on its tea, or on one of a dozen games of chess. Each face is at ease.

We walk past the men as they lounge in the shade of hanging trees, and walk up ancient steps to the *madrasa*. It is a large brick building, a small fortress built around a single courtyard. Its structure calls to mind the stalls of Esfahan, or the shrine in Mashhad. Peaked Islamic arches line the courtyard in two stories. Each alcove, so low that one needs to stoop to enter, houses a single wooden door of pale blue. In places, the walls retain shreds of blue tiles like those of Esfahan. The air of decrepitude, the crumbling bricks, the missing tiles, all make the place seem much older than the mosques in Iran, where the focus on religion, the care for the elements of the faith, has never ceased.

The Tajik caretaker of the *madrasa* emerges from a tiny office to inspect us. He is bent and ancient, with a sour look to his face, but he breaks into a smile when he finds we can speak his language: Tajik is an Afghan offshoot of Farsi. He offers us a room used throughout the ages by Islamic clergy and students alike.

The *madrasa* has no running water. The toilets are public ones outside the building, with no lighting, no sanitation, no cubicles, simply a trough over which one shits, alongside whoever else might be present. Although cooler than the day outside, its rooms are stiflingly hot. Yet despite these problems, it is one of the best settings for a guest house: when we creep into our white-washed room, tiny and ancient, with its peaked ceilings and tiny windows, we feel we creep into history. The feeling is akin to a stay in an ancient Greek monastery. What ghosts will sleep here with us tonight? I try to imagine the ancient learning in these walls, the scholars alone with their research, gaining knowledge both secular and religious. The feeling of time and place and history is a strong one.

Today Islam is not viewed as a religion receptive to learning and knowledge. It is seen more as a religion rejecting the modern world, an attitude typified by the fundamentalist readings of the Qur'an which claim that it and it alone contains all knowledge. The Qur'an contains all science, the extremists say, claiming Muhammad anticipated all the modern discoveries. Yet it is easy to forget that these claims, ones I have heard numerous times, have little to do with the fundamentals of Islam. They are new to the religion, modern reactions to the superior Western scholarship of the last hundred years. It was not always this way.

The Prophet made repeated calls to the importance of knowledge. "Seek knowledge, even unto China," he commanded, while in the Qur'an he appeals to al-Lah, "Oh my Lord! Advance me in knowledge!" For centuries Muslims would follow his words. As the early Muslim empires spread into new realms and contacted new peoples, the insatiable thirst for knowledge, to understand the conquered peoples, was understandable. But even when expansion ceased under the Abbasids, and the empire of Islam settled into five centuries of prosperity, the quest for knowledge continued; the Abbasids actively encouraged and organised one of the most significant flowerings of knowledge that the world had ever seen.

A story common in many books, one I believed for many months, describes how, following the Arab occupation of Alexandria, the Caliph ordered the destruction of the city's huge library. The supposed reasons for the act are that only one book was thought to be needed for the world of Islam. If the books contained what was in the Qur'an they were superfluous, while if they did not then they were ungodly. The story is apocryphal. The library itself had already been destroyed by internal dissension before the Arabs arrived. And even if it had not, the story would not ring true. Elsewhere, the standard Arab reaction was to translate all knowledge they encountered into Arabic.

Islamic scholarship drew on three ancient sources of wisdom for their inspiration: Persian, Indian and Greek. The Persians bequeathed a history of art, poetry and literature. The Indian world inspired astronomy, mathematics and eventually the decimal system itself. And in the Hellenic sphere the Muslims focused mainly on Greek philosophy – on the systems of Plato, Aristotle and Euclid, as well as Neoplatonic ideas – and the medical work of Hippocrates, but they drew just as keenly from Greek mathematics, astronomy, chemistry and physics. In less than a hundred years after initial contact, the Arabs had translated all the major Greek works into Arabic. It was only through such efforts that Europe could hope for its own Renaissance, when the gift of Greek learning was returned to it through its contact with the Muslim world in Spain and Italy. The Muslim colleges in Andalusia, home to the poetry, literature and learning of Cordoba and Granada, would provide a model for those at Oxford and Cambridge.

Built on such foundations, the era until the devastation of the Mongols was a time of Muslim genius. The philosopher ibn Sina (Avicenna) came from Bukhara itself at the end of the Tenth century, and is hailed as the greatest philosopher of the eastern Muslim world. Avicenna achieved the most systematic integration of Greek rationalism and Islamic thought, and contended that religion is merely philosophy in a metaphorical form that makes it acceptable to the masses, who are unable to grasp rational philosophical arguments. The physician al-Razi (known to Europeans as Rhases) came from Iran, and devoted himself to a meticulous study of medicine. He listed 176 methods of contraception and abortion, for which he found the support of numerous *hadith*. Omar Khayyam, best known as a poet for his Rubáiyát, was one of the greatest mathematicians we know about between the Fourth and Fourteenth centuries. Muslim analysis of history culminated in the work of ibn Khaldun, perhaps the greatest historical thinker of the Middle Ages, one of the first men to analyse the patterns of history. These thinkers were rarely specialists in a single discipline, more usually masters of many diverse fields: literature; medicine; mathematics; philosophy; astronomy. Islamic civilisation was producing Renaissance men centuries before the term was used in Europe.

Scholarship was not, of course, divorced from religion. Indeed, the growth of knowledge created an intellectual crisis for the Muslim Arabs, in which the men of religion, the *ulema*, felt threatened by both the philosophers and the Sufi mystics. Their differences were eventually resolved by al-Ghazzali, whose writing represents the zenith of Muslim religious thought. His major work, *The Revival of the Religious Sciences*, presented a unified view of religion, incorporating elements of the three sources formerly considered contradictory: orthodox Islam, mysticism, and the intellectualism of the philosophers. The work healed a rift in Islam that had threatened to tear it apart. It has been said of it that "if all the books of Islam were destroyed it would be but a slight loss if only the work of Ghazzali were preserved".

Yet if al-Ghazzali represented the zenith of Muslim thought, he also heralded the beginning of its downfall. Later in his life, al-Ghazzali's views became less receptive to the differing branches of Islam, and he worked to refute the Neoplatonic theories of many of the Muslim philosophers, such as Avicenna. Their ideas were seen as radical and abhorrent by most orthodox Muslims, as they rejected the doctrines of creation and immortality of the soul. Al-Ghazzali's *Destruction of the Philosophers* was, in many ways, responsible for the eventual decline of rational intellectualism in Islam: the man who had healed the rift in the religion would also be the architect of many of the arguments used in the rejection of modern knowledge. From al-Ghazzali's time onward, the emphasis on religion and religious forms above rational thought would only grow. In the end it would be the area of jurisprudence, not philosophy or science, which would dominate Islamic learning. In the end, it would be the orthodox men of Islam who would triumph over the philosophers and the mystics. Orthodox Muslim thought developed in parallel with the work of the philosophers, and centred primarily on the concept of Islamic legalism. It was seen as a way to preserve the ideals of the first Muslim community, and to structure Muslim life in a way worthy of the Prophet. After the leadership of the first four Caliphs, Muslims had found themselves in a different world, a growing empire far removed from Muhammad's original vision. The Muslims sought a way of preserving that vision, of forming rules of conduct that could guide them through a difficult time, one with little moral leadership. The most popular solution was an attempt to return to the ideals of the Prophet by enshrining his sayings and actions, the *hadith* and the *sunna*, into formalised legal codes. The laws that resulted were known as the *Shari'a*, and articulated rules of conduct for the community. In Islamic society, the term law came to have a wider significance than it does today in the West, encompassing both moral and legal rules. Consequently not all Islamic law can be enforced by the courts, as much of it depends on conscience alone.

By the Eighth and Ninth centuries, a bewildering number of oral traditions were in circulation about Muhammad and his early companions. These were collected, scrutinised and distilled to form the basic systems of the Shari'a. It was this process of scholarly examination of the hadith and the surviving records of early Islam, which would see the establishment of the four main schools of Sunni Islamic law and custom; schools of reason and religion that would spread through the Islamic world, and lead to the establishment of thousands of *madrasa* like the one we sleep in now.

In the wake of the establishment of these schools of thought, Muslims declared that "the gates of independent judgement are henceforth closed." It is this attitude that has come to triumph over the intellectual achievements of the great Muslim scholars. The *Shari'a* and the various schools of jurisprudence have remained; Islamic philosophy and science have not. The Muslim intellectual age lasted five centuries, but in the end it was overtaken by a desire for the forms of Islam alone, by a suspicion of free thought, which eventually led to intellectual stagnation during the decline of the last great Muslim empires.

The deterioration of independent thought within Islam continued well into the Twentieth century. Only twenty years ago, Saudi Islam supported the view expressed in the Qur'an that the world was flat. It is therefore understandable that today few people would associate Islamic history with culture and learning on a scale comparable to the ancient Greeks. Instead, many associate the religion with fundamentalist views of the world, rejection of modern learning, and fatalistic acceptance that all is the will of God. Given such a state of affairs, it is easy to assume that Islam is responsible for the intellectual stagnation of Muslim society, that today's problems can be blamed on the structure of the religion itself, but such an assumption is incorrect. Even a basic understanding of the history of Islamic learning is enough to show that the image of Islam as a regressive, backward-thinking religion is wrong. Islam was once a religion of knowledge, more so perhaps than any other major world religion. Of all the reasons for the current attitudes towards learning within Islamic society, Islam is not one of them.

Godless Pilgrim

Wednesday 12th July
Samarkand

It is now late afternoon. Kirst is outside, washing the desert from her clothes, conducting yet another languageless conversation with our host; I can hear her carbonated laugh dance over the sound of running water. We are so unalike. Kirst has a ready joy fermenting constantly just beneath the surface, and laughter is never far away. When she releases it, it is loose and free and almost mad, a barely-controlled hysteria that comes from close within, as though there was a short-cut in her brain between reality and delight. To me, one whose laughter is more likely to be gentle than crazed, someone able to consciously decide between laughter and silence, she is a constant wonder. Travelling with her has something of the fascination of studying an alien creature, one wondrous and beautiful and strange.

I lie, as I have done all day, on a narrow bed in a narrow room. I have spent most of the last twenty-four hours in a feverish delirium somewhere between here and the toilet; these grey walls are driving me mad. An unchanging image of joylessness: brown stain on the ceiling like a failed chemistry experiment; spider trapped between the fly screen and my glimpse of the apricot tree outside; three coffin-thin beds filling the floor. At least I have recovered enough to read, but I remain trapped by dizziness when I try to stand. I am filled with the mindless frustrated energy that comes with the tail end of an illness, filled with the claustrophobic desire for action that I cannot yet achieve. So I write.

This afternoon I have read most of Edward Said's *Covering Islam*, a critique on how Western media and scholarship have presented the topic of 'Islam', written two years after the Iranian Revolution. Said is the author of *Orientalism*, a seminal work that to many redefined the history of Western impressions of Islam. Historically, "Orientalism" has been a legitimate field of scholarly research. Orientalists earlier this century were as well versed in their subject – in its history, in its languages – as scholars of ancient Greek. Since Said, however, the term has come to mean something different: it has come to be widely used for the *mis*representation and *mis*understanding of Eastern cultures and society, rather than their legitimate study. This is in many ways a shame: to someone of my age, "Orientalism" has only ever been a pejorative term. Said is no doubt correct in his assessment of the prejudices inherent in the work of leading Orientalists, scholars who brought the attitudes of their time and culture to their work, but such flaws should not necessarily render everything they did invalid – divisions of this kind will always occur when one culture or society considers another one, separate and different.

Covering Islam is more concerned with society than scholarship, in particular with the treatment of Islam in the media; it is here where Said's concerns about narrow and misleading interpretations of Islam correspond more closely with my own. Of course, I too would come into Said's line of fire, not least for my liberal use of the term 'Islam' as though it were some objective entity, some readily observable state of existence or belief, something small enough to be contained in a single word. No word is powerful enough for such an entirety of history and culture and philosophy and religion of whole groups of very different people in very different places at very different times. In this, Said is correct. By using a single term for something so all-encompassing, my language is likely to be reductionist, inducing my readers to see 'Islam' as something uniform and limited, leading them to believe something that isn't true.

The same is true, however, for all such terms. 'The West' and 'Western civilisation' are no less poorly defined. These terms do not arouse resentment in the West because we are comfortable with them as hazy definitions which do not mean particularly much, as tags applied to notions that are at best vague and incomplete. The problem only arises when we consider something with which we are not comfortable, particularly other cultures and societies. We are not familiar enough with such things to know instinctively that the terms we use create a reductive view of the world.

This is especially true of Islam. Of all the terms we use to describe other cultures, 'Islam' is the most vulnerable to misinterpretation. No other term or concept can be used to denote so wide a set of beliefs, cultures, histories, politics and peoples. Christianity does not govern the totality of existence in the Christian world to anywhere near the same extent as Islam does for Muslims. Islam, as we hear over and over, is more than just a religion: it is an entire way of life. It is love and law, it is war and justice, it is politics and prayer. So when 'Islam' is used to describe one aspect of Islamic society, such as the treatment of women in one particular country, or the extremist violence in another, it is little wonder that its use only distorts how we see Islam as a whole. In many Muslim societies, as well as in the West, 'Islam' has become a political cover for much that is not religious, and thus any analysis of politics in Muslim countries is apt to taint the religion itself. Similarly, stories of atrocities and injustice in Islamic countries are liable to affect our view of the Muslim faith; they may even alter our impressions of individual Muslims themselves.

No such parallels occur in the West. Nobody links the latest mass-murderer with Christianity, nobody sees the latest fundamentalist Christian cult as characteristic of Western society as a whole.

We could explain this with the xenophobic streak present in every society, the fear and suspicion of something unknown. It is easy to be familiar with American society and culture when it bombards the world every day; other cultures are far more easy to see as villainous and threatening. A film like *Not Without My Daughter* can induce us to imagine all Iranians as villains, but we can ignore the millions of horror stories that emerge from our own cultures, ignore the films built on true-life terror that are made every day. The equation between individuals and societies, between politics and religion, is for some reason so much easier for us to make when the topic is Islam. And responsible for this, in many ways, is how Islam is presented to us on a day-to-day basis by the media. Through the years we have grown accustomed to thinking of the Western media as, on the whole, reliable and factual, and of the media of non-Western countries as leaning towards the propagandist and ideological. When Islamic newspapers scream about the disintegration of Western society, we are liable to ignore them, but when our television screens swell with images of screaming Muslim fanatics, we watch. Yet objectivity, factuality and accuracy are merely ideals, ideals which are rarely met, even if we hear the words so often we associate them instinctively with our own societies.

A major part of the difference between the ideal and reality is that almost all media corporations are profit-seeking organisations. Of course they are, we say: this is part of our society. But the ideal of presenting subjects in a balanced, objective way hardly ever converges with the drive to present a story that sells. News is entertainment, except in a few high-quality cases, and the news we see is the news that makes people watch; it has nothing to do with oft-quoted but rarely achieved idealised standards of journalism.

We all are products of our own societies, and we all instinctively know what type of story sells. Even my letters home have conformed to the rules of modern journalism. My letters are meant to entertain as much as inform, and it is entirely natural that the stories I tell will be as outlandish as possible. The same principles govern the Western media, only on a far grander scale.

This is the structure of media in a capitalist society, and its shortcomings are obvious. Where Islam is concerned, it means that the images we see most often are usually the negative ones. Sensationalist and amazing, and overwhelmingly negative. This means that the regular rendition of television pictures of 'Islamic' mobs, chanting for the destruction of the US and Israel, images of fanatics strapping bombs to their bodies in southern Lebanon, of fevered crowds screaming for their revolutionary leaders, of cruel punishments in Saudi Arabia – these images, along with our unfamiliarity with the topic, and its distance from us, limit 'Islam' as we know it to these characteristics alone. It is like viewing the entirety of American society through the hate-filled eyes of a bigoted redneck. Watching a crowd of Islamic extremists may not appear to be very different from watching a march of neo-Nazis or the Ku Klux Klan. Yet because these latter images are not the only ones we receive of America, we can dismiss them as the merest part of the truth; they exist, but hardly account for everything. Images of Islam, however, are so selective, so biased towards the sensational, that we can be forgiven for assuming that entire societies consist purely of screaming fanatics and oppressors of women. Why else would I have been staggered by the welcome we received in Iran? How else do I begin to understand why the simple sight of families picnicking happily together came as such a surprise? Even when one is aware of the dangers that writing about Islam entails, difficulties still remain. Intent on showing the often-neglected positive aspects of Muslim society, there is the temptation to overlook the negative side that we so often see. The great danger, and my greatest fear, is that I can easily be misconstrued as some kind of apologist for the religion, glossing over what is wrong with Islam in an attempt to show what is right. Such an interpretation is no better than depicting all Arabs as oil sheikhs or terrorists. The negative aspects do, after all, exist. They are not a creation of the Western media, just a fixation for them. In the wake of Said's work, a lot of Muslims jumped on the Orientalist bandwagon. With some justification, they placed blame for the problems in Islamic society on colonialism, on pre-Islamic customs, on Bedouin tradition, on the myopia of the Western media. Yet they must remember that Islam itself is also to blame. There is no doubt that it is a religion of many positives: the Qur'an *does* grant rights to women that they had never previously had; it *does* lay down a structure of law far more advanced and equitable than anything that had preceded it; the faith *does* create a culture of generosity and community spirit. Yet writers on Islam cannot ignore that the Qur'an also talks about beating one's wife, about death sentences for apostasy, or that there are justifications within the *hadith* for the horrific treatment of women in Arabia and Pakistan. There are aspects of Islam worthy of praise, but there are many aspects worthy of condemnation. The great challenge is to provide a balance between the two, to provide a view of the religion that in some way corresponds to reality.

Many Muslim apologists deny that such a balance is necessary, arguing that there is a difference between true Islam and Islam as it has been practised throughout history. Islam is not to blame for anything we see today, because what we see today is not true Islam. This is an excuse we have heard countless times throughout our trip. In Yazd we were even told that Ali himself was not a true Muslim, influenced as he was by those around him, that the only true Muslim in history had been Muhammad. If we were to believe these people, Islam is nothing more than the life of a single historical figure: the lives of over a billion believers and the weight of over a thousand years of history can be completely ignored.

This view is almost childishly simplistic. A religion is not a set of abstract ideals, carved into stone thirteen centuries ago and never since attained. If that is Islam, then it is not what this book is about. A religion is a living thing. Islam cannot be divorced from how it is believed and practised and lived; it cannot be divorced from the society it creates. When one judges Islam, one must judge how it is used today, how it governs the lives of its believers, not how a single man once lived his life.

At the risk of being labelled an apologist for Muslim injustices by Western readers, and labelled an infidel critic of the religion and part of the Western myopia by Muslims, I want to feel capable of such a judgement by the end of this journey. I want to convey the naked experience of an Islam that consists of far more than either the life and sayings of the Prophet or sensationalist images of fanaticism and cruelty. I want to show Islam as I experience it in the cultures we visit, in the people we meet; I want my own journey – this slice of life that is my own subjective truth – to provide a tiny glimpse of the kaleidoscopic reality that is Islam.

Thursday 13th July
Samarkand

Where knowledge begins, religion ends.
Ulugh Beg, viceroy of Samarkand, 1410-1449

The illness, whatever it was, has faded to no more than a handful of troubled dreams by the time night begins, and by morning it is gone. Yet while the delirium is a memory, the frustration of confinement is not: it is with delight that I finally leave our stifling room to explore the city once more.

On the outskirts of Samarkand, just beyond the old city walls, lies Shah-é Zinda, a mausoleum complex erected six centuries ago by Timur. At its heart is a tomb far older than the rest, that of Kusam ibn Abbas, one of the Prophet's cousins, the "Living King" after whom the mausoleum is named. According to legend, he was praying here when Zoroastrians crept up behind him and cut off his head. He finished his prayers, picked up his head, and jumped into a well. After that, his tomb became a place of Muslim pilgrimage, and it was the religious importance of the site that prompted Timur to build the necropolis that stands there now. This morning, beneath a clarion sky, we go to make a pilgrimage of our own.

Domes of ringing blue dance on the hills behind us as we walk down a final slope to the complex. One of them, though we cannot tell which, is an observatory built by Ulugh Beg, Timur's grandson. Kirst tells me his story as we walk, which she discovered yesterday while I was sick. Intensely secular, Ulugh Beg's only interest was knowledge. He could not really be called a Muslim, as he viewed religion as nothing but an obstacle to the attainment of knowledge, and was accordingly hated by the Muslim movement. He was a brilliant mathematician and scholar, a revolutionary in the field of astronomy: his observatory has a huge sextant for measuring celestial angles, and his tables remained the most accurate and complete in the world until the Seventeenth century. He developed his own cosmological theories about the revolution of the planets, and if the West had known about his discoveries it might be he, not Copernicus, who is regarded as the father of modern astronomy. (Copernicus, denounced by the Catholic Church as a heretic for declaring that the earth revolved around the sun, might have agreed about religion obstructing knowledge; the Catholic Church did not admit it was wrong to persecute him until 1984.) Ulugh Beg's attitudes towards religion would outrage most Muslims even today, and his fate is a fitting symbol for the decline of the scholarship that once lay at the heart of Islamic civilisation: his son, Abd al-Latif, a pious Muslim supported by Samarkand's religious movement, had him murdered in 1449. Yet it is not the ending of the story which disturbs me – it would seem inevitable – but that I am surprised that Ulugh Beg could have aired such views at all. They are not views I would wish to express publicly in Iran or Saudi Arabia today.

We reach the mausoleum. Its gates lead up fifty stone steps the colour of sand, into an open necropolis filled with an air of ruin and death.

Before us lies a narrow alley of octagonal stone tiles, guarded on either side by fierce walls of brick. The alley is all contrast – bright, dark, bright, dark – as carvings of sun and shade slant across the stone, lean on the ground. The shadows come from the domed tombs that begin twenty steps from where we stand; from there, they flank the path for at least another two hundred. Tall and crumbling, they bare their teeth at each other across our thin path of cobbled stone, a narrow chasm between high, crowding walls of grim brick and plaster. We walk towards the shadows.

The tombs vary in their states of disrepair. Each bears the tiles of Islam on its open facade: in dark blue and white, in simple diamonds, in interlocking star shapes of blue and gold, or delicately formed floral mosaics. White Arabic script, carved in bas-relief, twines with a raised pattern of blue leaf. The domes, of weathered brick and plaster, are uniformly crumbling; only a few still cling to the tiles of cerulean blue that laugh back at the sky across the city. In the alleyway a small taste of the necropolis's former glory is retained, but even here white plaster gapes at us – everywhere is the rough crime of decay.

We enter the first tomb through a peaked Islamic arch. Inside is bare and dark, and the cracked light that filters down from above is bodiless. Raw stone tombs emerge slowly from the gloom before me; they crowd a rough floor that is barely fifteen feet in any direction. The air inside the dome swirls, its sound a distant echo of the roaring of surf in a storm. Beyond the remotest echo is silence.

I glance back outside. Across from us is another tomb, identical in structure to the one we are in but far more decrepit: gone are most of the coloured tiles, leaving only the desert stone. A woman walks past, a flash of purple with a child at her side. Even from here I can smell her perfume. It reminds me of something distant, something lost, though I am not sure what it is. I stand for a moment, caught somewhere between a memory I cannot reach and a sound I cannot hear, swept by the sense of ruin of all that surrounds.

Outside, I realise that the woman has not one but two children with her. A tiny girl skips along beside her, a blur of movement of two legs, while the tortured limbs of cerebral palsy writhe in the baby's carriage beside her.

Fingers tight and claw-like wave absently in the air as the woman pushes her adolescent son slowly down the path. Slowly, peering into the gaping tombs, we follow.

At the end of the path we reach a large building, a final arch before a small courtyard. The building's door is heavy and wooden, carved with dramatic patterns in fine relief. A huge lock, larger than my fist, declares it closed. And before it, as though waiting for us, is the keeper of the tomb. He is a gruff, white-bearded man, very Uzbek in his skull-cap and long grey coat. His head is old, and when he closes his eyes his face holds as much life as a statue; he could well have been here for centuries. We wait, silent participants, while the woman asks him to open the door.

Soft sounds of mumbled prayer spill over us as we enter a short corridor, remove our shoes. The air is pulled tight with a kind of expectation that is difficult to recognise, one that neither includes us nor demands that we leave. No words are spoken as we follow the others into a large white room.

It is from here that the sounds of prayer come. Stone lattice grills in the walls admit sculpted beams of light from the world outside. They shine on to the two figures crouched at the room's *mihrab*, the alcove in the wall that directs their prayers towards Mecca. They are two women, their backs towards us, their bodies shrouded in white veils. Over their shoulders I can make out the glow of tiny candles. They do not acknowledge our presence.

The atmosphere feels dense and heavy, supersaturated with feeling, as though a careless whisper might precipitate a flood of emotion from the air around us. We follow mutely as the man unlocks two more doors, leads us to the inner shrine, to the tomb itself. It lies in its own room, a thin stone tomb cased in a carved wooden grill. The walls are of plain white plaster, bare; it has none of the drama of Iran. But it has all of the emotion. Wordlessly, the woman enters the shrine with its guardian, her movements slow and deliberate, as though acting out a ritual she has rehearsed many times. She bends, places her hands under the arms of her son, and lifts him out of the carriage. Then, with a slow sadness, she begins to half-carry, half-drag him around the tomb. His twisted legs drag on the stone.

The air in the shrine seems hermetically sealed. I dare not breathe.

I do not know how long curiosity holds guilt at bay; the moment is a private one but my eyes refuse to let my body move. Then, suddenly, I glimpse the woman's face. Tears stream in silence down her cheeks as she stumbles around the white slab of stone, as she cries with her soul to God for help. Something drops and gives way inside me. I feel a low sucking in the pit of my stomach as the full guilt of our intrusion hits. Unlike the wailing in Iran, it is impossible to doubt that this woman's tears are real, and her pain does not deserve the gaze of strangers. As noiselessly as we can, we make our way back to the entrance.

Pilgrims like this woman once came to Shah-é Zinda from all over Central

Asia. Now, the place has lost its glory, lost its hallowed place in Muslim belief, and the pilgrims no longer come in great numbers. Yet still, after all these years, they come.

We do not speak. We are both moved by what we have just seen, perhaps more so than by the religious hysteria that we witnessed in Iran. There, the feeling that filled us was one of awe; here it is one of sadness. The woman has touched us with her own grief. Written on her face were all the blunted dreams she once had for her child, all the struggle and heartache she was asking God to relieve. Together, they have slipped beneath my guard and claimed my heart.

I think back to all the Muslim holy sites we have visited, to the Indian Muslim pilgrims we met on the train to Mashhad. No doubt I will continue to seek out every holy Muslim site in Asia as part of this journey, my interest in the religion drawing me to every place of religious importance. As much as the Indians, as much as this woman, as much as any Muslim, I am on my own pilgrimage. But unlike any of them, unlike the countless pilgrims with whom my path will merge over the coming months, I am not a Muslim. My pilgrimage may be longer and more thorough than most of them will attempt, yet it cannot compare. I am a pilgrim without Islam, without a faith of my own. I am a godless pilgrim.

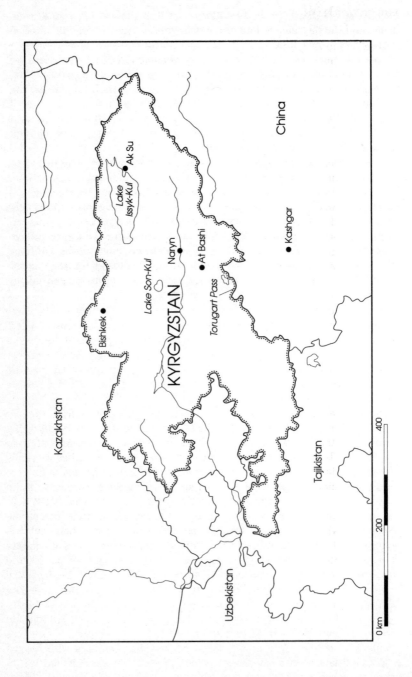

KYRGYZSTAN

Demon Drink

> Islam among illiterate people without mullahs cannot have roots; it is
> nothing but a sound, a phrase which conceals the old shaman notions.
> Ch. Valikhanov, Kazakh traveller to Kyrgyzstan, c. 1880

Karakol, 19th July

Dear Home,
We have been in Kyrgyzstan now for almost a week. Hopefully this letter
can fill you in a little on what we have been doing, and give you a bit of an
appraisal of the country – at the rate I have been sending these letters
home it is probably the last opportunity you are going to get. Kyrgyzstan
is a particularly interesting place to tell you about, because although in
many respects it is easy to like, it is sad in almost every way. Of all the
Central Asian republics it seems to have suffered the most from its eighty
years of Soviet domination and enforced atheism, and appears almost
completely emptied of original culture, apart from a handful of
meaningless artefacts: the men still wear traditional felt hats known as
kalpaks, and the Mongol tents known as yurts – which look like huge
steamed dumplings – still litter the landscape, even in the cities. There
seems to be, however, no trace of Islam, no sense of community beyond a
disturbing addiction to alcohol. Do you remember when we went to Egypt
and visited the Valley of the Kings? Something about Kyrgyzstan has the
same feel of some of those tombs, places that had been robbed several
times.
I am sure part of this impression of a lack of culture comes from the fact
that the Kyrgyz have dwindled to just over half of the population of the
entire country. Kyrgyzstan has never had an overwhelming dedication to
Islam – the Islamisation process of Kyrgyzstan's nomadic tribes was only
completed in the Nineteenth century – but the little that was once here
has been ruined by years of Stalinist social engineering. I wouldn't quite
say that the Soviets totally destroyed Kyrgyz culture, but what is left here
is a frightening distortion of its former self. On top of that, the ethnic
Russians who live here are just as dislocated from their cultural
background. Many have been here for generations and thus no longer
belong in Russia, yet Kyrgyzstan is soon to phase out its use of the
Russian language, and many of them must suddenly confront the fact they
no longer belong anywhere. With both sections of the population feeling
cut adrift in some way it is little wonder the place feels the way it does.
We hitched to Karakol with an ethnic Russian Kyrgyz named Volodia. He
was nice enough, and eagerly showed us his attempts to embrace
capitalism: failed billion dollar proposals for joint ventures with foreign
multinationals, written on tattered bits of paper in meagre English. Sort of
comic and sad, really, and we couldn't help liking him. Yet even he made

us question how prepared we are for Kyrgyzstan, when he introduced us to the Russian approach to alcohol. I guess this is frightening at any time, but after being so long in Iran I found it completely terrifying. Smashed bottles of vodka, drunken rages and wrestles, bleary lecherous attempts to grope Kirst – the transformative effects of the drug have never been more apparent. Volodia was a quiet and gentle man when he dropped us here yesterday, but after a bottle of vodka he and his friends had become hateful creatures smeared with violence. And as bad as our experience with him, was the shock of having it repeated with the native Kyrgyz population outside our hotel. Foreigners are a natural attraction for the red-faced leer of alcoholics in this country, and we couldn't even find refuge from them in our hotel; a pair of drunks from the street proceeded to follow us to our room. They are everywhere in Kyrgyzstan, these small, nut-faced men with their characteristic red eyes and drunken swaggers.
Seeing it all is, after a fashion, fascinating. If the people remain sober for long enough they can be really kind. But they can so easily undergo this sort of alcoholic transformation, and sharing no language with them makes us even more uncomfortable when we go outside. I suppose it is little wonder that we have so far liked the culture of Kyrgyzstan less than Iran.
I know alcohol is not necessarily a reflection upon culture or religion. I think there is a fair chance, though, that an Iranian would find what we have seen proof enough that Kyrgyzstan is a completely godless nation. They might not be far wrong. The Soviets actively encouraged atheism in all their Central Asian republics, and it has long been well established in Kyrgyzstan despite being almost unheard of in the greater Muslim world. We have certainly seen few signs of religion since we arrived. The sun is setting as I write this, but I don't expect to hear the call to prayer.
Tomorrow we plan for a trek into the mountains, hoping to be cold for the first time in months. I'm really looking forward to it. After that we will visit a celebration of Kyrgyz culture being held over near the Kazakh border before beginning our slow passage out of the country. Expect to hear from me when we reach Pakistan. Until then stay safe, and Kirst and I will do our best to do the same.
All my love,
Me.

Saturday 22nd July – Sunday 23rd July
to Ak Su

The old woman laughs. The engine, below her voice, is a wheeze of sound from somewhere in front. Here, in our darkened wooden box, it seems miles away. The woman shifts her weight on to the straw, leans against Kirst. With her mouth open, she is hideous. The black mass embedded in her gums looks like melted rubber; in the dim light the remains of her teeth have the glutinous consistency of molasses. And there, in the top

Ruined church in Ani, Turkey

One of the many portraits of Khomeini that fill the Iranian landscape, Tabriz

Kurdish woman risking punishment by showing her traditional clothes, Iran

Luxury hotel in Shiraz, Iran

Young girl in Mashhad, Iran

Ruins of Persepolis, capital of ancient Persia

Kirst in the Imam mosque

Turkmen women at the Sunday market of Ashgabat, Turkmenistan

Relic of the Soviet era, Kyrgyzstan

Shrine in Uch Sharif, Pakistan

Mendicant in Uch Sharif, Pakistan

Stilt houses, Sylhet, Bangladesh

Kushtia Sufi, Bangladesh

Islamic clock, Indonesia

Animist woman, Indonesia

Andrew and Kirst

left corner, a single gold tooth glints in the dark. We are in the back of a truck, bound for "Manas 1000", a celebration to commemorate one thousand years since the time of the region's most famous poet. Part of a national series of celebrations, Karakol's carnival is being held in conjunction with Kazakhstan, on the border, out where the steppe begins. I glance around the cabin. The metal door is locked behind me. Our only light, soft and aqueous, drains in to this blue-dark box from yellow perspex near the ceiling. We have been forbidden from looking out as we travel, the implication being that our presence in the back of the lorry is not completely legal. It is most certainly the barest form of public transportation around. The walls are made of cracked blue wood, smeared with mud, and a thin layer of straw on the ground is the only concession to comfort.

We are not the only ones in the cabin. An old shrunken man sits propped up against the far wall; he reminds me of a ventriloquist's dummy, so impassive and wooden he could be fake. Two younger men, both wearing the comical white *kalpaks*, crouch beside me lighting cigarettes rolled in newspaper. Three women sit on the hard floor; one nurses a baby. A thick jolt, and we are thrown into each other's arms, brief moments of hilarity. All, as they laugh, reveal gold teeth. The patterns are extraordinary – a checkerboard of gold and ivory for one, all gold on top for another – and the effect is mechanical, robotic. Gold teeth in Kyrgyzstan, the Soviet fashion: a disturbing sight to behold.

Kirst and I both sit on our bags. We have been hiking in the mountains for the last few days, and caught this ride from a tiny village away from the main highway. We must travel over a lonely pass, on this incredible disused road, before we reach the steppe, before we meet with the rest of the crowd. And so, bruised and dirty and shut in the dark, we pass an interminable morning.

In the past week every form of transport we have taken in Kyrgyzstan has broken down: every public bus, every hitched ride, every taxi. This truck is no exception. We hear the complaint of the engine during the climb to the pass, sense the rise and then fall in height, feel the unspeakable shudder as the motor collapses into itself. All sound and motion ceases; we are stuck. A rod is pulled, a handle is thrown, and finally, after three hours of darkness, the light of the outside world floods our pathetic cabin. We emerge into a landscape of dreams. Our road, lonely and pale, stretches off ahead towards Kazakhstan in a straight ribbon of dust. On either side is the flat land of a small valley; hills a few hundred feet high rise around us. They are smooth and grassy, a single version of green. And there are no trees. We have touched the steppe, reached the land of Mongol horsemen and white doughy tents. The earth is naked and empty, so bare it is scarcely real. It is as though whoever designed this world was interrupted before they could finish. Grass and road and sky and hills, nothing else. It is so clinically pure it could be a nightmare; it could just as easily be heaven. The grass bends beneath a petulant wind.

Barrels of white wool have been dumped in the sky, their shadows flee from us across this low landscape. We follow them along the road, leaving our fellow travellers behind, vainly trying to flag down a lift in a group of ten.

Like the Kyrgyz behind us, we cough in the dust of appeals refused. But I do not mind. This artificial landscape, with its dreamlike simplicity, has bewitched me, and I am happy just to be here. Kirst is just as buoyant. I know, however, that our happiness owes itself to more than just our surroundings. We are both filled with an awareness that what we are doing should be cherished before it becomes a memory and a loss. If only we could retain this feeling every day of our waking existence: it remains far too often only in the domain of travel. The traveller knows, more than anyone else, that they must look now, for they will never see that face, that town, that child playing in the dust, again. When I travel I hold the magical awareness of the transience of existence, of the importance of the moment. This moment – now! – will never come again. The awareness is tragically easy to lose when surrounded by a world that is familiar, when each moment is the same as the next, unheeded and lost.

The carnival, when we arrive, is well under way. The billowing hills flatten to an open plain, vast and endless. Dust, its austere scent mixed with that of the grassy plain, hangs permanently in the air above cars and buses, above people and horses. Horses without number. It seems at first that over half the crowd is mounted; some are children who can be no older than five. The sound of galloping hooves comes at us from everywhere, as spectators and participants race each other from one part of the plain to another. The sound evokes hordes of Mongol raiders in my somewhat-too-fertile mind's eye.

The carnival is low and spread out, and it is difficult to identify a focus. On the far edge of the plain, strung out beneath power lines, is a thin line of hundreds of yurts, their regimental column bringing to mind the tents of an invading Mongol army. To our left, lies an impromptu market. To our right, hastily-erected stands for the few spectators content to remain still. In the centre of the plain, a whirling column of dust rises into the air, tossed by the hooves of horses as they tear the steppe, part of an endless race. And before us, the biggest crowd of all, gathered around two men on horseback trying to wrestle each other to the ground. It is to this that we go first.

The air around us is excited and feverish. Horses and their riders crowd around, and the hot stench of horse urine fills the air. The game, simple and violent, seems to be one that has no winners, only a variety of losers. After each bout the crowd erupts, galloping in all directions, shouting and whistling and fighting amongst themselves. It is an uproarious orgy of confusion and mischief, one that only ceases for the beginning of the next bout.

It is difficult to imagine we are in this country because of its connection to Islam. This celebration is of the horsemen of the steppe, the descendants of the Mongols. It has nothing to do with religion; it is an attachment that goes back to long before the time of Islam. It has been estimated that in 1200AD, the time of the Mongols, Central Asia contained half the world's horse population, and the Mongol love of horses was a major factor in their victories throughout the world. Their armies were not large, and were not especially well armed; it was their vast numbers of remounts, and their extraordinary skill in the saddle, which made them the conquerors they were. Their passion with horses, judging by the shouts and mounted revelry of those around us, lives on in Kyrgyzstan. This is a celebration of national culture, and it is far more recognisably Mongol than Muslim.

We blunder off towards the yurts. It is in them, treated to successive bouts of wordless hospitality over cups of green tea, that we spend the rest of the afternoon.

When we emerge from our third tent, late in the afternoon, we find that the world outside has changed. We have planned to camp here on the empty steppe, as we have been told the celebrations will continue tomorrow. But now, in fading light, most of the yurts are being dismantled. The steppe is emptied of crowds, and the air tastes of threat.

We stalk gingerly across the field. Around us the hooves of horses thunder as before, but now their riders are out of control, fleeing mounted police. A wild-faced man, hair flying, swoops past a pair of strollers, spits at them. His face is aflame with alcohol, his eyes are a fierce red ruin. These men have been drinking all day. Near the empty stands, small groups huddle in the grass near their horses, singing and drinking warm vodka. Figures lie face-down in the dirt like half silted-up ships. A man staggers towards us, his face purple and raw. He yells wetly, waving an empty bottle of vodka at the sky.

A scream. Behind us, two men fight; the eye of one pulses with blood. A hundred metres further on, a group of ox-like men shout at each other, violence spattering their words. We turn, return to where we have left our bags by the yurts, skirting yet more comatose figures on the way. We do not respond to the shouts that sail at us across the open space; we know why they come. Through it all, surrounded by all this mess and violence, we are aware that we are the most conspicuous people on the steppe. And we cannot communicate with anyone.

I am no longer accustomed to hard drinking. I am used to the peace of Iranian society without alcohol, and any kind of inebriation seems alien and strange. What surrounds us now terrifies me. Imagine a world where heroin is the accepted drug, where junkies sprawl everywhere in the grass, only worse, for heroin is not a drug of violence. More than ever before in my life, I am frightened by alcohol.

We scramble for our bags, race in the dying light to the road, hoping to plead our way on board one of the few buses still rolling out of this now savage place. The plain has drained itself of people and only the drunken remain. It is an immense relief, then, when the man who approaches us on the roadside seems to be sober. He is small, like most Kyrgyz, with an air of having been put together rather haphazardly, and his moonlike face suggests mildness. With grunts and gestures, he indicates that he can find us transport back to Karakol.

He leads us to an old yellow bus, filled with smiling Kyrgyz. We climb on board, and crouch on our bags in the aisle.

Relief and gratitude fill my heart, yet even now we cannot escape the spectre of alcohol. The bus begins to move forward, preparing to leave, and then the cabin explodes into violence. Our moon-faced saviour is back on board, and has seized Kirst's arm. His face is like a clenched fist, one ready to swing at anyone on board. The woman beside me flicks her throat and rolls her eyes; this is the Kyrgyz signal for drunkenness, and is something we have been seeing far too often.

The other passengers leap into the aisle, begin shouting furiously, shove their bodies between the man and Kirst. Behind them all, I can only watch. The man turns and batters the bus driver, a flurry of punches around the head and shoulders. A fat woman tugs at his arm, and he turns his assault on her. Three men roar to their feet, climb over Kirst, lunge at the man. Hammering blows force him out the doors; he shouts back at us, his angry rebuke drowned by the screams of the fat woman. I can feel my body shake.

The bus doors close. We begin to leave the nightmare behind.

We have travelled less than a hundred yards before a drunk – at first I think it is the same man, but it is not – kicks the doors in, swinging his fists to force his way on board. We are rolling out through a cordon of violent drunks, and anything moving is a beacon demanding their attention. I crouch up the back, remembering the feeling of creeping out through the fights at football games. The difference, of course, is that we share no language with these people, do not understand their culture, and are lost on an empty plain at the edge of the Kazakh steppe.

Daylight has become a green gloom by the time we finally begin the climb away from the plain. I glance back as the chaos behind us continues. I am sickened and saddened, terrified of alcohol's power to destroy a culture. I am tempted to be relieved that we have escaped, but the journey is far from over. In the darkness, our driver transforms what should be two hours of travelling into six with the gradual consumption of a bottle of vodka. Glasses of *kumis*, the Kyrgyz national drink, made of fermented mare's milk and tasting of rotted salami, vanish down the throats of all the passengers. I watch despairingly while a day of drinking continues into the night.

Yet we cannot complain. We feared for our safety on the steppe, frightened by the ferocity that surrounded us. We fear for our safety now, frightened by the intoxication of the man at the wheel on this narrow highway. But this is what we asked for. We wanted our journey to the steppe to offer a glimpse of Kyrgyz culture, and that is what it has done. Savage and frightening, it will be difficult to forget.

Monday 24th July
Lake Issyk-Kul, near Karakol

Here, in this anonymous village on the lake, in this tiny house, we peer back into Kyrgyzstan's past, sift through old sepia photographs, faded and nameless. A Muslim grandmother, veiled and discreet, stands beside a tiny hut. A father, laden with Russian military medals, peers out past my cheek. Young men, their heads bulging in Russian fur hats, prepare for war. Links to a past long since fled.

The photographs belong to Mahabat, one of the women from yesterday's bus. She has insisted we stay with her, in this house of three rooms which holds her sister and brother and mother. Mahabat is typically Kyrgyz: ebony hair, deep dark almond-shaped eyes. She has a gentle face. She gathers the photographs together while a Russian game show blares in black and white crassness on television.

Mahabat is a student of medicine, struggling to enter one of the lowest-paid professions in Kyrgyzstan. Compared to her Western counterparts she seems unlucky, but as a Muslim she is fortunate: the literacy rate among Soviet Muslims is almost one hundred per cent, a stunning departure from the other Muslim nations in the world; to be an educated woman in most Muslim countries is a rarity.

Mahabat cooks us a meal in what amounts to the kitchen, a single hot plate suspended on some bricks on the floor. The toilet is a hole in the ground at the bottom of their garden; running water does not exist. The conditions are no different from millions of places around the world, from thousands of places I have stayed myself, yet I am still surprised. I keep expecting more from what was once one of the world's superpowers.

After yesterday it is a relief to be entertained by this woman, by her brother and sister, to be given the fragile gift of an evening of laughter. We communicate in clichés plucked from the Russian-English phrasebook we purchased in Samarkand. It is an evening of "would you care for some more tea" and "it's raining cats and dogs", a time filled with giggles at the absurdity of communication. After the oppressive nature of what confronted us on the steppe, the purity and innocence of it all is comforting. This is the first evening we have spent with Kyrgyz when alcohol has not reared its fearsome head.

We give thanks to God before dinner. Our prayers end with the muttered word "*Amin*", as we drag our hands over our faces to symbolise the ritual washing before prayer. For the first time, an indication from the Kyrgyz that we are still in the Muslim world; I had come to think of it as a completely faithless nation. Of course, such rituals may mean nothing for the rituals of religion often pass into culture and survive long after religion is gone. The Soviet scholar I. Basgoz argues of Kyrgyzstan that "even though certain Muslim practices like recitation of prayers after a meal continue, they have lost their religious significance. It would be a mistake to consider them the continuation of Muslim practices. People view them as a part of traditional life, an ethnic heritage".

Islam's more recognisable rituals, the 'five pillars' which are the acknowledged fundamentals of the religion, seem to have disappeared. The pillars of Islam are the elementary rules by which Muslims can claim to follow the path of Muhammad. They are the *shahadah*, faith in the existence and unity of God, and Muhammad as his Prophet; *salah*, the five daily prayers; *sawm*, the fast during the month of Ramadan; the annual *zakat* tax to re-distribute wealth to the poor; and the *hajj*, the once in a lifetime, pilgrimage to Mecca. All demand far more than the people of Kyrgyzstan are able to give. We have yet to be woken early in the morning with the call to prayer. The zakat no longer exists, and with a history of isolation and now poverty, the *hajj* for most Kyrgyz is impossible. The pillars that Muslims throughout the world use to identify their faith have gone from Kyrgyzstan. For eighty years, they have been crushed by Soviet occupation and the country's isolation from the rest of the world. Now all that remains is softly spoken thanks at mealtimes, hands brushing the face before food, an act whose significance is as much cultural as religious. All that remains of Islam are relics, dead and worthless, like poor trinkets from an exhumed tomb.

Outside, in a thin drizzle, I walk delicately over planks of wood, suspended over a drowning garden, to the toilet hut at the back of their garden. The garden is filled with apple trees, their green apples as stunning as mad impressionist art. In dim blue light, I peer at them through cracks in the door, listening to the sound of a cow bellowing at the rain. I feel happy. After an evening of gentle joy, the very existence of the world seems a cause for rejoicing. I walk back to the house smiling.

Inside, the tranquillity of the evening has shattered; its sweet purity vanished. The family sits, subdued, in the company of two Kyrgyz men who are obviously drunk, their faces red and their mouths full of gold. They laugh and shout at my entrance, knock over glasses and slap Mahabat's thigh. I sit as the front door opens, bearing a huge woman, barefoot with matted hair and covered in mud. She swaggers into the room, bringing with her the cold blue rain, and faces us with a gruesome leering grin. The air around us tightens; this is Mahabat's mother. She sits beside me, her breath so bad it almost makes me retch. Mahabat, before an image of life and enthusiasm, stands and takes our plates, her movements as stiff as an ancient mannequin. She leaves us alone with the drunks.

Burnt, Frozen

Thursday 27th July
to Lake Son-Kul

Our plan has always been to travel to China directly from Kyrgyzstan, through the Torugart Pass to the south. It is a good plan, with all the romantic allure of remote mountains and Cold War animosity, but it has one major flaw: it is illegal. The border is a zone of confrontation – due, we are told, to a nuclear installation on the Chinese side – and is closed to tourists unless they have approval from the Ministry of Tourism in China itself. A restricted area, eighty kilometres wide, smothers the only approach to the pass, the lonely road south through the town of Naryn. Yet while the crossing is illegal, it is not impossible. We have heard stories of tourists crossing from Kyrgyzstan being detained in no-man's-land, of stubborn Chinese refusals to grant entry to any foreign nationals, of people being stuck for days. Yet some have made it across, or have at least travelled in the direction of Torugart without returning. We like to imagine the border as a place of romance and danger, and the challenge of bluffing our way through appeals to us both. The illegality only adds to its appeal. We recognise we might need to camp in no-man's-land for a day or more, and with no public transport the journey to the border may be long and difficult. So although we have a week remaining on our Kyrgyz visas, we have already turned our attention south.

We do, however, feel there is enough time to visit Lake Son-Kul, described to us in Bishkek as a "magical place". It is extremely high, at three and a half thousand metres, nestled in a huge plain in the mountains, and is one of the most remote and inaccessible places in Kyrgyzstan. It lies just off the road to Naryn.

We spend the early part of the morning hitching to the turn-off to Son-Kul. Mornings are the only safe time in Kyrgyzstan, the only safe time to be on the roads, the only safe time to be a foreigner in public. By noon the drinking will have begun, and by late afternoon many of the drivers we beseech for a ride will be drunk. The turn-off is a dead place, of dry rock wedged between craggy hills. The mountains rise all around us, dry and impersonal; the sky is deep and blue and far away. The main road sweeps past us, climbing and curving until it is out of sight. The way towards Son-Kul hurries up a rocky hill and vanishes just as quickly. Our world is bounded by rock, and we are provided with neither vegetation nor water. At least we have shade, in the form of the rusting remains of what was once a bus stop.

Kill time, kill time.

We wait for seven hours. In that time only three cars pass on their way to Son-Kul; all are full. The monotony is a thick sludge draining into my brain, slowing all my thoughts. By early afternoon we have begun to derive enjoyment from throwing stones at other stones.

Stand and stretch. Sit, wait. Stand again.

At five o'clock, when seven hours spent lodged in this landscape of tormenting boredom are finished, we decide that trying for Son-Kul any longer would only be a waste. We would only arrive in the evening, and must leave tomorrow if we want to ensure we reach Torugart with time to spare. Our day at the lake has been replaced by hours of standing by the roadside. We move our bags to the road to Naryn.

Why is it predictable that a car, containing the local police chief and his wife, chooses this moment to sweep towards us slowly and turn towards Son-Kul, when we have not seen a vehicle for the last four hours? Why does it seem inevitable that, having just decided that going to the lake today would be foolish, we accept their offer of a lift? I am staggered by our own stupidity.

Once moving, however, my spirits rise. We are sure to see enough of the "magical place" to make the journey worthwhile. Days are long, and I am confident we will have a couple of hours of daylight left once we arrive. I picture a small alpine lake, surrounded by snowy peaks, clear and beautiful. I see our campsite, near the tents of the mountain nomads, and can clearly see the road south beckoning towards Naryn, towards China. The dreariness of the day lifts as I imagine the beauty of the scene; even the drab green landscape around us begins to seem interesting.

> Flat tyre
> Punctured spirits
> At the roadblock
> We wait
> For a pump

The twelve soldiers at the roadblock, an hour from the turn-off, could be red-faced highwaymen or rebel soldiers in a civil war, such is the motley disorder of their uniforms. Why twelve men are required to man a single wire pulled across a lonely road I do not know. They are all drunk. This is only natural for no matter how remote we may be, we are still in Kyrgyzstan. Leering at us with greedy red eyes, the soldiers rifle through our bags, demanding gifts of the things that interest them. They thrust plastic bottles of *kumis* under our noses. They demand we sit with them on the grass while they drink vodka, cackling with the intoxication of both alcohol and their control over us. An unwanted evening begins to pour into the valley.

The green world around us is completely in shadow by the time the wire rises and we begin the final climb to the lake. It is up a vast slope, green but empty, like the steppe. Near the top, at the approach to a kind of pass, the land is scattered with drifts of snow. When we reach it, when the world of Son-Kul spreads itself out before us, my head is dizzy with the effects of altitude. The woman in the front of the car vomits.

Ah, but should we complain? Finally the vista of Lake Son-Kul fills our vision. It lies in a wide open plain, grassy and treeless, a billowing sheet of green. At its edges the land slopes upwards slightly to form a shallow bowl. There are no snow-capped peaks, no towering mountains; we are too high for any to rise dramatically above us. Just an enormous shallow lake in the centre of the plain, one which looks more like land in flood than anything permanent, an immense puddle not normally there.

The most worrying aspect of this empty landscape is that it offers no evidence of habitation whatsoever. Now I see why we saw so few cars, because from here the landscape is completely devoid of life. I cannot see how we might plan to escape such a world. I am happy enough to have seen the lake from this distance and I have no overwhelming desire to get any closer. But it is too late, the moment of decision is already past. Our driver has left the road, our only lifeline to the outside world, and we bump through the long grass towards the lake.

The landscape of Son-Kul, I realise after twenty minutes of bouncing through land that is not as flat as it seemed from the pass, is deceptively huge. Already the road, the pass, and any recognisable landmarks, have vanished. I clutch at anything I might use as a reference, but the shapeless earth melts and changes, avoiding my mental grasp. I am left with the sickening conviction that we could get lost even on an open plain. And still, as the lake grows further away, not nearer, the place remains incredibly, impossibly, frighteningly uninhabited.

Darkness has begun to fall all around us, bringing with it a sinister feel. We are far from any road, from any sense of safety, so it is a relief when we finally reach the lake to come across a single yurt beside an abandoned building of brick. The building is filled with broken glass, the whole area is built on a dusty expanse of dung, and the people in the yurt seem just as abandoned as we feel. Yet their presence is reassuring. The police chief surrenders us to this place, indicating that he may return in a week, and vanishes into the gathering darkness. I feel senseless and numb, more isolated than I have ever felt before, even on long mountain treks. We are in the most isolated part of one of the most isolated countries in the world, and I can see no way out.

The temperature plummets with the darkness, and I can suddenly see how drifts of snow could exist on the hills around when the days here are so hot. Arriving in clothes of thin cotton, we scramble in our bags for any warmth we own. As we do, dirty-faced fishermen with wild hair emerge from the darkness to shake our hands, before vanishing just as silently. Children with faces all lumpy with warts come to gape, but before long the cold drives them away too. We wedge ourselves into our tiny tent, trying not to breathe the smell of horse dung and rotting fish, and shiver our way to sleep.

Friday 28th July
Lake Son-Kul

> Travel is a foretaste of hell.
>
> Proverb of ancient Turkestan

I cannot believe this place could have been so cold. The sun, close and merciless in these mountains, roasts us against the shelterless plain. The only "magical" aura belonging to this land comes from its status as a kind of hell.

Son-Kul is more swamp than lake, and the number of insects that inhabit the land around us is staggering. A black maelstrom follows us wherever we go, swirling and stinging; before we have even fully emerged from the water after our only swim, the swarm settles to lance our wet skin. A species of mosquito as large as my hand, which can bite through two layers of clothing; horseflies with eyes of evil metallic green; dozens of others we cannot name, all hateful. The assault is far worse than anything I have experienced, even in Africa. I have never had to apply insect repellent to my entire body before – to my scalp, to my buttocks, to my groin. If I miss even a patch of skin no bigger than a coin it is bitten in minutes; my legs are lined with strips of bloody bites. Our only escape is inside the tent, in the suffocating heat of a nylon tomb flayed by the sun. We have no shade, no relief, but anything is preferable to the torment haunting us outside.

A hawk whirls overhead, its shadow hunting us in two dimensions.

The land around us is empty of vehicles, empty of people, empty of hope. We have no explanation of where the fishermen of last night have gone, and only the screaming children remain. For nine hours we have stayed here, full of despair. We remain stuck in this God-forsaken place, facing the prospect of a second night on an insect-infested heap of dung, and the very real danger of being unable to make it to the Torugart pass before both our Kyrgyz and Chinese visas expire. What frightens me now is that I cannot even imagine being able to leave. From time to time we hear the sounds of vehicles in the distance, and we race out of the tent, waving and screaming. But it is in vain. The vehicles never materialise. The plains remain empty of everything except the sound, and even that disappears before long. And so we sit, we write, we sweat. My skin is tormented by the sun and covered with sores, and I wonder if there is anywhere on earth more unpleasant than Lake Son-Kul in July.

Adding to the despair is the cruel feeling that we have lost sight of the purpose of this journey, that we have been betrayed by the cultural void that is Kyrgyzstan. I have never felt further from the living reality of Islam than I do today. A week beyond China lies Pakistan, land of the pure, land of both the best and worst of Islam; it is there that we should be. A great surging panic seizes my throat, will not let go. Stuck firmly in this hateful place, the journey has become rudderless and lost.

The tension of being trapped affects us both, affecting the way we interact. Laughter at our predicament one moment; an argument the next. We argue about religion, about Christianity.

I have been unprepared for the effect that my investigation into Islam has had on my views of Christianity. Delving into the theological sections of university libraries was a new experience for me, exposing me not only to Islam, but to Western scholarly research into the origins of the Church and to how outsiders might view the Christian faith.

Jesus features prominently in the Qur'an. He is one of the prophets of God, a miracle worker, a man "strengthened" with the Holy Spirit. Muhammad was the last in a long line of prophets – 124,000 of them – many no more than good, exemplary people. Jesus is one of the most important of these prophets, along with the likes of Abraham, Isaac, Job, Solomon and David, but to the Muslims he is no different. The prophets did not claim divinity. They were humans entrusted by God to spread the word, both by deed and speech. Indeed, Muhammad often emphasises his own humanity. Unlike Jesus he is no miracle-worker; the Qur'an is miracle enough. To the Muslims of Arabia in the Seventh century, Christianity was simply a wayward cult, one that grew from the following of a single prophet, a man who was not, and did not claim to be, divine.

Then God will say: "Jesus, son of Mary, did you ever say to mankind: 'Worship me and my mother as gods beside God?'" "Glory to you," he will answer, "how could I ever say that to which I have no right?"
The Qur'an, 5:115

To the Muslims, the doctrine of the Christian faith was one entirely flawed. The idea of both the Trinity, and of a unitary, all-powerful God having a 'son', was abhorrent. To the fiercely monotheistic Muslims, with their savage opposition to idolatry, the process of worshipping manifestations of God was bound to be offensive. They knew that such teachings were not part of Jesus' original message, and with Muhammad's religion pitted against such concepts from the very beginning, the Qur'an expresses bewilderment at what it views as nonsense again and again.

The Messiah, Jesus the son of Mary, was no more than God's apostle and His Word which He cast to Mary: a spirit from Him. So believe in God and His apostles and do not say: "Three". Forbear, and it shall be better for you. God is but one God. God forbid that He should have a son! His is all that the heavens and the earth contain.
The Qur'an, 4:172

To Muhammad, the only God worthy of worship was far too great to be divisible in this way. For humans to claim to know something of God was sheer sacrilege, a profanity that had inspired him to break with the traditional Meccan faith in the first place, so it was little wonder the Muslims found the concept of the Son of God so offensive.

The Muslims had ideological reasons for disbelieving that Jesus had ever claimed to be divine. Jesus is a major figure in the Muslim faith, and it is only to be expected that Muhammad would wish to refute any claims of his divinity. Ideological reasons notwithstanding, however, many Western scholars would agree. Such names as the best-selling theologian Karen Armstrong, John Hick, and even the conservative scholar Vincent Taylor have all written on the subject. As the theologian Geza Vermes writes, biblical scholars generally accept that Jesus never claimed to be divine.

This discovery came to me as quite a shock. It was like discovering that scholars had unearthed the origins of the universe a century ago, while the rest of the world continued to ponder the question without an answer.

What surprised me most was that most of the academic work is written by believing Christians. They are bishops, theologians and priests, all with a profound belief in their faith. I had expected such figures to be anarchists, striking from the outside with suspect motives and hidden agendas. Instead, these are men and women who are willing to withstand the harsh glare of historical research, and who wish to strip away the historical accretions of the Christian religion in order to make their faith more relevant to a changing world. They have reduced Christianity to little more than a faith in God, and wish to focus on what Jesus' real message was. Yet their faith is unmoved in the establishment that has existed for two thousand years, on what they claim is invented doctrine. Many accept Jesus as a *symbol* of the divine and ineffable transcendent reality, not in any way linked divinely to God, while still insisting that the Church is a valid institution. Of such a state of affairs, the theologian Michael Goulder writes: "In the eyes of philosophers, the Christian faith has become intellectually disreputable because it no longer asserts anything."

There are a number of aspects to the argument about the divinity of Jesus. That he never asserted directly or spontaneously that he was the Messiah is commonly admitted; the term "Son of God" was never intended to denote divinity, and the term Jesus often used for himself, the "son of Man", simply stressed, it seems, the weakness and frailty of the human condition. Jesus went out of his way to stress that he was a frail human being who would one day suffer and die. The extensive work of scholars over the last forty years indicates Jesus did not claim to be divine.

The basis of the current research lies in what we now know of the historical context of Jesus' life. The Jews had long been expecting a Messiah, an anointed one, the deliverer of mankind. Ever since the rule of King David – who as both monarch and spiritual leader, founded the first independent Jewish kingdom in Jerusalem – the conception of such a figure had been as a Davidic Redeemer; a man endowed with the combined talents of soldierly prowess, righteousness and holiness, and one who would herald a new era for the Jews. The Messiah was expected to be a descendant of King David, and in both the Old Testament and the New Testament the Messiah is referred to as the Son of David. Any man who claimed, or was proclaimed, to be Messiah in the inter-Testamental period was going to have his claims understood along these lines.

The identification of Jesus, not just with *a* Messiah, but with *the* awaited Messiah of Judaism, was fundamental to early Christian belief. The literal Greek rendering of the Semitic Messiah, *Christos*, would lead to the term 'Christian' within a generation of the crucifixion of Christ. 'Jesus the Christ' would be used so frequently in the Gentile regions evangelised by Paul that it would become the shortened 'Jesus Christ' and even simply 'Christ'. Jesus rarely claimed the title for himself, but his Messianic status was the main issue of the early teaching of Christianity. In fact, Jesus preferred the appellation 'prophet' to that of Messiah. This term was, however, discarded very early by the Church, investing Jesus with the title 'Messiah' from the beginning. And it was this title that remained, despite the fact it had little meaning to the Gentile world which would adopt the new religion with such fervour.

Jesus was not, however, the political Messiah envisaged by the Jews. It was assumed by all Jews of the period, including those who taught Jesus, that when the Messiah came – the bold, soldierly leader they imagined – he would remain the quintessential Jew, true to Jewish Law and tradition. Jesus, however, saw himself differently. He saw himself as a prophet, God's vice-regent, able to do as he pleased. And he pleased to preach and act on the principle of love, to proclaim a kingdom based on love and nothing else. It is to these teachings, the original teachings of Jesus, that the theologians of today wish to steer their faith.

It must be remembered that the concepts of the time, the language used, were all Jewish. Jesus was a Jew, and never envisaged his mission as having a wider, Gentile, content. Accordingly, the language that was applied to Jesus must be considered in this light. And it is not the title of Jesus as Messiah that caused problems for the new religion – indeed, at the time, Rabbi Gamaliel declared this doctrine authentically Jewish – but the interpretation of him as the Son of God. It is this idea that has so appalled both Jewish and Muslim audiences for centuries, one that seemed responsible somehow for the amazing spread of the religion into the Gentile world, and which would eventually require the convoluted doctrines of the Trinity to support it.

The 'son of God' was a concept familiar to Jews of the period. It was a common term; to the Jews, fierce monotheists, it did not indicate divine nature. In the Old Testament, the thoroughly human figure of the Davidic king was thought of as God's son: "I will be to him a father, and he will be to me a son". For both King David and the awaited Messiah, this is a way of expressing intimacy with Yaweh, the Jewish God. Yet the phrase was even more widespread than a simple expression of intimacy. Numerous examples exist in Jewish literature of rabbis and other holy men being spoken of as God's sons, and it was often used simply to mean Israelites in general. Every Jew could be called the *son of God*, but the title came to be preferably given to the just man, and especially to the most righteous of all just men: the Messiah.

Jesus is often alluded to as the Son of God in the New Testament, a title understandably equated to a notion of divinity. Yet Jesus was proclaimed Son of God in the Jewish sense, in support of his role as Messiah. He never alluded to himself as the son of God; the doctrine of sonship never played a part in the public proclamation of him as a prophet. What did separate Jesus from other mendicants of the time was his use of the term *Abba* to address God, a term normal for a human child to its father, unheard of in such a context. Apart from this, there was little declaration at the time that Jesus was divine. Not even the Synoptic Gospels of Mark, Matthew and Luke, so called because they provide the same general view of the life of Jesus, written long after Jesus' death with the intention to convert rather than record, attempt to bridge the gulf between the term *son of God* and God himself. To identify a contemporary historical figure as divine, a man teaching at the time, would have been inconceivable to a First century Palestinian Jew. Conditioned by centuries of staunch monotheism, the claims of a man of the era to be the incarnation of God would have been impossible to preach, let alone believe. Even Paul, a Jew at home in the Greco-Roman world of pantheistic myths, shied far away from such a claim.

The decision of the followers of Jesus that he had been divine took time. Indeed, the doctrine that Jesus had been God in human form was not finalised until the Fourth century. It was only when Gentiles began to preach the Jewish Gospel to the Hellenised peoples of the Roman empire that the hesitation with regard to the divinity of Jesus vanished. The restrictions of language and culture were gone. Paul had been unable to push the image of Jesus beyond "the image of God" and "the stamp of God's very being", but in the Second century, Ignatius of Antioch was quite content with describing Jesus as "our God" and "the God who bestowed such wisdom upon you." More and more, the emphasis came to be placed on the divine nature of Jesus, the increasingly holy figure, until we are left with the paganisation of today, exemplified by the agreement to constitute the World Council of Churches upon the doctrinal basis of "acknowledgement of our Lord Jesus Christ as God and Saviour". In what purports to be a monotheistic religion, God himself is no longer worthy of mention.

Jesus, the Jew, a man of unwavering monotheism, would probably have been appalled by such developments; we can never know. We can, however, be certain that the teachings of the Christian faith came to be founded not on the pure language and teaching of the Galilean Jesus, nor even from Paul the diaspora Jew, but from a Gentile interpretation of the Gospel transformed by its collision with the pagan Hellenistic world.

Such an eventuality should not surprise. The founder of Buddhism, Gautama, was a historical figure just as real as Jesus. He lived in north-east India about five hundred years before the birth of Jesus. Renouncing his wealth to seek spiritual truth, Gautama eventually attained enlightenment, and travelled far and wide to preach his message. He made no claim to be divine. He simply preached a message of peace and love, of the goal of elimination of egoism in order to be able to merge with a transcendent reality. After his death, however, Mahayana Buddhism would develop, at around the same time as Christianity. In it, the Buddha came to be revered not as an ordinary mortal, a man who had preached an important message, but more as a god, an earthly incarnation of heavenly power. The parallels with Jesus are obvious.

No doubt Muhammad was aware that Christianity had moved far from its origins as a true monotheistic faith. The Christians had their valid views, yet they had strayed:

People of the Book! Do not transgress the bounds of truth in your religion. Do not yield to the desires of those who have erred before; who have led many astray and have themselves strayed from the even path.

The Qur'an, 5:77

Central to Muhammad's message was the unity of God; even a vague idea of the origins of Christianity would have been sufficient for him to reject it as blasphemous.

I mention what I have read to Kirst. *Who are these scholars? This is mere interpretation of history. Why do you trust them? The authors have hidden agendas. All this sort of research is ideologically driven.* I understand her reaction completely: if the positions were reversed, it would be I who would be questioning her sources. These are sacred issues and scholarship on such matters is not to be trusted.

Yet we have to ask why we react in this way. If I were to tell her the latest findings from the last forty years of Egyptology, or archaeological research into the origins of the human race, she would be fascinated. We would have a lively discussion, even if the scholars disagreed with what she had learnt as a child. She would never feel that her preconceptions outweighed scholarly opinion. She would never give precedence to a two thousand year old book, a book written to convert, over modern research. And she certainly wouldn't make the same excuses for Islamic history. How deep does our cultural bias go?

Saturday 29th July – Monday 31st July
to Kashgar

...stripped of political rhetoric of "the achievements of socialism" and "benefits of fraternal assistance", the fate of Soviet Central Asia represents perhaps the most tragic and least reversible example of the failure of the Soviet experiment that, in the name of ideological goals, led to near destruction of a region, its people, and its culture.

Teresa Rakowska-Harmstone
Foreword, *Soviet Central Asia*

The unease, the helplessness, and the presence of alcohol around us, always, always.

We escaped Son-Kul late in the afternoon, hitching a ride in an army truck. We were crammed into the cabin with half a dozen crazed drunks – driver included – for twelve hours, as we made our way through dizzying mountain roads in the darkness, terrified out of our minds. In the loathsome town of Naryn, taxi drivers so drunk they could hardly stand harassed us for three hours as we waited for a lift south. In At Bashi our companions were the police, forcing us to drink warm vodka despite our protests and demanding thousand-dollar bribes to take us to the border. At the edge of town, a one-armed alcoholic joined us for our thirty-hour wait for the first truck to the border, becoming progressively agitated as we refused to drink with him. And unsmiling youths gathered to drink and spit and stare, hounding us with their eyes and blowing kisses at Kirst. By the time we reached the border, with its great coats and Kalashnikov rifles, its clouds of steam billowing on Russian breaths, we were desperate to escape it all, desperate to escape Kyrgyzstan.

And then, of course, came the battle to be allowed out of the country, the day-long wait in the face of Chinese intransigence in the thin air of no-man's-land, the bribe which finally bought our entry into China. Only then were we truly free of Kyrgyzstan.

It is difficult to believe that we originally entered the country as part of an investigation into Islam. I am aware, of course, that people drink in many Muslim countries, even if not to such a soul-destroying extent. Behind the alcoholism, however, Kyrgyzstan is a nation that has had its cultural fabric destroyed, its knowledge of itself obliterated, by eighty years of Soviet rule. More than all the other nations of Central Asia, Kyrgyzstan has been ruined by Communism. It has no reminders of the place it once was, no artefacts to serve as cultural anchors for society. Eighty years ago the land was a place of Muslim nomads; now it is a place of sedentary alcoholics with no obvious devotion to God. The Soviets have left the country with nothing. No economy, no pride, no culture, no religion. To travel in Kyrgyzstan was frustrating, at times horrifying, but to contemplate it now simply makes me sad.

PART THREE
SOUTH

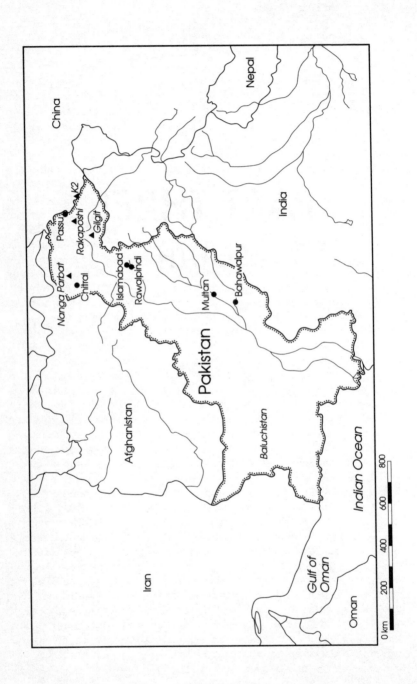

PAKISTAN

Dark Roaring White

Sunday 6th August - Monday 7th August
Passu

The universe, in Passu, is made of rock.
It is rock without scale: tilted, ruthless. Monolithic and grey, judgmental and mean. It once lay at the bottom of the sea, now stands without explanation, owning us as much as we own it. When the Indian subcontinent collided with the rest of Asia around fifty million years ago, it was this rock that was caught in between.
These mountains belong not to the Himalayas, that most famous offspring of India's inexorable march north into Asia. The 'roof of the world', the high land that encompasses Tibet and the mountains of Nepal, is the archetypal result of a collision between two continents. Like the join where two masses of soft clay are pressed together, the land in the Himalayas has buckled and been pushed skywards, a vast tropical plain thrust into the thin atmosphere of altitude, transforming it into the world's highest desert, sterile and lifeless. The leaning titans around us are lifeless too, but they could never belong to a plain, no matter how high. They belong to the Karakoram range of northern Pakistan, home of the densest concentration of high peaks anywhere on earth.
The Karakorams did not behave predictably in India's fifty-million-year-long, slow-motion encounter with Asia. Most of India slid into and beneath the bigger mass, pushing it high enough to form the Himalayas, but in the region of Pakistan the top layer of the continent was shaved off, peeled away from India in a layer of hard rock by the colossal might of Asia. This rock, sheared upwards like wood shavings or shards of ice, was thrust just as high as the Himalayas, but in a chaotic jumble of broken peaks and jagged angles. The scars can still be seen in the mountains around us: the strata in the rock are more often vertical than horizontal; the knifelike ridges are snapped and pointed; the peaks are screaming points of granite. All on a scale alien to human thought.
This process sculpted the Karakorams into the most jagged mountains in the world. And here, in the most northern areas of Pakistan, this mountain range is at its most brutal. Here it strikes three other ranges – the Himalayas, the Hindu Kush and the Pamirs of Tajikistan – to create a place of frightening scales and massive differentials in height. Further down the valley the peak of Nanga Parbat awaits us, its six and a half kilometre leap from summit to the adjacent Indus gorge the sharpest elevation difference found anywhere in the world. Its south face is an unbroken four thousand metre wall so sheer that no snow can cling to it. To the north is K2, the most difficult climb on earth, surrounded by the longest glaciers outside the polar regions. And around us, filling our vision, the glacial spines that surround the village of Passu shine like living flesh in the morning sun.

They lie across the valley from us. Separating us from them is the Hunza river, a roaring channel of water the colour and opacity of wet cement. Dense and dark, it churns violently over the rocks, so clouded it could be man-made. It is a vast clashing chaos of grey, a pulverised mountain descending from heights we cannot imagine, more rock than water. And above it, calling like a gutter full of wind and sighs, comes the gaping sound of the air as it follows the river down the valley.

Passu itself seems unaware of the drama surrounding it. A tiny village of no more than a few hundred people, Passu is peaceful in the way that seaside towns are peaceful. Confronted by a scene so monumental it mimics infinity, something in the soul eases, flattens. We explore the town's narrow lanes all morning, full of a delicate joy.

The lanes of the village run between tiny plots of vegetables, fruit trees and golden wheat. Glorious apricot trees droop over the paths, depositing their coloured treasures at our feet. All the plots are hedged with loose piles of large stones, the raw material found everywhere we look. There is a sense of tradition and permanence expressed in these stone fences and buildings, of time fixed, frozen. Apart from the narrow highway following the river valley both north and south, we could be in another century.

The road is part of the Karakoram Highway, the famous KKH, a treacherous ribbon carved into the mountains between China and Pakistan, and we lie at its farthest northern extremity, one of the last Pakistani villages before China. With the vast unknown mass of Pakistan stretching south from where we stand, I cannot convince myself we have truly entered the country. China is gone, but Pakistan seems not yet with us; this place is so remote, so tiny, so unexpected, that I do not feel we have seen anything of the country.

Even the villagers contribute to this feeling. My image of Pakistanis is of dark-eyed men, their women shut out of sight. Here, however, women and girls are everywhere. Both sexes are clad in the flowing garb of the national dress of Pakistan, the *shalwar kameez*, baggy pants and an overlong shirt in an identical colour. The men's are drab – grey, brown, blue, cream – but the women are bright flowers, their brilliant pink or blue or green clothes contributing rare colour to an otherwise grey landscape. Many of the older women wear tall, multicoloured pillbox fezzes, draped with a thin white gauze; everyone we encounter offers us a broad smile.

I am startled to find that these northern skins are far more fair than I had expected. Many heads are brown instead of black; some could almost be called blonde. They are the genetic relics of Alexander's conquests, the results of his encouragement to his troops to intermarry. In pockets throughout Asia such faces can be found, yet they always come as a surprise, an oddity in the dark skins of everywhere else.

It is the presence of women in public, however, that I find most intriguing. Much of Pakistan is still ruled by the law of purdah, the cultural tradition of Muslim India that has had Muslim women in complete seclusion from the time of the Mughals to the present. I had not expected to see many Pakistani women outside any of the major cities, and I had certainly not expected to see any walking the streets unveiled.

The reason, I discover when we return to the guest house for the evening, is that the people of Passu, like most of the people of the Hunza valley, are neither Sunnis nor Twelver Shi'ites. These people are Ismailis.

Karim, the button-faced owner of our guest house, explains the difference in simple terms.

"Ismailis have bright minds. Not like Shi'a. The Shi'a don't want their women to be free. Ismailis are well educated. They have good jobs."

"That is the only difference?"

"That is the only difference."

We sit on the front steps of Karim's tiny guest house, watching shadows as huge as mountains steal our valley from us, bringing with them a glacial chill.

I look at Karim. His head is bald and shaved, a smooth bronze dome above his small features. His face is hard, suited to the landscape that made him, as though beneath his skin there is nothing but bone. Yet it is a hardness that reflects his life, not his heart: his soft brown eyes carry a gentleness in them, his smile a warmth. Like everyone we meet in this tiny village, his presence makes me happy; after the rough welcome of Kyrgyzstan and the indifference of China, the people of northern Pakistan have come as a relief.

The difference between Ismailism and other Muslim sects is, of course, more complex than Karim claims. The Ismailis began as a splinter group of the Shi'ite sect in about 765AD, following a dispute over who should succeed Imam Ja'far as the spiritual leader of the Shi'ite community. The vast majority of Shi'ites supported Imam Ja'far's younger son Musa, whose line would continue until the twelfth Shi'ite Imam. Those who supported his eldest son, Isma'il, became a persecuted minority, a sect which only managed to develop and retain its radical ideology through a rigid code of secrecy – a masonic-style hierarchy operating at the fringes of society. These Ismailis, as they quickly became known, believed their seventh Imam, Isma'il's son Muhammad, to be the last in a direct line of descent from the Prophet, and are often referred to as Seveners.

The fortunes of the Ismailis were varied. Their most famous successes were in North Africa in the Tenth century, when they established the glorious if short-lived Fatimid dynasty, building the new city of Cairo as their capital, and erecting the great mosque of Al-Azhar as the centre of their faith. (Al-Azhar was converted to Sunnism centuries later, becoming one of the first universities in the world, a place of Islamic learning and jurisprudence that still dictates the way of life of most Sunnis today.) Splinter groups were also well-known: a group known in the West as the Assassins established a stronghold in the mountains of northern Iran in the Twelfth century, carrying out terrorist acts of assassination against Sunni religious and political leaders. The Crusaders recorded the fear with which the group was regarded throughout the region, and took the group's name and reputation – and, indeed, the very word *assassin* – with them back to Europe.

Ismailism stagnated as a minor heresy after the Mongol invasions, however, and it was only in the eastern lands of Islam – in India, in Pakistan – that it would eventually prosper. Here, for centuries, the Ismailis have remained a close-knit group, clinging to their beliefs, surviving in pockets, isolated islands in a vast sea of Sunnism. And here in the Nineteenth century, with the aid of the British, the Ismailis acquired a leader. Hasan Ali Shah was a former provincial governor of Iran, on the run after unsuccessfully attempting to seize power of the country. In Pakistan he helped the British in their attempts to control the frontier tribes; his reward would be to become the spiritual leader of the Ismailis, the first in a religious dynasty claiming descent from the Prophet through Isma'il. His title: the Aga Khan.

Today's Aga Khan is Hasan Ali Shah's great-great-grandson, Prince Karim, a man who commands the respect of Ismailis all over the world as their infallible spiritual leader. His photograph hangs in dozens of places inside our guest house. Huge messages of welcome adorn the mountains opposite us in the valley, marks of a visit he made to Passu five years ago. Schools and community projects throughout the valley bear his name, and we have already gathered some idea that it is the attitudes of this man which have today made Ismailism so noticeably different from other forms of Islam. The progressive views of a single man have moulded the views of an entire society, in a religion rarely noted for its liberal attitudes. The Aga Khan's influence over the Ismailis of Northern Pakistan is as significant as that of Imam Khomeini in Iran.

What makes the Aga Khan so interesting, however, is not the views he holds, but who he is and how his views could possibly influence anyone in this lonely valley so far from anywhere. For the Aga Khan lives not in Pakistan but in Switzerland, enjoying a lifestyle appropriate to his status as one of the world's richest men. He was born in Geneva, not India or Yemen; his companions are not religious men but celebrities and film stars. That such a man should retain any credibility at all with a man like Karim astounds me.

When I ask about the signs in his honour across the valley, Karim looks pleased.

"It was the happiest day for Passu when the Aga Khan came," he says. "He is a great man."

"Is it difficult to follow a man who lives so far away?" I ask. "It must be difficult for the Aga Khan to understand what life is like in Passu, when he lives in Switzerland."

"Oh no, not difficult at all. Our Imam can understand. He is a great man." That phrase again. Karim looks directly at me, his face shining with pride. "Our Imam is the world's seventh richest man." The statement lacks any trace of resentment, any hint of anything other than pride and respect.

"But don't you think he should live closer to Muslims, maybe live somewhere like Karachi?"

Karim looks aghast. He shakes his head quickly, as though trying to rid his mind of the suggestion. "Oh no!" he says. "Karachi is too dangerous. And what would happen if he got sick? No, it is much better that he lives in Geneva. He has Indian parents, so he knows what it is like here. And from Geneva he can organise. Red Cross, World Health Organisation, everything is in Geneva. So he can organise to do good for Ismailis in Pakistan."

Karim stands and walks into the garden, beckoning us to follow. It is lush and manicured, an ordered green amidst the chaos of rock. It speaks in faint echoes of Pakistan's colonial past, of the British passion for efficiency and order. Karim stops at the gate and gestures to a low stone building a hundred yards away.

"The Aga Khan school. Every village, he makes schools like this. He makes many things. He makes dams, he makes water pumps. And not just Ismaili villages; other villages too. He is the best leader for Ismailis."

We return to the steps of the building, where a small boy – sombre, cheerless, professional – has brought us tea. It is the sweet milky tea of India and East Africa, a sudden departure from the green leaves of Central Asia, another remnant of the British tradition. It makes me smile: I can no longer decide if such things are out of place in this fairy-tale world or not. Karim is eager to continue the conversation, to convince us of the strengths of his religion. I am content to listen, to try to harvest some sense of the shape of this man's belief, of how it can be governed by a man so far away.

"Ninety-nine percent of Ismailis are educated. This is a very special thing for Pakistan. We are a very intelligent people. Our Imam says that education is *the* most important thing. This is why he builds schools in all the villages." His eyes dart; he has just seized an idea he knows will impress. "Our Imam says if you have to choose between educating son and educating daughter, you must choose daughter. Why? Because she will educate her children, and so we have an educated society."

"Soon you will go to Gilgit. Ismailis are the majority in Hunza, but in Gilgit, we are the minority. We are a minority everywhere. And you will see, you will see it is better with Ismailis. In Gilgit there is Sunni, Shi'a and Ismaili. All together, and often fighting. And after Gilgit, not many Ismailis. You know why? Because we don't want to conquer. We are happy with a stable population, our Imam tells us. Not like the Shi'a, they want to breed and breed and conquer the world with babies. We have family planning, but the Shi'a, they just breed."

The Islamic world has staunchly opposed international efforts to reduce poverty through the introduction of family planning. I have to admit that finding it here, in one of the smallest villages of Pakistan's far north, comes as a surprise.

"Does the Aga Khan tell you that family planning is part of Islam?" I ask

Karim. He nods. "Our Imam tells us it is better only to bring children into the world if we can care for them. God does not want us to have children if we cannot care for them. If you think, it is clear. This is not what the Shi'a think, but they are wrong. They say the Qur'an is against family planning, but the Qur'an is from God, and God is not cruel."

The Aga Khan was born and educated in the West, so it is little wonder that his teachings are more palatable to Westerners than those of other Muslim leaders. Yet I still marvel that this poor Pakistani peasant, a world away from Geneva, has taken his words so closely to heart.

Beyond what Karim tells us, I cannot judge to what extent such teachings have penetrated the rest of Passu's population. But we cannot help notice the visibility of Ismaili women in public, something else Karim claims is the doing of the Aga Khan. This aspect, at least, is one we can judge for ourselves. All the reading we have done has suggested that women in rural areas of Pakistan are shut away from sight, virtual prisoners in their homes.

"You will see, when you go south. You will see no women. They are in *purdah*; they must not be seen. But here, you see women. You see? You see everywhere. Ismailis are much better for women than Shi'a or Sunni."

Karim finishes his tea and excuses himself: he must prepare our meal. It is the last we will talk with him of religion, yet he has provided an important glimpse of the diversity of Islam. Karim has offered us a reminder that Islam should never be viewed as a single entity, homogenous and monolithic. The reminder is a valuable one.

We walk to the river while evening falls, watching as the unbounded expanse of sky collapses into the mountains. We encounter villagers on the way; all stop to greet us and offer us precious smiles. I may have to wait until further south to see the differences between the various branches of Islam in Pakistan, but I already know one effect religion itself has had. Tonight, for the first time in a month, we have returned to an environment where God means something, in a place unclouded by alcohol. Not only can we be unworried about what each encounter might bring, we can rely on it to be pleasant. The simplicity and innocence of such an atmosphere is an incredible relief.

Tuesday 8th August – Saturday 12th August
Mt. Rakaposhi, the Hunza Valley

> Three of these days
> spent
> climbing to Rakaposhi,
> that huge icy stare seen from the road,
> a passionless ancestor swallowing our valley whole.
>
> Three days
> caught between heat

and ice
and rock
and space.

With an ill dizziness comes uneasy sleep:
troubled by dysentery and altitude, dry and confused and awake
I find   I dream
    tearful passions,   of a lower time,
    the skin beneath the earth.   of a higher place.

The implacable glacier, a vision as we climb,
is a train of white tombstones,
a melancholic regiment of frozen syllables,
broken remnants of pure ferocity
marching down the mountain.

We climb through a transient green
– alpine, hungered –
trailing our exhaustion in elegant streams
up to the clamorous ridge,
up to the ridge where we first
devour
the glacier
with our eyes.

Beyond us
forty football fields of ominous ice,
an Antarctic world of an unwelcome scale
dusted with grey like a tarnished mirror.

Above us
the momentary whiteness of the peaks, smooth and
unvanquished   and cool
Quarrelling stones
and savage valleys
quench us from the outside world.
And as we watch, we see the monster decay,
a slow-motion

               puff

ten tonnes of snow and ice
noiseless substance
as it yearns towards the void.

Below us

at the broken feet of the towering earth:
a marsh of stones and mosquitoes,
the meagre bowl where we camp.
We sit and breathe the air, frozen colour
while

Around us
filling the valley with their chill
are humbled shadows,
the sinister echo of all that surrounds,
and the obscure sound of avalanches
absent noises
mumbled sadness
disconnected from the chaos that we see
detached from all motion
sounds alive and of their own creation.

(the peak,
so cruel
so mortally white)

and then
down we come
three days after we began.

In Purdah

Monday 14th August
to Gilgit

> Live like Ali. Die like Hussein.
> Sign on the outskirts of Gilgit

Gilgit is where Ismaili dominance comes to an end. The sign, nailed to a
stray poplar in one of the many villages that cluster around Gilgit, is a
declaration that we have returned to a land that is shared by Twelver
Shi'a; we know it is also home to large numbers of Sunnis. It is an area
tainted by sporadic outbreaks of sectarian violence, a town where the
easygoing feeling we found in the north begins to fade.
Gilgit is also where I am forced to address a topic I have long avoided but
can no longer ignore. I am forced, finally, to consider the treatment of
women in Islam. No investigation of Islam can be complete without some
consideration of how the religion treats its women, and nowhere could be
a better place to do so than in the tribal areas of Pakistan. In Gilgit, for the
first time on the entire journey, we have encountered a place where
women are hidden.

At the edge of town lies one of the hundreds of police checkpoints that litter the landscape here: the war zone in Kashmir is never far away. Our minibus is waved through just after midday, and we begin the process of lurching through pedestrian crowds and stalled jeeps to the centre of the town.

Gilgit is a tourist town, the largest metropolitan centre in the north. It sits in the heart of Pakistan's most mountainous region, almost at the juncture of the three rivers – the Indus, the Hunza, and the Gilgit – that carve the world into such furious terrain. It is close to all the region's major peaks, is conveniently well-supplied, and forms a logical base for the thousands of tourists who descend on the north in summer, here to organise anything from simple treks to well-organised assaults on the world's highest peaks. It is also like nothing I expected.

I had imagined Gilgit to be on the verge of becoming a city, somewhere with some semblance of infrastructure, a place of ordered busyness with a sense of its own future. Instead, we are met with a disordered town, dirty and shapeless. We arrive after two days of flash floods, during which many of the surrounding villages have been evacuated, and Gilgit retains an atmosphere of total confusion.

We climb out of our minibus into the sudden mud near Gilgit's market and traipse through the greedy streets to our hotel. Welcome to the Madina Guest House, Gilgit's largest traveller's hang-out. It is a place designed around the dope-smoking sub-culture of travel in Asia, around ease and convenience and the total exclusion of the outside world, around banana pancakes and Western breakfasts, around those who come to Pakistan for its mountains, those content to drift through the days between treks in a confined and Westernised sanctuary in the heart of Gilgit. It is the kind of place which often sets my teeth on edge, probably because it is a reminder of how unexceptional we are; being confronted by scores of travellers just like ourselves detracts from the uniqueness of our own experience. Yet I find it surprisingly agreeable. We are, after three months without contact with other travellers, starved of communication and their presence comes as a welcome surprise. It is here, seated comfortably in a shaded courtyard, that I drink milky English tea while I write.

Sounds, unstifled noise from the streets outside, come to me over the compound wall. These were the streets we had to walk through on our way here. They are lined with parked jeeps, clogged with patient trucks waiting for their loads, their air full of a sense of commerce hoping to happen. We came through market streets, past crude stores painted blue and green, selling everything from biscuits to bicycle pumps, from fuel to freeze-dried food, selling carpets and silver and cloth and pots of stainless steel. Traffic moves randomly through it all, through the mud and dust and rubbish; dogs and ragged crows pick at piles of accumulated waste. Outside there are men selling slices of cut melon and coconut, waving away the flies with filthy pieces of rag, crowds of men busy with their lives, all in their dusty *shalwars*. The odd sight of a policeman directing traffic with impeccably white gloves, the sprawled chaos of a frontier town, a casual streak of slowness through everything, a feel of captured lazy mountain air. And one thing more – with every step, there is the awareness that Kirst's is the only female face in sight.

A few women brave the streets with their husbands, browsing in the stores, while others drift by in the dry silence of government vehicles. None show their faces. All conform to the fundamentalist 'ideal' of Islam, their faces hidden by white veils, their eyes peering out at the world through craven slits in the fabric. These are the 'women of Islam'. It is the lives of these women which causes so much outrage in the West.

For many years it was veils such as these that formed my image of what a Muslim veil had to be, an image inspired by films of sultans, harems and dancing girls. I know now that the original veil covered only the hair, that Quranic injunctions regarding veiling do not mention the face. In fact, female pilgrims performing the *hajj* are forbidden from veiling their faces in this way. They must wear simple white robes, with a veil which covers their hair but which leaves their faces and hands and feet exposed to the world, in the way of the chador of Iran. Muhammad never decreed that women should cover themselves completely. The behaviour in Pakistan today, and in dozens of other countries around the world, stems not from Islam as it was envisaged by Muhammad, but from subsequent reinterpretations of ancient customs. Even in Saudi Arabia, where veils like these are common and where many women now wear gloves to be more 'Islamic', the covering of women's faces in this way was not required before the discovery of oil.

In the south, Pakistan's Islam is overwhelmingly detrimental to the status of women. It has been this way for centuries. *Purdah*, the principle of seclusion from public scrutiny for all women, was a tradition of the Indian Mughal Empire. Reformers throughout this century, including Pakistan's founding father, Muhammad Ali Jinnah, have railed against the practice, yet in rural areas it remains in place. Many houses are surrounded by eight- to ten-foot-high *purdah* walls. Each family compound is designed around protection and seclusion. All rooms face inward, and few ground floor windows face the outside world. Those that do are either built close to the ceiling, or are frosted to prevent passing males from catching a glimpse of the women inside. In the NWFP, the North-West Frontier Province which borders Afghanistan, it is illegal to build a house with windows overlooking those of another house.

Most of Pakistan's customs have little to do with Islam. Their origins are tribal, not religious. Yet as history has shown, Islam has a knack of incorporating misogynistic practices into its doctrine, and most Pakistanis today believe their attitude towards women comes directly from the Qur'an itself. Today, it is the forces of Islam which are most resistant to social change.

The honour of the Pakistani Muslim family is believed to reside in the chastity and modesty of its women, who are secluded in their homes for much of their lives. Their husbands and brothers perform all public chores, such as going to the market to buy food. The custom is known as *chador va chardiwari*: "the veil and the four walls". It holds that a woman should go out only three times in her life: the first time when she is born; the second when she is married and taken, weeping, to her husband's home; the third when she dies and is taken to be buried.

Paradoxically, while such a culture is built around the idea of the value of one's wife, women in Pakistan are treated appallingly. Husbands leave them penniless for other women, capitalising on Islam's unfair divorce laws; wives can be killed or mutilated on the slightest suspicion of sexual misbehaviour; young girls are molested by their religious instructors. The crimes are dealt with leniently; custom takes a tolerant view.

In the nomadic areas of Baluchistan in Pakistan's south, women accused of compromising their honour have been known to hang themselves from the low, single beam of their tents. Baluch tents are so low that they must bend their knees in order to hang until they die. The courage needed to face such an ordeal is staggering. These customs are most savage in the tribal areas of the country – in southern Baluchistan and in the NWFP, both of which border Afghanistan.

The women themselves are taught to believe that their lot has been dictated by God, that the sanctity of their honour as well as their second-class role in life has been decreed by Muhammad. This is not the case. Both the *hadith* and the Qur'an contain passages to make these women outraged at their treatment: legislative passages dealing with their rights under Islam, to divorce, to inheritance, to equal rights. "Treat your women well and be kind to them," Muhammad had said. "Men and women are as equal as two teeth on a comb." Yet none of this is explained to these women. Their faith is strong but they are illiterate, and unable to read the Qur'an for themselves, they have no way of knowing how Muhammad intended them to live their lives. Their religion comes, instead, from what the men of their community tell them. And what they are told is rarely to their benefit.

The irony is that Muhammad was one of the world's greatest reformers on the behalf of women. Women were among his first converts, and their emancipation was part of his mission. He abolished sex-discriminating practices such as female infanticide common among Arabs at the time, admonishing them for their dismay at the birth of a girl. He re-wrote the marriage laws in favour of women. He introduced laws guaranteeing women the right to inherit and bequeath property, and the right to full possession of and control over their own wealth. Islam may well be the only religion to formalise the rights of women, and to legislate ways to protect them. We often associate Christianity with the West and thus, by association, with a more progressive attitude to women's rights, but this is misguided. Such rights are a social phenomenon, not a religious one. Christianity, for the greater part of two millennia, has been a deeply misogynistic religion, despite the teaching of Jesus about equality of the sexes. After his death, the existing patriarchal system asserted itself once more, and the Church became and remained an overwhelmingly patriarchal institution.

The process was similar for Islam. As Islam expanded, even more horrific social customs than the Arabs had ever encouraged were incorporated into the religion. From India to Africa, Islam proved receptive to dozens of practices which reduced the status of women in society, gave men even more control over them, or otherwise countermined Muhammad's appeals to Muslims to treat their women well.

Female circumcision is a case in point. It is frequently described as an "age-old Muslim ritual", and even encouraged by some members of the Islamic clergy as *sunnat*, a commendable act in the eyes of God. Yet the practice is not mentioned in the Qur'an, and even the *hadith* – the less-than-reliable recordings of the life and sayings of Muhammad – mentions it only once, disapprovingly.

Female circumcision seems to have originated in Stone Age central Africa, travelling north down the Nile into ancient Egypt. It was here that Muslims first adopted the custom. Even today blunt stones may be used for the operation, followed by the sewing together of the vagina with desert thorns. There can be few crueller practices found on earth. Yet in many areas Islam adopted it, in the same way that dozens of other practices came to be incorporated into the religion. Such flexibility lay at the heart of Islam's phenomenal success. Female circumcision is now practised in many African countries, as well as Pakistan and India. It has reached as far as Malaysia and Indonesia, and is even common in rural Saudi Arabia. It is not only Muslims who undergo the procedure – both Coptic Christians and animist tribes in Africa have adopted it – but it was the expansion of Islam that spread the practice to the world.

The custom of polygamy in Islam is very similar. The incidence of polygamy is now rather low in the Muslim world, but in the past it has caused untold damage to the status and lives of Muslim women. The passages in the Qur'an regarding polygamy were recorded shortly after a major battle, in which many of the Muslim males had been killed. Muhammad's intention was to provide protection for widows and orphans, who would have been left destitute unless the surviving males took additional wives. The rules are quite demanding:

> If you fear that you cannot treat [orphan girls] with fairness, then you may marry other women who seem good to you: two, three, or four of them. But if you fear that you cannot maintain equality among them, marry one only...
>
> *The Qur'an*, 4:3

> Try as you may, you cannot treat all of your wives impartially.
>
> *The Qur'an*, 4:130

The Qur'an – never a strict, consistent treatise – is often like this, seeming to contradict itself in many places. Muhammad received his revelations over a period of twenty years, and the views and attitudes presented in it were bound to change. Yet the emphasis is clear: polygamy is only permissible in exceptional circumstances.

In the pre-Islamic period of Arabian society known as the *jahiliyya*, polygamy was a recognised institution for both sexes. Polygyny and polyandry: both men and women were permitted multiple spouses. Muhammad condemned both practices. His introduction of polygyny was not a reversal to pre-Islamic customs, but came from his concern for the welfare of widows and orphans.

A generation after Muhammad's death, when the early Islamic Caliphate was seized by the Umayyads, wealthy males used their influence with the *ulema* to have the passages of the Qur'an interpreted in such a way as to re-introduce the practice of polygyny. Polyandry for women, however, remained outlawed. The preconditions were ignored; instead of marrying unprotected widows it became, and remains, a custom for men to take young, unwed women as their subsequent wives.

Islamic history is littered with such examples of political or personal concerns overriding those of the religion itself. Genital mutilation and polygamy are but two. Dozens of customs contributing to the repression of women have spread through the Muslim world. And where they are practised, their proponents justify them as being part of Islam.

Why has this happened? Why has Islam, more than any other major religion, proved so receptive to anti-female attitudes? Many Muslim feminists focus solely on how the religion has changed since the time of Muhammad, exonerating 'true' Islam, finding fault with how the religion has been manipulated but not daring to criticise Islam itself. They argue for rights within Islam, not a rejection of it. Even Western writers adopt a similar argument, selecting passages from the Qur'an which demonstrate Islam's *pro*-female stance, illustrating Muhammad's desire for reform. They conclude Muhammad would be appalled by the situation of today, that his reforms were limited by the society of the time, and that he would no doubt have wanted his changes to continue. They argue for a continuation of the spirit of the religion, instead of its traditions. Jan Goodwin writes: "For political ends, the Prophet's intent regarding women is both misinterpreted and misapplied, and his sympathy for women's rights is frequently no longer reflected in the law and practices of modern government." Of course, such arguments carry little weight with the orthodox *ulema*, to whom the Qur'an is the revealed Word of God: perfect, unchangeable. If God's revelations dictate that a woman's inheritance should be one-quarter of a man's, then that is what God intended for all eternity.

The arguments of such writers – Muslim and non-Muslim alike – are far too narrow. It is far easier to attack the practices that have arisen since Muhammad, to attack 'inauthentic' Islam, than to criticise Islam itself. It is thus tempting to select only those passages which show the Qur'an in a pro-female light, as this stresses how far Islamic cultures have strayed from the original religion. But there are worrying passages in the Qur'an, passages which should not be ignored, passages which have allowed misogynistic attitudes to flourish as part of Islam for centuries. It is to these passages the mullahs point when they argue for Muslim tradition. The interpreters of religious texts within the world of Islam – almost exclusively male – emphasise Quranic passages that reinforce Islam's patriarchal aspects while de-emphasising its clear injunctions of equality and justice, but it cannot be ignored that the passages to which they refer do exist. Islam itself provides fuel for the misogynistic fire. The Qur'an may grant visionary equality in many places, yet in others it displays contradictory signs:

> Men have authority over women because God has made the one superior to the other, and because they spend their wealth to maintain them. Good women are obedient. They guard their unseen parts because God has guarded them. As for those from whom you fear disobedience, admonish them and send them to beds apart and beat them. Then if they obey you, take no further action against them.
>
> *The Qur'an*, 4:34

One of the most controversial issues regarding women in Islam is the dictate that they be veiled. A passage used to support the seclusion of women is given in the surah entitled "The Confederate Tribes":

> Prophet, enjoin your wives, your daughters, and the wives of true believers to draw their veils close round them. That is more proper, so that they may be recognised and not be molested.
>
> *The Qur'an*, 33:58

Feminist writers often interpret this to be intended only for Muhammad's wives, as the revelation came at a time when the intrusion of his followers into his private life was threatening to overwhelm him. Yet the inclusion of the "wives of true believers" cannot be denied; it has helped assist those who have wished to segregate women for a thousand years.The point is not that Islam is inherently misogynistic. It possesses too many reforms in favour of women, places too much emphasis on equality for that. It does, however, retain many attitudes understandably present in Seventh century Arabia. These attitudes, by virtue of the Qur'an as a divine, unchangeable document, have become enshrined in the religion, written in stone. And it is these attitudes which have allowed the repression of women to prosper in an Islamic context for centuries.
Here, in the sluggish heat of northern Pakistan, I know I have only just begun to confront this side of Islam. Iran may be a place of misery for many women, but Pakistan is far worse. And tomorrow we begin a journey

to Chitral, the most isolated province of the country. Chitral, one of the last regions to fall to the British, was only fully incorporated into Pakistan in 1949, and is a place where tribal law and custom still dominate. The journey alone will expose us to the broken lives of women in the wild regions of Pakistan; the destination promises to be even worse. When we cross into Chitral we will enter the North-West Frontier Province, a place where Pakistani law and human rights count for nought.

Chitral is a valley province, sealed from the outside world by two high passes, both closed for most of the year. The Shandur Pass, at 3810 metres, is the gateway to Gilgit; the Lowari Pass leads south, to Peshawar. The road we will be taking tomorrow is not a major one, merely a track that splits from the Karakoram Highway to follow the Gilgit river west. It is a journey of only one hundred and thirty kilometres, yet it is meant to take three days. This is an indication of how bad the road must be, a measure of the isolation of Chitral. Our guidebook describes the journey as "sphincter-tightening". Until we cross the Lowari Pass south to Peshawar in a week's time, we will be in the land of remote and tribal Pakistan, where Islam is at its most frightening.

Tuesday 15th August – Wednesday 16th August
Gilgit to Mastuj

"A woman in village Ghulamullah was attacked with a hatchet after she disobeyed her husband and stepped out of the house..."

"Tariq Ismail stoned his mother and wife to death in Daira Din Panah on a petty issue..."

"Four armed persons abducted a young girl, Naziran, and her minor child, and sold them to a sweetmeat seller..."

Pakistani newspaper reports

A long and tiring first day, and now a rewarding morning, climbing to the village of Phander. Our road takes us through fields of corn and wheat, lodged haphazardly throughout this rocky landscape. Women and children work in the fields, cutting the wheat by hand, tying it into teepee-like bunches. It seems women can be visible when there is work to be done. The women are shrivelled, hunched and tiny, easy to mistake for children from a distance. All wave to us as we pass. Men, women, children.

Rock fences and lines of poplars encase our road on the last stretch to Phander. The world has become hard, jagged slate. It is black and sinister, a solemn substance that speaks of ash and utter ruin, and at the edge of the village it becomes a saddened district of nameless graves of gravel and sharp stones. Thin jagged tombstones, mounds of razor stones. Many of them are tiny, clearly those of children.

Phander offers lunch, rest, a view of a valley beyond. In spite of my tiredness, I am extraordinarily happy: the morning of welcome has touched me, and I am startled by the intensity of my joy. As I devour my quota of fried paratha bread and tea, I do not realise that the welcome is almost at an end.

After Phander we move away from the river, twisting into the grey hills. The way to the Shandur Pass is forever upward, slow, inexorable. We round a blind curve to confront the smiles and waves of a handful of young girls in brightly coloured shalwars of blue, orange and pink, wedged into the rock like a crop of mountain flowers. Like all the girls in the North, their trousers match their flowing tops, uniform in their bright simplicity. They keep waving long after we are gone.

This is the last friendliness we will see for a long time. The villagers after Phander become noticeably more grim; before long, the first stones are thrown. My happiness fades: in village after village we dodge the large stones launched at us by children from the rocks above, and I find I like the people less and less. We have heard tales of the southern stretch of the Karakoram Highway, of cyclists being stoned by villagers who deem cycling obscene. Indeed, most places in Pakistan consider a woman sitting astride a bicycle so immodest it deserves a stoning. Here, the issue cannot be modesty but instead a pure hostility towards outsiders. Perhaps such an attitude is the only reason these fierce mountain tribes have been able to survive for so long. Whatever the reason, we do not need to wave much in the afternoon.

The final steep climb to Shandur is far from awesome: a jumble of sharp stones, then a wide open area of green peat bogs, populated by cattle and miniature goats. And then, within minutes, down again.

Welcome to Chitral.

Plots hedged by poplar and plum:
　　　lonely green bright
　　　fragments of life.
Towering mountains rise around us, black and eternal,
　　　tangled, austere. We thread their canyon
　　　　　amid the cold smell of ancient stone, withered
　　dust.

　　　　　rock surrounds
　　　　　high as cloud.

　　In fields
　　　　　and in opaque villages: judgmental
　　stares.
Hostility beats around us like the sea.

shadows: bitter eyes: silence.
Caught.

In Mastuj, even our driver feels the threat
as hawk-faced men crowd the jeep to glare, to
spit, to swear.
    A crawling unease tightens my flesh.

We are glad to escape to the only guest house in Mastuj, where a rug-covered floor and walled courtyard offer welcome refuge. The animosity we find here has more to do, of course, with local customs than with any global Pakistani attitude towards foreigners. Until this journey, Pakistan remained consistent with the hospitality we have found in most countries of Islam, and other travellers have told us hospitality – in general – is what we should expect. The atmosphere outside the guest house walls is disquieting, but we will be gone tomorrow. As darkness drowns the world and we gather to eat around a single gas lantern, the welcome of Chitral begins to concern me less and less.

Instead, my thoughts return to the issue of women: not to women and Islam in general, but to the status of women in Pakistan itself. I have seen nothing, this afternoon, worthy of concern in its own right. Injustice is impossible to gauge from a distance. Even in the village streets there is nothing to fill me with outrage. After all, the women are hidden: I cannot be outraged by lives I cannot witness. But it is their very absence which concerns me most. It is a reminder of all I have read. In villages throughout this darkened valley, women endure the kind of lives which touch me with horror. Pukhto proverbs tell the story. *Husband is another name for God. For a woman, either the house or the grave.*

Iran may spring to most people's minds as the world's worst oppressor of women. A few well-publicised incidents have given it one of the worst international images in the world. To me, Pakistan's image had always been different. Benazir Bhutto, its former Prime Minister, was enough to ease my qualms about the country: about freedom, liberalism, equality. The reality, of course, is far more complex, far more cruel. In Pakistan, the possibility of a female leader means nothing to the rights of the country's women: Bhutto was as far from the lives of rural women as Kirst and I are. The comparison with Iran is a useful one. I had felt that the grim image of the Iranian chador was a ready symbol of all that is wrong with Islam; Benazir Bhutto a symbol of what is right. To Muslim women in Pakistan, however – indeed in many of the stricter parts of the Islamic world – an Iranian woman riding her motorbike to work, even with her chador gripped firmly between her teeth as it billows out backwards, is a figure to envy.

The current state of affairs for women in Pakistan has not come about overnight. The Western world associates the last fifty years with significant advances in social conditions and human rights, but this has been the case in few Islamic countries: the same period has seen an almost uniform slide backwards, into the ways of the past. And in few countries has the social regression been worse than in Pakistan.

Fifty years ago, Pakistan was only just emerging as a country, as the predominantly Muslim areas of India sought their independence. The driving force behind Partition was Muhammad Ali Jinnah, head of the Indian Muslim League, now revered in Pakistan as the *Qaid-i-Azam*, or "Great Leader". He was the country's first governor-general, and can be called Pakistan's founding father with some justification.

Jinnah envisaged a secular state for Pakistan: in 1947 the Islamic movement was far less powerful than it is today. Like Turkey's Atatürk before him, Jinnah called on his fellow Muslims to "take along your women with you as comrades in every sphere of life." He was an ardent opponent of many of Pakistan's tribal customs, noting that there was nothing in the Qur'an which required women to be confined. "We are the victims of evil customs," he said. "It is a crime against humanity that our women are shut up within the four walls of their homes like prisoners."

Jinnah might well have been able to mould the new nation to his views. Atatürk had created a secular state in Turkey out of the Ottoman Caliphate; in Ismaili Hunza we have seen for ourselves how the attitudes of a single man can shape a society. Unfortunately, it was never to be. Jinnah lived only just long enough to witness the establishment of his dream. He died only a year after Pakistan was born.

During the next thirty years, Pakistan became a country of coups, corruption and martial rule. With increasing poverty, civil chaos and wayward leadership, social conditions in the country stood no chance of progressing. The tribal areas remained uncontrolled and violent, as the economy stumbled the people turned to Islam for a solution.

Islam has always been a religion of return, of revival. In the face of hardship, Muslims do not abandon their religion; they instead turn to it in droves. Islam is a complete system for living one's life, decreed by God; if such a system is failing, goes the argument, it can only mean that one's faith is not strong enough, that God's ideal has not been attained. And thus the failure of Islam in Pakistan was cause to become more religious, not less. The cycle continues: the further Muslim countries sink, the louder the call becomes. And in Pakistan, this meant the forbidding rise of the fundamentalist Islamic movement. Thirty years after Pakistan's troubled and painful birth, religion had become the most powerful force in the land.

From Partition to the late 1970s, social reform in Pakistan had gone nowhere. In retrospect, this might actually have been a modest achievement. In 1977 General Zia ul-Haq, with the support of both the military and the by-now powerful Islamic movement, seized power from Benazir's father, Zulfikar Ali Bhutto. In his first speech to the nation, Zia claimed legitimacy on the grounds he was "fulfilling Pakistan's divine mission of becoming an Islamic state." It was a grave indication of what was to come.

Zia proceeded to turn back the clock on every aspect of social life. And in almost every case, it was the women of Pakistan who bore the brunt of his reforms. He decreed that the testimony of two women in court hearings was required in court cases to equal that of a single man's. In compensation cases, the value of a woman's life was similarly deemed equal to only half that of a man's. New laws were passed on obscenity and pornography, fostering a culture that associated women with obscenity, immorality and corruption. The Ansari commission, set up by Zia to 'Islamise' Pakistan's political system, recommended that the Head of State be closed to women and that female members of the National Assembly be over fifty years of age and have the permission of their husbands to participate. Zia advocated the return to the "veil and the four walls", to a complete absence of female visibility. If women were harassed, killed or raped in the streets, it was because they had provoked these actions. The theologian Dr Israr Ahmad, a man selected by Zia for the country's governing Federal Council, announced on state-controlled television that nobody could be punished for assaulting or raping a woman until an Islamic society had been created. Police brutality increased; stories became common of sadistic rape and torture at the hands of the authorities. Women were powerless to prevent what was happening to them in their own country; many were too poorly educated to understand the crimes being perpetrated in the name of Islam. Indeed, many could only submit when they were told that all such laws were in the cause of Allah.

The most insidious of all laws introduced by Zia related to *zina*, sex out of wedlock. The laws were written so that such crimes encompassed adultery, fornication and even rape, and the maximum punishment became stoning to death for those who were married. For others, the punishment is up to one hundred lashes, and ten years of imprisonment. Islamic law relating to the crime of adultery requires as sufficient proof that there be four witnesses "of good repute" to the act. The passage in the Qur'an makes it clear that this is to prevent slanderous claims of adulterous behaviour – those who falsely accuse somebody of adultery without four witnesses are guilty of a crime themselves. Incredibly, Pakistan has twisted even this decree to the detriment of women. Women who are raped require the same four witnesses. As it is even less likely that four male witnesses of good repute will stand by and watch a rape than simple adultery, it is almost impossible for a woman to satisfy the law. Then, cruelly, the law rules that while her accused male is thus not guilty of the rape, the woman is an admitted adulteress, and is prosecuted and punished. A cry of rape is no different from a public admission of illicit sex.

The laws made it clear what the attitudes of both the government and the *ulema* were towards women: women were helpless, without rights.

According to one national women's rights organisation, seventy per cent of all women in police custody are physically and sexually abused. And just as shocking is the fact that three-quarters of all women in jail are there under charges of *zina*.

Zia was bad for almost all Pakistani women, but it was the country's rural women who suffered the most. The 1985 Pakistan Commission on the Status of Women concluded that "rural women in Pakistan [are] treated as possessions rather than self-reliant, self-regulating humans. They are bought and sold, beaten, mutilated and even killed with impunity and social approval. They are dispossessed and disinherited in spite of legal safeguards [and] the vast majority are made to work for as long as 16 to 18 hours a day without payment... the average rural woman of Pakistan is born in near slavery, leads a life of drudgery and dies invariably in oblivion."

With such a situation for the lives of over seventy-five percent of Pakistan's women, the presence of a woman at the head of the country seems paradoxical. Yet the situation of women in Pakistan is far from uniform, with conditions varying remarkably depending on geographical location and class. Pakistan has its privileged few, as well as its middle class, and women born to these classes fare substantially better than their rural sisters. The strongest backlash to Zia came from such women, as they realised just how fragile their hold on rights was.

Benazir Bhutto, however, was more than just one of Pakistan's upper class. Social status alone could never overcome her handicap as a woman, not even as one riding a wave of dissatisfaction with Zia's rule. Benazir was not elected because of her own record or political philosophy, which was deliberately vague, but because she was the daughter and political heir of her father – the former Prime Minister Zulfikar Ali Bhutto – who is now designated as a *shaheed*, a martyr for Islam. His portraits are everywhere, and his birthday has become an occasion for official celebration. Pakistan's paradox owes itself to political legacy, not social justice.

Since Zia, matters have not improved, despite two periods with Benazir Bhutto at the helm. Bhutto's campaign pledge to repeal Zia's *zina* laws was popular, but after her election it became clear that women's rights were of secondary importance to the need to maintain a delicate balance between various political forces.

Bhutto's party had no majority, and had to strike deals with the smaller parties, including those representing conservative religious values. She never managed to repeal a single one of Zia's Islamisation laws. And in 1991, in between Bhutto's terms, the country passed a *Shari'a* law bill, declaring Islamic law the supreme law of the country, taking precedence over the constitution. It may have taken fifty years, but Jinnah's hopes for a secular state were finally dead. With very little fuss, and none of the outrage that accompanied the transition in Iran, Pakistan became an Islamic Republic.

Iran's overnight transformation was a burst of violence, a drama played out on the world stage that captured headlines and shook the world. Pakistan's transformation has been far more insidious. Its adoption of the worst of Islam has been slow, but it has been thorough. And along with the plight of Pakistani women, it has been largely ignored by the world.

Such a blind spot is only natural, and no different from how I view these isolated northern regions: it is far easier to be outraged about something one can see. If I were not aware of how Pakistan treats its women – of stories of police brutality and rape, of brides being burnt alive, of molestation of young girls, of the heartless rule of a law which can dismiss all such injustices as natural – then the absence of women on the streets of Mastuj would not trouble me at all.

Assault On The Senses

Saturday 19th August – Monday 21st August
to Peshawar

The humidity. Senseless. I drip. We washed our clothes forty-eight hours ago and they are yet to dry. The pages of this diary have absorbed enough moisture to have buckled. Smoke and noise and moisture: Peshawar is an impossible place.

Our journey to Peshawar, from the town of Timargarha in the north, is in a bright red mini-van, its rear emblazoned with the words, "God Help Me!" in large gold letters. A cry from a panicked passenger, perhaps. We climb into the back, sweating; it is only seven in the morning but it is hot already. This is not the dry heat of the northern mountains but something far more oppressive, something wet and horrible.

In the front seat sits the only other woman in the van. To us she is nothing but a pale violet *burqa*. The *burqa* is an image of repression, a full body cloak of extremely thick material, with a woven grill over the face. Everything is left to our imagination; the only thing that does not bear contemplation is how hot she must be. As we move further south, the air begins to crush us, a wet animal filling the van with its stifling presence, and the woman spends most of the journey slumped against the car door.

We are on the final leg of our journey from Chitral, the journey that takes us out of Pakistan's remote mountains and into mainstream Pakistani society for the first time. Yesterday, as we crossed the dramatic Lowari Pass, we hit the great mass of hot and wet air that is South Asia's monsoon. The change has been dramatic, debilitating. The monsoon clouds will, over the next four months, move south and east with me as I travel towards Indonesia. I know I shall be caught in a world of obscured sunlight, epic storms and constant damp for months, but for the moment I do not care. The transition from the arid country of rock and sunlight in the north is too sudden, too exciting. We have entered a different world. The landscape opens before us like the ocean, and I am captivated by the

Peshawar plain as our road skirts the side of a cliff towards it. Suddenly the world is emerald, a rain-softened landscape of rice and wheat grown in fields wet and green. Its vibrancy boggles an Australian mind accustomed to months of sand and rock. My image of Pakistan is of a desert country, filled with the dust we expect of Iran and Uzbekistan, or of the lunar landscapes of the mountainous north. Such lusciousness comes as a shock.

The highway strikes through villages bursting with life; I struggle to absorb it. Mango sellers beam over their golden wares; minivan drivers shout at passengers in motionless traffic jams; food vendors – snarling, shouting faces lunging in the window – hawk ice-cream and roasted corn. White cows graze on the platform of an abandoned railway station beside the goods office, solemnly ruminating the trials of their own existence.

Shaded by trees, we follow the railway tracks south, tracks lined with a market of canvas tents, a river of drifting pedestrians. Buffaloes plod along the road, struggle through the fields. Huge and black and graceful, imbued with a kind of lazy elegance that comes from the slow deliberation of their movements, they are gorgeous. We move on, following bundles of large sheets of tobacco on the back of a truck.

And then we hit Peshawar, a face hitting a fist.

From the bus station at the edge of the city we travel inwards on a bus decorated in psychedelic detail: trimmings of tin and tinsel, jangling chains of silver metal dragging on the ground; flashing fragments of mirror and chrome; wooden frames hand-painted in colours so bright they would do a five-year-old proud. Birds, vines, sunrises, crazed images from favourite Pakistani films: all are loud, all are gaudy, all have an irreverent quality that laughs in the eye of authority. A collage of excitement, manic colour and bad taste. We squeeze into one of the thousands of such beasts that dominate Peshawar traffic, peering out in awe at the chaos around us. Each moment the realisation that we have thus far seen only a tiny fraction of Pakistan assaults me like the thousands of car horns that echo around us. This is a *city*, teeming with life and noise and pollution and energy, everything on such a scale that the traffic on the way in suddenly seems peaceful. On foot, Peshawar demands effort simply to stand still.

Noise and fumes, the streets crowded with moving metal. We battle with the heat, consuming mangoes, mango juices, cokes and green tea as we explore the streets after finding a hotel. Shop-fronts spill onto the footpath, and traffic both pedestrian and vehicular collides on the roads. Auto-rickshaws coughing black fumes trail us wherever we walk, blocking our way across the streets, their drivers bullying us in the hope of a fare. Touts lean from the multicoloured buses, trying to argue us on board no matter which direction we are walking. "*Chalo! Chalo!*" they scream – "let's go" in Urdu. Dental surgeons gather on soot-stained corners beside vast grinning pictures of dentures and cut-away faces advertising their wares. Dirty yellowed plastic teeth beneath glass cases. Nameless Afghan restaurants clang with noise, roaring fires at their entrances; street-side hawkers offer everything from pens to plastic bags, combs to Afghan scarves, and twigs of fibrous acacia, splayed at the ends to be used for cleaning teeth. The shredded sounds of a city. Melon sellers waving away the flies. A few rare women, their *burqas* shielding them from both the world and any semblance of comfort and freedom. Kirst walks before me in the crowds, as this seems to reduce the number of men who sneer or grope or bump against her, the challenge of my gaze deterring all but the most insistent suitors. Sugar cane crushers; sellers of mango and lime juice; coppersmiths banging away beside raging flames; decaying filth. Sliced coconuts; grapes and pomegranates sold in plastic bags; ragged crows haunting the garbage. My God the heat. Close, impenetrable markets, labyrinthine and alluring. Gaudy women's garments made of silver and gold lace; vegetables and spices; silver and brass and copper; carpets and cloth and shoes; nuts and grain; the stench of offal. Noise and smoke, noise and smoke.

And there is a crazy violence to it all, a violence that seems to taint everything in Pakistani society but which seems stronger here than anywhere else. It may come from Peshawar's proximity to the Pukhtun tribal areas of Pakistan close to the Afghan border, which are subject to no law beyond their own. Or it may come from Peshawar's status as a war town, centre for most of Afghanistan's *mujahideen* groups and home to many of the war's refugees. People without a home, without any sense of the future, can possess precisely the kind of desperate energy that assaults us on the streets of Peshawar; they can just as easily resort to desperate, brutal solutions in their efforts to survive.

It is not generally recognised that seventy-five per cent of the world's refugee population is Muslim. Poverty, war and unstable governments are the rule in the Islamic world, from Algeria to Bangladesh, from Afghanistan to the Sudan, and with the highest growth rate of any major identifiable group in the world, the problem is only going to become worse. Pakistan, for example, had a population of 30 million when it was created in 1947; in less than half a century this figure has quadrupled to over 130 million. Muslim societies have a population growth rate of three per cent – twice the world average, and a rate which sees its population double every twenty-three years. More than 80 million Muslim children are born every year: one hundred and fifty a minute. Far too often the world they see is one of chaos, war and increasing poverty. And as the Afghan children of Peshawar's refugee population are finding, it can also be one without a home.

The Afghan war has been one of the more tragic conflicts of the last few decades. This is not because more people have died than anywhere else, because more homes have been destroyed, or because more people have flooded into neighbouring countries; Afghanistan is no worse than countless other conflicts in these respects. What lends the war in Afghanistan its tragedy is that it has changed Afghan society forever. Even with the war ending, with the Afghan refugees crowded into tent villages all along the Pakistani border beginning to return home, there is no chance that they will be able to resurrect the society they once had. The rise of Islamic radicalism that has accompanied the war has severed the country completely from its once tolerant past. How this has happened serves as a grim warning for the future of moderate Islam.

For years Afghan *mujahideen* groups were hailed in the West as 'freedom fighters', valiant opponents fighting to free their country from Soviet oppression. Money from the West, principally the US, flowed into rebel groups, channelled through Pakistan and Peshawar. Pakistan made huge political mileage over its status as a Western ally in a region of Soviet influence, and it was widely acknowledged that many in the regime made millions by skimming the gun money as it went through.

Perhaps less well known, however, was that Saudi Arabia funded American aid to Afghanistan dollar for dollar. And the Saudi aid came with strings attached. While American money was being channelled through Pakistan, Saudi Arabia funded the resistance movement directly, giving it far greater control over where its vast sums of money went. The Americans funded any groups opposed to the Soviets, and the Saudis only gave their money to groups that were as arch-conservative as they were. Moderate *mujahideen* groups did not stand a chance. As the funds were spread more thinly, these organisations either vanished or changed their allegiance to the fundamentalist resistance leaders who could keep them supplied with arms. In the latter part of the war against the Soviets, moderate groups had difficulty paying their phone bills, let alone trying to fight a war.

There were other conditions applied to Saudi money. Their deals often included the supply of puritanical Wahabi fighters, there to proselytise as well as fight. The Wahabis were extremely well funded and well armed, and their influence over the Afghan soldiers was immense. The irony was that Wahabism was completely alien to the people of Afghanistan. Eighty per cent of Afghans are Hanafi Muslims, one of the more moderate Muslim sects and one completely at odds with the fanatical strictures of Saudi Wahabism. The Wahabi doctrine is radical and regressive: Wahabi-trained guerrillas have been implicated in the World Trade Centre bombing and in terrorist acts in Egypt and Algeria. These are the men who tried to destroy the tomb of Muhammad because it encouraged improper Muslim worship. Their attitude to the West, to unbelievers, to a flexible interpretation of their religion, is just as uncompromising and just as dangerous. Remaking a society and a culture that was once the darling of the hippy tourist trail, where women walked proud and unveiled down the streets of Kabul, has been one of the more frightening and far-reaching effects of the war.

The effects of Wahabi proselytising could be seen most clearly in the refugee camps based around Peshawar and the Khyber Pass. Anti-West sentiment, for example, was flamed by fundamentalist clerics under the dominion of organisations that had been funded by Saudi Arabia. Relief agencies received death threats. An Australian agency had a warehouse burned to the ground by an angry crowd after being incited by an extremist mullah who claimed that soap was only being given to female refugees because Westerners in the agency wanted to have sex with them. Pamphlets circulated claiming that the Western women employed by relief agencies were suffering from AIDS and had come to Peshawar to infect Muslims.

More dangerous, however, were the changes within the insular refugee society. Fundamentalist teachings became common; radical interpretations of the Qur'an became the norm. A people once renowned for its progressive attitudes was now issuing *fatwas*, or religious rulings, banning women from "wearing perfume or cosmetics, going out without their husband's permission, talking with men other than close relatives, walking with pride, or walking in the middle of the sidewalk."

Now, as civil war rages still between rival Islamic factions, there is not a moderate Afghan group to be seen. It is entirely likely that when these Afghan families *do* return to their own land, they will not only be returning to a country of shattered buildings and broken roads, but to a country whose society has been remoulded in the image of Arabian extremism. They will have left an open society, Islamic but tolerant; they will be returning home to an Islamic republic fuelled not by authentic Afghan Islamic ideals, but by the burning extremist fervour espoused by the Wahabi fundamentalists of Saudi Arabia.

At issue, of course, is more than just the fate of the Afghan nation. The radicalism of the refugee camps spills over into Pakistani society; the feverish puritanism engendered by the war walks the streets of Peshawar itself. The long-running instability across the border has had an effect on Pakistan, particularly in these western regions, and it has not been a positive one. A rise in Islamic fundamentalism has only been part of the problem. Lawlessness and violence are infectious diseases, and the spread of guns and violence and drugs and crime and radical politics from these extremist areas has affected the rest of the country. In Karachi, over ten thousand people have died in the last four years as a result of fighting between rebel groups and the government. Areas of the city are subject to martial law; others have been brought to a standstill by gunmen opposed to the government, and residents flee to the northern mountains to escape the violence. In the southern province of Sind, banditry and kidnappings have become so common that many roads are not considered safe without an armed escort. The problems in these areas have been growing for years, but now a steady supply of arms flows from the regions bordering Afghanistan, raising the stakes considerably. When we leave the NWFP, we can expect to be searched by police.

For its own part, Peshawar and its surrounding province are practically lawless. The tribal areas were never fully subjugated by the British, and have traditionally been subject to no laws other than their own. As a result, they have become the heart of Asia's gun and drug trade, channelling drugs from the poppy fields of Afghanistan – now the greatest heroin producer in the world – to the West, as well as producing the guns and bazookas and mortars that keep the fighting going in both Afghanistan and Pakistan's South. The government is belatedly trying to rectify the problem, but without much success. Just before we arrived, a group of German tourists were kidnapped in protest against government plans to impose the rule of law in the region.

Now, as we lie in our grey hotel room beneath the futile turnings of a fan, listening to the wearying madness outside, I wonder how anyone can live in such a city, in such an impossible environment. Pakistani society is in trouble: with corrupt government, little rule of law, and economic stagnation, it is little wonder a fury permeates. Noise and smoke and dust and violence, everything with a dangerous edge. Heat and damp, rubbish and poverty, and the dazed misery of existence. The cacophony from the streets outside is the lament of a desperate society.

My God the heat.

Tuesday 22nd August – Thursday 24th August
to Lahore

The cadaverous early morning light is too feeble to illuminate our corridor; our room is dark and ripe with damp when we wake to the sounds of Peshawar's chaos. Pukhtun hospitality obstructs our departure: several complimentary cups of green tea and cobs of roasted corn with a pair of shoe salesmen we meet in the street means we arrive at the bus station far later than expected.

I note, as we board the minibus that will take us as far as Rawalpindi, that there are advantages to being a woman in Pakistan as well as disadvantages: the crowd on board shuffles around to give Kirst a seat by the window so that she does not have to sit beside any strange males, while I am given a stout wooden stool with no back and have to lean forward all journey. As consolation Kirst offers me the gleeful laugh she reserves for all my misfortunes; if I wasn't here she wouldn't realise she was being treated differently. Even such points of politeness, however, are apt to remind me how sexually repressed Islamic culture can be. In Egypt, fundamentalists teach that men should not sit on a bus seat vacated by a woman for at least ten minutes, until her body heat is no longer apparent. In 1992 the Egyptian author Farag Fouda was killed for criticising such fundamentalist excesses.

Like Fouda, like almost all commentators on Islam, I use the word 'fundamentalist', and have done so extensively throughout these diaries. 'Fundamentalist', however, is a poorly-defined term, understood differently by different people, despite being used extensively by all. Such is the nature of language: a word can be so widely used it can creep insidiously into everyday communication, no matter how misleading, how inaccurate, how poorly-defined it may be. 'Fundamentalism' was originally a Protestant Christian idea, referring to the belief that the Bible possesses complete infallibility as the revealed Word of God, rejecting the notion that human motive, thought and creativity could have influenced its text. It is derived from a series of tracts entitled "The Fundamentals", published in the US between 1909 and 1915. The application of the term to Islam, however, makes no sense. To every believing Muslim, the Qur'an is already the revealed Word of God, so a movement based on this belief is hardly revolutionary. When applied to Islam, 'fundamentalist' means very little.

Many of those who write about Islam today seem unaware of the origins of the term. Some shy away from its use but for other reasons, most notably that it implies a return to the 'fundamentals' of the religion. They believe that this implication of a return to the essence of Islam is erroneous, that fundamentalists are far from the faith preached by Muhammad. 'Fundamentalist', to them, is a term to be avoided as it grants a legitimacy to an unyielding, bigoted, and often violent section of the Muslim community. Some prefer the term 'Islamist', but to me this grants an even greater legitimacy to the movement, placing it at the heart of the religion. 'Extremist' is probably the most accurate term, but like it or not, 'fundamentalist' has slipped into the English language. Most would associate it with a regressive, literal and narrow interpretation of religion. No matter what its limitations, the term conjures a definite image, an image close to the one I am trying to convey, and this alone makes it a useful one. If I were, ultimately, required to provide a workable definition of fundamentalism, it would probably be the one suggested by the Islamic commentator V. Shonia, namely that Islamic fundamentalism is politics based on Islam.

Our journey is along Pakistan's Grand Trunk Road, the main highway of a country of 130 million people. It is a road steeped in history. Once – under both the Mughals and the Raj – it was the main axis across the subcontinent, a ribbon of life and commerce stretching from Kabul to Calcutta. With such a pedigree I find it disappointing: a ragged strip of asphalt through country of boisterous green, crumbling at the edges and barely wide enough for a pair of buses. We hurtle along at a murderous pace, our progress foiled as a result of the frequent checks by police for weapons and drugs, shadowy symptoms of what goes on further south.

We cross the Indus river, wide and grey and soundless. It marks the border between the NWFP and the Punjab, and the transition between the two regions is sudden and noticeable. In place of the ubiquitous blue and green chequered *mujahideen* turbans of Peshawar are now handkerchiefs, wool scarves, bright cotton prints. Sudden genetic variation amongst the men: mixed with the hawk-nosed Aryan tribesmen of Afghanistan are skins as dark as those in Africa. For the first time in urban areas we see women's faces: *burqas* are gone, replaced by thin white scarves draped elegantly over raven hair. The scarves are Islamically proper, yet after our time in the NWFP the fact that they reveal women's faces is enough to shock us. We pass the pedestrian crowds slowly, gaping.

I note that everyone who squeezes into our cramped van voices a single mantra as they do so; the same phrase is muttered reflexively as they clamber out. In Pakistan, this phrase is spoken before commencing any task. A driver might mutter it before moving out into traffic, a farmer before leaving for the field, a carpenter before picking up his tools. It is *Bismillah ar-Rahman ar-Rahim*, the phrase prefixed to every *surah* in the Qur'an. *In the name of God, the Compassionate, the Merciful.* It is recited as part of prayer by millions every day, a reminder of the presence of God in every act, that every action is performed for al-Lah. It is uttered almost subliminally, a reflex action so basic it emerges as a mere grunt on the tide of breath. Often the phrase is just a sigh of "Bismillah", but however it is spoken it is constantly before us, a persistent reminder that God rarely leaves the awareness of the believing Muslim.

Pakistan continues to surprise us for all around the land is green, glowing emerald beneath a sky the colour of black eyes and blueberries. The monsoon has truly begun and the day is heavy with unshed rain. Lightning flashes in the distance are a surprising orange, the colour of ripped flesh. When the fist of heaven finally cracks, hammering us with rain that drives the air into the ground, our bags are retrieved from the roof of the van, and with the kind of Pakistani treatment of foreigners we have become used to, the three men in the seat in front insist on nursing our bags for the rest of the journey to Rawalpindi. We can love the Pakistanis for their hospitality as much as we hate them for their attitudes towards women and their leers at Kirst.

We see little of either of the twin cities of Islamabad or Rawalpindi, being dropped instead in the mud of Pir Wadhai bus station between the two. We are travelling directly to Lahore, and find another bus immediately. Stopstartstopstartlurch through heavily polluted suburbs, dense with signs in English advertising everything from law schools to cinemas, tin workshops to fortune-tellers, tyre stores to institutions that declare themselves as "amusement and marriage" centres. Horse and buggies known as *tongas* clipclopclipclop by. A snake charmer draws a crowd. The smell of decaying vegetables and the shit of dogs and humans and buffaloes is strong enough for us to be thankful we won't be staying in these suburbs when we return. We hope. A lone man with a pelican, the crowd even larger for such a strange beast so far inland. A barefoot child sells used dentures on plastic sheeting in the dust.

On to Lahore through angry terrain. Swallowed by the thick air.

Friday 25th August – Wednesday 29th August
Lahore

> A mystic place between time and shadow, the shrine
> of Ali Hujwiri, the Data Ganj of Lahore, this country's

holiest Sufi saint. Devotional scenes
as purple and distraught as Iran: barefoot crowds,
the wailing ash, the tears of beggars and women.
A garland of flowers around my neck, silver biscuits at my feet.
An impenetrable scene, both physically and spiritually:
the crush of bodies, the mystic's tears. The warm call of Sufism,
that yearning jewel of interest I carry
must now wait
till I am alone.

My heart is without borders:
I cannot accept
that Kirst must leave.
We inhabit the dark palaces of our hearts separately,
more distant now than ever, and avoid the future completely.
Silence is preferable
to the abandonment we both expect to feel.

Thursday 30th August
Rawalpindi

My diaries have always been a record of *whats*, not *hows*: what I do, what
I think, not a description of how I feel. Any impression of the pale thread
of emotion is far too elusive, far too difficult for me to catch. I know from
earlier journal experiences, however, from trying to reach back to
discover a previous me, that emotion is what I require. Especially on this
day, of all others. Some say that nothing other than God can be an
adequate image of God; I sometimes feel the same way about my
emotions. I know I cannot recreate the texture of these feelings in mere
words, yet I owe it to a future me to make the attempt.
Today was the day that Kirst left me.
A grey blend of fear and grumpiness descends on us in the morning as we
pack. The unknown future, still impossible to envisage, hangs about the
halls of our thoughts, dulling our conversations even if it is too poorly
defined to bring sorrow, and we move through the morning feeling vague
and disembodied. I simply cannot picture how my life will change in the
hours to come. I am an automaton, soft and hopeless, drifting through a
sea of disbelief and impoverished imagination.
It is Kirst who brings on the change. As we move to the door to leave, she
gestures back to a card on the bed.
"You have to read it when you get back," she says.
The gulf between the present and a lonely future is abruptly bridged.
"When I come back" has suddenly become a time I can visualise. A card
on a pillow, a message from a future only hours away, waiting for me. I will
return to the hotel room, I will open the card, I will read. And I will be
alone. The future pierces the disbelief. The image of loneliness that has

been impossible to visualise is now distressingly clear. A hard sob escapes my lips, a jagged beginning to the howl that follows it, filling me, filling the room. Kirst looks on aghast, unprepared for anything like this. The roles of our relationship have been set for years: I am the comforter, she the one who should be the one crying. She can offer no words. She stands mute, her arms stiff and useless at her sides, watching me with big wet soft eyes. She waits for the grief, the slip, the craziness, whatever it is, to subside. Her gaze reveals an astonishment as strong as mine at this hidden emotion, not knowing whether to plead with it to stay or be thankful when it goes. As the gobbling sobs fade, I know that this lapse has shaken me badly. The assault was completely without warning, and I feel I can no longer trust myself, that I no longer have any idea of what lies in wait within me. I want to tell Kirst how I feel, to convey a sense of the loss that her absence will bring, but words and ideas slip between me and the feeling. Love and loneliness, both imperfect emotions, neither of them the right shape for the vessel of language.

Kirst's own reaction to leaving, minutes later, is just as surprising. Crammed tight in a gaudy Suzuki on our way to the airport, her nerves spill as a hiccuping giggle over her teeth, growing to become a manic, almost deranged squeal. My final taste of laughter. Travel alone may be superior to any other form when it comes to exposure to foreign cultures and receptiveness to new experiences, yet these benefits come at a stiff price, the loss of the constant laughter, the perpetual humorous delight in one's surroundings, that only comes when experiences are shared. Our belief in a final hour together vanishes at Rawalpindi airport. A jostling crowd of men and women in *shalwars* is gathered at the entrance to the building, peering past the grim guards who keep them at bay. Only ticket holders, we are told, are allowed into the terminal building.

The bite of disappointment is severe. We have saved our final goodbyes for the airport, have entrusted our final time to this place. Not that anything significant could ever be uttered in a foreign airport, but to be denied the opportunity seems terribly cruel. Our final words must be said as we are washed by the grasping tide of a Pakistani crowd, shoved on all sides by strange dark men.

The final goodbye is brief and strange, insufficient for any meaning. A truceless moment sandwiched between two journeys. Kirst offers me a smile submerged in sadness and then is gone, in to combat the chaos of bodies and baggage that reigns within the building. As her back retreats down the dim corridor I retain a vision of her pale blue eyes.

What surprises me most, as I turn away from the terminal building, is that I suddenly feel nothing. I have said farewell to Kirst in foreign lands before; those times I felt nothing right up until the moment of departure, only to be bereft all the more savagely for not having prepared myself for being apart. This time the wave of emotion subsides like the sad sucking of a tide going out, leaving me with a yellow emptiness in my heart.

I suddenly feel very old.

Trails Through The Dust

Monday 4th September
Multan

Asceticism is not that you should own nothing, but that nothing should own you.

Imam Ali

I wake, confused, after an afternoon sleep to recover from the overnight bus trip. Reach out for Kirst. Several minutes pass before I realise where I am, a sleep-laden limbo time of distress. In the days since Kirst left I have coped best in the daylight hours; only moments of weakness and confusion drive something frail and hopeful to the surface, something crushed when I remember I am alone.

I am alone now not only on my journey, but also as a tourist in this city: with the well-publicised lawlessness in Karachi and the surrounding province of Sind, few tourists venture into the south. I have certainly seen none. For the most part there is little to attract them here, to this flat plain of dust and heat and violence, when the awesome mountain landscape of the north remains available. Unlike them, however, my travels are not governed by exquisite landscapes or by comfort. The four days in Islamabad as I extended my visa were spent taking stock of the journey thus far and planning the rest of the trip. I am here to look for Islamic mysticism.

Multan was among the first places on the subcontinent to fall to Islam. When the armies of the early Arabs took Sind early in the Eighth century, converting at the point of the sword and slaughtering the Hindu warrior caste, Multan was transformed from a place of Hindu pilgrimage into a Muslim centre overnight. Islam took a long time to spread into the rest of the subcontinent, but Sind has been part of the world of Islam from the very beginning, and Multan itself has been an attraction to the mystics and holy men who have characterised Islam in India for centuries.

It is to follow these men that I have come. Sufism was responsible for the spread of Islam to most of the subcontinent; apart from conquests like that of Sind, the widely-held notions of Muslim armies always converting upon pain of death are false. Even the mighty Mughals could not truly convert their subjects by force. It was the wandering mystics who were the real champions of Islam in South Asia, men who spread a message of *sulh-i-kul*, peace with all, who were flexible enough to bend Islam to a Hindu mentality. Sufism remains, to many Westerners, the most inscrutable part of Islam. It is one thing to understand what Sufis are; it is another to understand what they believe. This is probably because Western Christianity, of all the major branches of monotheistic religion, was the only one never to fully accept mysticism. Our societies are not geared to an understanding of the philosophical constructs and mental

169

discipline that drive a true mystic. In contrast, Judaism, Eastern Christianity and Islam all at some time embraced their own forms of mystical tradition. Until the returns to stricter religious interpretations this century, it was the God of the mystics, not the God of the orthodox and literalist clergy, who eventually became normative among the faithful in all three faiths. The lack of a mystical tradition may, in some ways, explain the popularity of Eastern religions such as Buddhism with Westerners during the past decades.

Sludge underfoot, the stench of effluent, and the grey-green heat of the monsoon, wet and solid. I walk towards the centre of the city, in search of the shrine of a Sufi sheikh known as Rukn-i-Alam. I stride through a torrent of abuse and harassment with a black umbrella above my head to protect me from the sun (it sounds strange even to write, but portable shade is a Pakistani fashion in these southern furnaces, and a damn good idea. Shopkeepers hiss; bystanders laugh and jeer; beggars pluck at my sleeves; young boys taunt. For once, after weeks of such treatment with Kirst, the harassment is a relief. It means I have to consider that we have been misinterpreting its intent all this time; maybe the treatment is for being a foreigner, not for being a woman.

After the hammering crowds at the tomb of Ali Hujwiri in Lahore, its alleys jammed with the faithful and with shopkeepers and beggars wishing to profit from them, the shrine of Rukn-i-Alam comes as a surprise. It stands erect in a courtyard on its own section of hill, a sentinel above the rest of the sprawling city, tall and domed and desolate. The beggars are far fewer than I had expected, yet they still number more than the faithful who have come to pay homage to their saint. A crowd of stunted limbs and empty eyes gathered at the gate, a slow trickle of believers, and me. I leave my shoes with a man sitting beneath a plastic awning. Efficient and dignified, he ties my shoes and numbers them with the grace of a professional. Only a dozen others line his vast shelves, clearly intended for a much larger crowd.

I walk across the hot stones of the courtyard to the monument. It recalls Samarkand: the pink stone and elaborate architecture of Lahore have given way to the austerity of pale brick, the lifeless colour of the desert. A blue geometric mosaic adorns its upper reaches, narrow pillars and pointed arches of sky and sand preserved in tilework. Yet the building is less inspiring than I had hoped. It impresses because of its age rather than architectural splendour; it is far from being an image in stone of the wonder of God. I trail behind a young Pakistani couple, clearly tourists themselves, to the entrance.

The interior of the building is almost completely deserted. A ceiling high and wooden, two stooped women laying wreaths on a tomb in the centre, the empty echoes of silence. I am disappointed. The walls are bare, and despite the splash of colour that is the tomb, draped in pink cloth and rose petals by the absent faithful, an air of abandonment hangs over the place.

The other shrines I visit in the city are no more enlightening. They are dead places, empty of the faith at work I have come to find. I think I shall leave tomorrow. Multan is not what I expected, and the sooner I finish with this part of Pakistan the longer I will be able to spend in Bangladesh. Bangladesh, the great unknown: I am still to meet anyone who has been there. I can only hope that the Sufism which was responsible for the spread of Islam through its lands still remains.

Sufi mysticism, like the mysticism of all the monotheistic faiths, began as a reaction to an anthropomorphic vision of God, one that was emerging from early Islamic orthodox doctrine. All three monotheistic religions developed the idea of such a personalised God, and it seems natural, particularly in the West, to associate a personalised God with the concept of monotheism itself. The words of the Qur'an, and of the orthodox teachings of both Judaism and Christianity, create an image of God who does everything we do: he loves and hates, punishes and rewards, creates and destroys, sees and speaks and hears. Christianity took such personalism to extremes: it made a human person the centre of its religion, and developed the notions of sonship that were inevitably bound to emphasise the idea of a personalised God, a God about which we can claim knowledge, a God we find possible to imagine. It may even be that without some degree of identification and empathy of this kind, religion cannot exist. The remote First Cause of the philosophers draws few worshippers, while a personalised God possessing qualities with which we can identify has spawned religions which have lasted thousands of years.

A personalised God, however, can have serious shortcomings. God can become a mere idol carved in our image, a being no greater than our own imaginations, hence an inevitable projection of our own prejudices, needs and desires. The belief that God 'plans' means that a major catastrophe or personal tragedy can make him seem callous and cruel, uncaring and unworthy of worship. A personalised view of God is inherently reductionist: God becomes limited as a result of our own limitations, fails because of our own failures in understanding. If nothing other than God can be an adequate image of God, then a literalist image, constrained by its very dependence on language, is doomed to failure. It is from the limitations of language and conception that mystics have turned, seeking a more fulfilling, transcendent and spiritual version of God. And their influence has been more significant to Islam than to any other of the monotheistic faiths.

Muhammad's primary concern was with the practical aspects of his revolution, with the establishment of a just and ordered society for the Arabs. He and his closest companions, however, retained a balance between what the Muslims called *dunya*, the worldly aspects of life, and *din*, religion and a life of piety. Muhammad led the life of a near ascetic, living simply in mud brick quarters and enforcing austerity on his household, and the Qur'an itself contained many mystical overtones. The mystical foundations of Islam were laid from the very beginning.

The incredible rise and spread of Islam in the centuries after Muhammad's death changed society too quickly for many people. The initial piety of Muhammad's vision was quickly lost beneath the weight of wealth that came with Islam's success on the battlefield. The rise of the Shi'a was itself a reaction to the wealth and hedonism of the court. The Caliphate had focused on *dunya* at the expense of religion, and the Shi'a and many groups like them called for a return – a call heard even today – to the austerity and piety of the early Muslims, a revival of true Islamic attitudes and ways of life.

During the Eighth and Ninth centuries, one such group was focused on this return in an ascetic and spiritual, rather than revolutionary, manner. They attempted to return to the simpler life of the very first Muslims in Medina, dressing in the coarse garments made of wool that were supposed to have been favoured by the Prophet. The Arabic word for wool is *suf*, and these ascetics came to be known as Sufis. Their clothes, at a time when silks and brocades had become the fashion of the wealthy, were a symbol of their renunciation of worldly values and their abhorrence of physical comforts.

The Sufis would never rebel against the established order in the way of the Shi'a or the Ismailis. Their effect, however, was just as profound. Their motto of peace with all drew followers from all walks of life and religion. The Sufis rejected the supremacist doctrine developing in the orthodoxy, who had begun to see Islam as the one true faith, the only path to God, and who focused on the passages of the Qur'an deriding the other religions. To Sufis, any path to God was valid. God was a God of love, not justice and retribution, a God anyone could experience if they looked deep enough within themselves. Indeed, Muhammad was an inspiration to the Sufis, who hoped to experience God in a way similar to that experienced by Muhammad when he received his revelations.

The Sufis developed the techniques and disciplines which have helped mystics in almost every religion to achieve a transcendent state of consciousness. Fasting, night vigils, trance-like chants, singing and dancing – all were part of the Sufi repertoire, all designed to bring the Sufi mystic closer to a vision of God, to a union or reunion with the Creator present in all things. Descriptions of incredible scenes of Sufi worship have long amazed me. They are what I have missed in Multan, what I hope to find in Bangladesh.

Sufism was frowned upon for centuries by the *ulema*, for its idolatrous notions of union with God, and also for its tendency to encourage withdrawal from society and solitary contemplation. Many Sufis believed that the most perfect communion with God came only when the soul was in a state of quiet, ceasing to reason or to reflect either upon itself or upon God. Following such beliefs had led many mystics to withdraw from society, seeking God from within. This behaviour was in conflict, as the *ulema* saw it, with the Prophet's injunctions to Muslims to take an active part in their own society. The instructions in the Qur'an were clear: there should be no monasticism in Islam. The Eighth and Ninth centuries were thus a time of great conflict. The major orthodox jurists were teaching Islamic jurisprudence in a formal, dry and legalistic manner, while the Sufis saw their role as keeping the spirit of the religion alive, rather than conforming to the form and ritual of the state religion that was ominously taking shape. It was not until several centuries later that the split between the two schools would be resolved, and it was only then that the Sufis would really begin to spread their message to India.

Sufism was perhaps strongest as a movement in Iran, yet nowhere was it more important than on the Indian subcontinent. Conversion by the sword gave Sind to Islam under the Umayyads, but the massive bulk of India proved impossible to overcome in such a swift stroke. It would be the Sufis, not the conquerors, who would make the greatest inroads. With their tolerance of other creeds, the Sufis were far more receptive to established beliefs in the regions in which they preached. In Hindu India their doctrines met a receptive audience: the travelling Sufi *faqir* bore a remarkable resemblance in teachings and appearance to the Hindu *yogi*. The principles of asceticism were already a part of Hinduism, so with Sufi thought bent to local conditions, their words were bound to strike chords with the established spirituality of the region. Even under Muslim conquerors it was the Sufi orders who could claim much of the responsibility for conversion; as the Mughals pushed Islam into less populated areas such as Bengal, the Sufis were creating pockets of hybridised religion, their beliefs a combination of pre-Islamic custom, superstition, mysticism, and the teachings of Muhammad. These pockets would remain dominant for centuries, until the communications revolution of this century came to wash a storm of Arabian orthodoxy across the world, a return to strict and pure Islam, a revival of renewal and reinterpretation. I only hope that the dearth of believers in Multan is not an indication that I have come too late.

I return in darkness to my hotel. A dire place of rats and damp shadows, it grows out of an air-conditioner mechanic's workshop like a tumour. The owner and his flunkies greet me in the courtyard, invite me to sit and watch television with them. Their interest is focused mainly on the shrunken old man who has wandered the hotel courtyard all day. He is small and mostly absent, a man unlikely to cause anyone harm. Remembered stories of molested male travellers have sounded in my head all afternoon, as the rest of the staff have been unable to resist fondling him. A joke, a laugh, a grope of his groin, a degrading desperate feel to the whole thing. Until now I had wondered if I was just being over-sensitive, but it seems I was not. They bring him before me, the young receptionist giggling as he tries to yank down the old man's trousers. His older brother laughs.

"You want to fuck him? Fuck fuck. Very good."

Laughter from all. The night continues in this vein. The young boy rubs his groin into the old man, who stares uselessly at the television. Before long I can endure it no more, can offer no more forced and polite smiles, and return to the sluggish heat of my room. If only the desperate edge to these men would vanish. If only I could convince myself that all this was good-natured fun. If it wasn't for the constant undercurrent of anger and sexual repression in Pakistan's society, it would be a marvellous country. Its kindness, its hospitality, its friendliness towards total strangers, are at times astonishing. So I am saddened that I lie in my bed instead with thoughts of the harassment, the stares, the cruelty to women and the men outside.

Tuesday 5th September
Bahawalpur

This day: long, tiring, yet ultimately rewarding; the first time I would have been able to describe a day this way since Kirst left. And as added entertainment, the persistent assumption of people I meet that I am Japanese.

I am destined for one last Sufi monument before turning towards India. The tiny village of Uch Sharif, stranded on the edge of the Cholistan desert, was once a centre of religion and culture comparable to Multan. It spawned one of the most important Sufi sects of the subcontinent, was home to dozens of *madrasa*, and drew the faithful from around the world. Those days are long since past. Now it hosts only the very faithful or the very committed: pilgrims, mostly, to its handful of Sufi shrines and sometimes, very rarely, a strange and wayward traveller.

The countryside between Multan and Bahawalpur, the nearest large town to Uch, has an element of rural Iran about it, all angular mud compounds and date palms. Unlike Iran, however, sudden greenness is here, in clumps of irrigated vegetation that taunt the arid climate to do worse. Fields of cotton line the road close to the river, along with an eclectic mix of palm, eucalypt and acacia. Yet always, beyond them, sand dunes raise their stubborn heads, reminders of what the land would be like without those glaciers hundreds of miles to the north. They are not the dunes of a sandy desert, but are instead the pale grey of the Indus: this is where all that pulverised mountain has come.

The most bizarre sights of the journey are of massive white colonnaded mansions, odd combinations of Southern plantation and Greek ruin, several modelled directly on the US White House. In a context of desert poverty, they are extraordinary. I can only use large industries or wealthy landowners to explain their presence. Rural Punjab and Sind are overwhelmingly feudal, and the great land owning families of the region still exert enormous power over their subjects. The Bhutto family is one of the most important, part of a system that owns tenants and villagers in a way unheard of in the West for centuries.

Bahawalpur is a revelation after the mud and filth and steely damp of

Multan. Bright and small, a well-preserved city thrusting from the desert, I like it even before I stride under the huge pink Farid gate which once marked its entrance. Guarding the gate now are giant fruit stalls, a restaurant, a pair of youths selling pakoras pungent and spicy behind bubbling oil. Hotel Al Hamra, down a laneway on the edge of all this narrow chaos, is described as "only for those on the tightest of budgets" by my guide book, but it is far superior to what I had to endure in Multan. Even the weather here reigns supreme. It is bright and clear, the breath of the desert, with not a hint of the monsoon grimness and hanging skies of further north.

Back outside, choking on my first taste of *pakora*, I learn the fate of those who pause a moment too long in Bahawalpur. I am besieged by well-wishers wanting to shake my hand – and not let go – and talk, despite the town's near-total lack of English. In ten minutes this happens to me no less than a dozen times, and I am pressed by a crowd pining for somebody able to translate. The almost frantic eagerness to be friendly reminds me, for the first time in months, of Iran and it pains me how crippled I am without language.

I am buoyed enough to try for Uch Sharif immediately, despite fears about the lengthening shadows. My spirit is soaring; nothing can go wrong.

Uch is smaller still: the same Persian feel, an even greater lack of English. It is only fifty kilometres from Bahawalpur, but the journey involves two buses, the second breaking down on the outskirts of town. The sun is savage, bright, and the empty sky gleams, cleaves my spirit just as open. I walk the rest of the journey, brave beneath my umbrella, gathering stares as I go. Such attention worries me no more. On my own it is impossible to resent the glares of these dark-eyed men; it was only when the attention was directed at Kirst, overtly sexual, that it was offensive.

Uch's main street leads directly into its bazaar, small and manageable. It is a semi-thoroughfare, denying cars but admitting a parade of bikes, scooters, bullocks and tractors. Iron workers bang furiously at glowing metal and hanging plastic awnings protect dusty vegetables from the sky. I push through the usual mixture of turbans and *burqas* and white scarves shielding all but the eyes of these women from the world. Exclamations as I pass: mischievous, real. Beyond the bazaar, in the narrow alleys traced with tiny gutters of flowing effluent, I am lost in minutes. The stares are hesitant here, suspicious even, particularly from the older faces. I ease my passage with frequent *salaam wa leikums*, the ubiquitous Muslim greeting: *peace be upon you*. The phrase is recognisable anywhere in the Muslim world, but here it is a key, a magic spell that works to unlock these tight, suspicious faces to reveal the smiles hiding behind them.

The tomb I seek appears from nowhere, the narrow streets obscuring until the last moment the hill on which it sits. This is the tomb of Bibi Jawindi, wife of the Sufi saint Jalal ad-din Bukhari, a man largely responsible for the rise of the important Suhrawardiya school of Sufism on the subcontinent. Bukhari's tomb lies in Uch as well, though I have already realised I shall not find it. The town may be small but it is a maze, and nobody responds to my queries of his tomb: all direct me here instead.

It does not matter for this place is inspiring enough. Uch Sharif means "high place", and from this sudden plateau of dust amongst the warren of bricks, I can see the surrounding countryside. My gaze goes out over pale mounded graves, shards of brilliant blue tile still clinging to some of them, to a world of green and sand. The vista is rich with emerald cotton fields, a wall of palms offering yellow dates to the sun, glistening black buffaloes bellowing out their complaints to the world. The tomb is a ruin, half destroyed, swept away years ago by the waters of a flooded Indus. Octagonal like the ones in Multan, it manages to be far more inspiring, far more exquisite, despite being nothing more than a half-cracked shell. A facade of delicate blue and dust, a structure of intricate patterns woven from the colours of desert and sky. The tomb is as dead as the broken graves all around: I was never going to find Sufism here. In the other tombs of Uch, perhaps, but not this journey, not me.

And yet I am not disappointed. I stand and turn in the dust, arms wide, breathing in the sun and sand and green and brick and stone. I am nowhere; it is fabulous. This meagre place is of poetic simplicity, a village of insignificance far away from the tourists of the mountains, the travellers smoking dope at the end of their mountain treks. I am a universe away from anywhere, sunk deep in myself. For reasons I cannot fully explain, I feel full of joy.

Then, it seems, my day-long journey is over. My expedition to this remote little village, isolated really only in my imagination, is complete.

It is not the only journey finishing. The limits of my exploration of Pakistan end here, at this rough outpost at the eastern limit of the Arab empire. Pakistan captures the feel of an Arab world, a world that finishes in these deserts. Onward then, into an Islam no longer of sand but instead of quarrelling jungle and heavy tropical air, to an experience of an Islam born not of Arabia but of India. With its deserts and its history of early conquest, southern Pakistan can fool itself that it is as much Arab or Persian as it is Indian. As I turn back towards Uch Sharif's tiny bazaar, I know that this is the last taste of such a culture I shall have. The journey, as far as Pakistan is concerned, is complete. All that remains is time on buses, as I make my way overland to Delhi, and then on to Calcutta and Bangladesh. I am turning, closing inside, looking onward. How appropriate that today, at the furthest limit and end of the journey, I began to read E.M. Forster's *A Passage to India*.

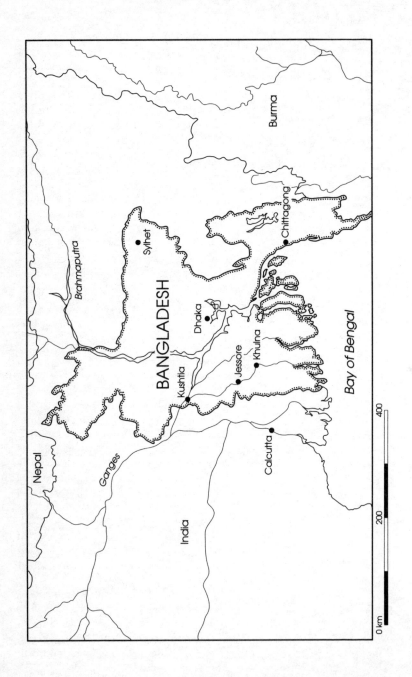

BANGLADESH

Cross Borders

Tuesday 26th September
Calcutta to Jessore

Through the blurred train window I watch Calcutta's scrabbling suburbs pass, and after them the lumpy brown villages of West Bengal. The houses are pictures of true poverty, set in densely packed piles of rubbish, their roofs plastic sheets weighted by stones. Scenes frozen: children cowering under black plastic sheeting; a legless man selling cigarettes in the rain. A woman holds out a naked baby while a pariah dog waits hungrily to devour the yellow faeces as it hits the ground. To Muslims, dogs and pigs are equally unclean; it is easy to see why.

The heavy rain that began last night, an emphatic escalation of the daily monsoon weather, has not eased all through the morning. It has meant that the first five trains to the border today were cancelled, and as a result my compartment is filled with the terrible odour of over a hundred bodies. I am lucky to be near the window, to be able to breathe even a slice of the air from outside, as the heat inside is frightening, my very own Black Hole of Calcutta. Of course, the condition of the train does not improve our comfort: this is the only train journey I have ever experienced where passengers needed to open their umbrellas inside the carriage.

From time to time the rain eases, and I am rewarded with views of the breathtaking rice-paddy green of West Bengal. Here, unlike Central Africa, there is no red ochre earth to break the pattern of colour, and unlike Indonesia no terraced mountains smash the uniformity. Here there is only dark emerald land and a sorrowful sky: flat, grey-blue, dramatic.

We arrive at the border town of Bangaon – a place as dark and grim as the day – just as the belly of heaven splits, and I haggle for a rickshaw in the instant mud and hammering rain. A rickshaw-wallah agrees to take me the five kilometres to the border itself, though the sight of his frail body struggling through the downpour with my much larger frame while I remain beneath his painted blue canopy fills me with a naive guilt all journey. Even through his sodden clothes I can feel the suffering of his bones.

Our muddy road takes us through swamp, hidden from the sky by rows of giant peepul and teak. A banyan tree, dark and wise, reaches downwards with its myriad roots. The trees greet each other above our path; in their branches is wind and the sound of surf.

Everything remains dim as the rain continues to fall; it comes down in grey priestly folds with no persistent form, lashing at everything. The landscape on either side of the road appears to be drowning: huts of bamboo squat low in stagnant water. A sludge of green floating everywhere. Small brown children wade through the muck, stop to look at me. The fetid water creeps into their homes, and continues to rise with the rain. Sounds: the rain scraping on the canopy, the squelch of tyres in the mud, the rasp of the rickshaw-wallah's breath. Despite the misery of the scene, its dark drama is as beguiling as art. The landscape shifts perspective as we move, and I gaze upon a painted world.

The Indian Civil Service has been described as being neither Indian, nor civil, nor even a service. I am inclined to agree. My final moments in the country are spent dealing with stultifying inefficiency, intimidation, and requests for bribes. I weather them all with the cheery stubbornness that seems to work best in such situations and, after a little over an hour, I am granted permission to leave the country. I shoulder my pack for the short distance through no-man's-land. I walk towards Bangladesh, to the poor cousin of Pakistan, to the final part of my journey in South Asia. I am, after a three-week Hindu hiatus, returning to the familiar world of Islam.

Neither the jungle that surrounds, nor the low green customs building that emerges from it after only a hundred yards, give me any indication that things have changed. When the most important question from the customs officers who gather around me is whether or not I am a Muslim, however, I know I have arrived. I am asked for baksheesh just as blatantly as I was across the border, but for the first time in weeks the use of half-mumbled Arabic phrases receives a positive response. At the immigration post a dozen steps further into the country I feel even more at home: the forms are waved away by the superintendent, and I am invited into his office for tea and biscuits. Earnest interest in my welfare comes as a surprise after India, and I stay for half an hour to discuss politics with him and two journalists, both of whom decide to visit me later in Dhaka. Handshakes and frequent *salaam wa leikums*, smiles and welcome. I am surrounded by Islam once more, by things I know; the feeling is akin to putting on a welcome old boot. It is late afternoon by the time I begin the walk to the border town of Benapol.

Benapol. It suddenly seems possible for a place to be more decrepit than an Indian village. Everything is low and grey and crumbled; signs are faded and stores are empty. The buildings were once painted, but have long since lost their colour to poverty and the monsoon; the black damp of the jungle seeps from every wall. The colours are those of India but even more drab; the people are those of West Bengal but even more aggressive. My path is down the town's single main street, lined with the trucks that attend every border, and I suffer the gazes of hundreds of compact Bangladeshi labourers captivated by my presence. Interest in me is something new for I have become accustomed to the general indifference of India, where tourists are a tribe in their own right. Here, the immigration forms have already revealed that I am the first Westerner to enter this way for ten days.

The labourers' bodies are those of the southern version of Indian man: small, dark-skinned, delicately boned. Hard men and poor, teeth at all angles, glassy eyes. Each one calls to me as I walk, with the tone of mischievous children seeking attention. Unlike the welcome given to me at the border post, it is an act purely for their own entertainment, provoking jeers and laughter amongst their fellows; none wish to speak to me. I walk on.

It is four o'clock. I stand alone in this makeshift town as the rain begins once more. I have no wish to stay in Benapol, and need a bus somewhere, anywhere, anywhere that will get me into the country. The only available buses will take me no further than Jessore, the first town inland, but this is fine: I will have at least escaped the border.

The journey begins in gathering gloom. The road, and hence our progress, is so clogged with bicycle rickshaws that it becomes clear we will not make Jessore until night. I gaze out at the land that will be mine for the next month, trying to get some sense of it, to gauge its character. The darkness plays with me; everything is dreamlike, ephemeral. The road is lined with black ghosts, bamboo huts selling spare parts, medicine, sweets. From each, no matter what they sell, hang bunches of bananas, small and blackened. Behind the huts are sometimes rice paddies, sometimes jungle, sometimes swamp. I am left with the impression that everything I see is transient, could be gone tomorrow; the manlike shapes drifting along the road seem scarcely real. Occasionally we pass settlements, too small to be called villages; in several I see real, solid buildings peeping through the damp growth of the jungle. The wrath of far too many monsoons has defeated these structures, covering them with a black-green jungle mould. It gives them an ancient, ruined, majestic air, as though they are in the process of being swallowed by the jungle just like an ancient Angkor Wat or Borobodur.

It is late, as expected, by the time we arrive in Jessore. I see little of the town. A cheerless cinema, a ferment of buses and rickshaws, half-finished buildings sprawling onto the mud. I wade through the rickshaws, searching for a hotel. I can find nobody with English to help me; after India this change comes as a shock. The hotel, when I find it, brings Africa to my mind. A cramped room of muddy cement, spiders and mosquitoes filling the air. The smell of damp is of books or clothes shut in a cellar for fifty years; it stings my nostrils. There are, however, differences. In Africa the mosquito nets were empty veils waiting for their brides, pale hanging ghosts with a strange and sad kind of beauty to them. Here they are grubby grey screens useless and full of holes, distressing to touch.

I lie now inside the net which forms a box around my bed, listening to the unbounded night outside and scribbling my diary in between power failures. Four this evening. The scene is perfect: the croak of frogs from beyond the window reminds me of the swamp that seems to have engulfed the world; the occasional peal of thunder or flash of lightning is simply the monsoon reminding me how firmly I am in its grip. I look across the room. My bag, my clothes, all my belongings are thoroughly soaked. The rain here is inescapable. And the monsoon will continue to follow me, as it has done since Peshawar. By the time I reach Indonesia I shall be screaming for sunlight and dry air, sick of the constant smell of moisture and rot, desperate to escape the five months of low skies and unrelenting rain.

Of course, of all the countries in which to be travelling during the monsoon, there are few worse than Bangladesh. Its rainfall is staggering: just north of the country is the Indian town of Cherrapunji, the second wettest place on earth. Even more debilitating, however, is the combination of geography and circumstance that ensures that Bangladesh is the most flooded country in the world. The country lies on a vast alluvial plain, a landscape of shifting river courses and accumulated silt, formed from the juncture of the two greatest south Asian rivers, the Ganges and the Brahmaputra. Bangladesh is, in effect, the largest river delta in the world, a sombre terrain as flat and featureless as the sea, ninety per cent of which lies below a height of ten metres. It collects monsoon rain deposited all over the subcontinent, from both Nepal and India, and in the monsoon months up to a third of the country lies underwater.

This flooded water world is Bangladesh for five months of the year. The floods render millions homeless; they destroy livestock, agriculture and settlements; they ruin communications and roads and health; they are the source of the impermanence and decay lying at the heart of Bangladesh. The floods, however, contribute only a fraction of the sadness that sours this land.

Bangladesh has suffered some kind of calamity – famine, flood, cyclone, earthquake – every year for the last two decades. Sixteen cyclones every ten years, tearing at the country from the Bay of Bengal during the monsoon. In 1965 it was ravaged by a cyclone with the power of ten three-megaton Hydrogen bombs. In 1970 the damage was even worse: in one of the worst natural disasters of this century, a cyclone claimed the lives of over half a million people. The quiet wingbeat of tragedy, a country of helpless deaths.

A year after the 1970 cyclone, the country began its struggle for independence against West Pakistan. I am of a generation only ever aware of Bangladesh as Bangladesh, not East Pakistan, just as my images of Iran have only ever been of the war and of fanaticism, never of the Shah. I have no memory of the united Pakistan, formed at Partition from the predominantly Muslim areas of the subcontinent, no memory of a single country split in two by thousands of miles and a hostile India. It was an unworkable concept, and 1971 was the year that East Pakistan began to demand its freedom.

In the time since Partition, West Pakistan had funnelled development funds and foreign aid to itself, despite a higher population in East Pakistan, at that stage producing the majority of cash crops for the country. The Bengali population was downtrodden, oppressed by what they saw as unjust Western domination. The culmination of their frustration came when the West Pakistan government declared that Urdu, and only Urdu, would be the national language. The Bangla language movement gave birth to a push for independence. Bangladeshi identity was rooted in the concept of language: the new nation would be called "Bangla Desh", or "land of the Bangla speakers".

The war with Pakistan was one of the most brutal of the Twentieth century. It was also a reminder of the ideological insanity of the Cold War. The US could interfere in Vietnam yet ignore the fact that Pakistan, an ally, was systematically slaughtering its own population in an internal conflict just as bloody. Few countries have a symbol on their flag to represent the blood its children shed at its creation, but Bangladesh does. Napalm was used to destroy whole villages and stories of atrocities abounded as the army of West Pakistan attacked the poorly-armed population of the East. Ten million people fled to India. The ethnic overtones of the conflict were as sinister as they have been more recently in the Balkans: systematic rape was used in an attempt to destroy the purity of the local population, to ruin the concept of the Bengalis as a separate people. Unlike the Balkans, few mass graves were dug; the bodies lay piled instead in fields for the vultures.

The full story of Bangladesh thus does not make for happy reading. The country was first sucked dry by colonialism, and then by Pakistan. Two ruinous cyclones forming two of the worst natural disasters of the century, and then a tragic war, one which left the country physically and emotionally destroyed, with one of the worst economies in the world. The story, however, continues. Floods in 1974, the entire grain harvest destroyed resulting in widespread famine. A coup d'état and a state of emergency. An election a few years later, an increasing emphasis on Islam and Arabic, riots, a decade of political turmoil. With more floods in 1988, three-quarters of the country was inundated and thirty million people left without homes. Thirty million. An economy which may as well have not existed. A cyclone in 1991, 120,000 people killed, millions more homeless. A population growth rate as high as any in Asia. A tiny country, a speck on the map, yet the eighth most populous country in the world, with easily the highest population density of any country apart from microstates like Singapore. It is three times more crowded even than the tumultuous swarms of India.

The country's largest foreign exchange earner – by far – is the money sent home by those who have left. Its largest cash crop is jute, the result of the British emphasis on single-crop economies, used to produce twine and sacking. Bangladesh is thus left with little with which to fill one with hope: an economy based on repatriations and twine, used to support one of the largest, most poorly-educated populations in the world, in a country with no infrastructure, one cursed by disasters, sinking further and further into the silt on which it stands.

I listen to the sounds of the rain outside, to the lament of sadness on the wind. Bangladesh, an unloved country, a place where all the dreams are rotted. I wonder what it holds in store.

Wednesday 27th September
Jessore to Khulna

I do not like Khulna. The place has struck me as a miserable town of unlikeable people, although after only a single mud-spattered afternoon I know I haven't really given it a chance.

The city lies on the edge of a region known as the Sundarbans, a vast area of the south-west delta that forms the largest mangrove littoral in the world. The region is virtually uninhabited, an impenetrable fortress of twisting estuaries and swamp. The last remnants of the jungles which once covered the subcontinent are here, jungles which took the original Aryan invaders of India a thousand years to hack through on their way from Pakistan. Bangladesh will be my first taste of how Islam has adapted to an environment utterly unlike the deserts where it was born. As an introduction to a country of jungle and swamp and water, Khulna is as good a place as any.

It is not just history which makes Islam a religion of the desert, but its very form. The descriptions of heaven in the Qur'an dwell longingly on "gardens watered with running streams". Passages discuss the value of a man's camel, and the shifting sands of the desert can be felt in its words. To the people of Persia, with deserts of their own, or to those of Central Asia or of Egypt, the call of such a religion must have been strong. Iranians hunger for gardens as though it is their version of heaven here on earth. The merest patch of green sends them into raptures; I think back to the many times we passed families picnicking on the median strips of major roads.

The Qur'an takes on a different meaning, however, for people of a jungle land, places of perpetual green, to whom water is a curse as much as a blessing, river people forever at the mercy of flood. A desert culture could easily accept a literal interpretation of the Qur'an, could forever be prone to fundamentalist interpretations of the religion. To the people of Bangladesh, however, a strictly literal interpretation of the Qur'an does not make sense. In Bangladesh, from the very beginning, a re-interpretation of the words of Islam has been required.

In Khulna I have already seen that modesty means something different than in countries closer to Mecca. The veil here is uncommon, children roam the streets without clothes, and the half-naked labourers I pass would be a shocking sight anywhere else I have been. In Iran, by contrast, even short sleeved shirts are deemed immodest. Islam, when presented with Bangladesh's environment, was forced to change; if it had not done so it would not have survived.

Thursday 28th September – Sunday 1st October
Khulna

A fevered dream of begging for food; nightmares abstract and angled and bitter. Confused and frightened in the darkness. My hotel room breathtakingly small, a damp cave of broken glass and cobwebs. Cold fever, icy with sweat; scared. A tangled night. Something I have eaten. Pure death.

Sounds of doors opening, of hacking and spitting as people rise for dawn prayer. A relief to see daylight. Didn't know what kind of hell I had reached.

Aching and bruised from fever, an illness stamped into my body. If I am going to feel this terrible I refuse to stay in this place.

Move to the Park Hotel. Wood panels and starched sheets. Shame I feel far too ill to enjoy it. Dizzy. Sleep.

Afternoon. I feel better, I think.

Up here on the fourth floor of the hotel, the jangle of thousands of bicycle rickshaws floats up to me, disconnected from the world. Another political demonstration outside. Bullhorns, chanting. Third one in two days. People protesting against the government. Rain sounds vicious.

Ugh. Worse. Heat terrible but I freeze. Most people under sheets and fan, and here I am sopping with sweat in my sleeping bag but still cold. Head pounds if I move. I wonder how I ever got through diseases like this before. Delirious.

Alone.

Another day. Weak.

Starving yet I constantly feel as if I will vomit, food and bile pressing upwards on my lungs. So constipated. In three days all I produce is a tiny piece of brown hardened leather, covered with a kind of yellow jelly. I pick it up. If I didn't know where it came from I could have mistaken it for some foreign delicacy. Quenelle. Biltong. Confectionery.

Struggle outside for the first time. Man in the mud-stained back room of a street-side pharmacy agrees to see me. No doctor, but I don't have the energy to go further. Only a few thousand doctors for a population of 130 million. A crowd of twelve people push inside to watch him examine me. Oh Bangladesh, a crowd wherever I go. The verdict: "viral fever". What does that mean?

I have bought a ticket for the steamer to Dhaka. Can't stand feeling this way. A decent doctor in the capital, surely.

I have now eaten nothing for four days. Caught a glimpse of myself naked in the mirror. The victim of a liposuction operation gone horribly wrong, the flesh removed as well as the fat. The skin on my arms is all wrinkled, as though it doesn't know what to do with itself.

The worst wave of today's illness has passed, can sit up now to write. What is there to say. Wallow in self-pity. I dare not make plans for the rest of the journey, as I feel too depressed to do anything but go home. Would dearly love not to exist. What is there to say.

The Blue Poetry of Oblivion

Monday 2nd October – Tuesday 3rd October
to Dhaka

> Kill me oh my trustworthy friends,
> for in my being killed is my very life.
>
> from the *Mathnawi* of Jalal ad-Din Rumi

I know I have been losing weight for two months, ever since a stomach bug I picked up in Lahore, but this last week seems to have broken me completely. I am so bony now I feel more comfortable squatting than sitting – sharp bones line both my back and my buttocks. I run my hand down my spine; it feels reptilian. I have the body of a prisoner of war. Thank God my cabin has no mirror.

I sit alone on the deck of the steamer to Dhaka, one of only two passengers in first class. There is little difference between our deck and the ones further back. First class is only differentiated from second by price and thus smaller crowds, but in Bangladesh any escape from the crawling press of bodies is the greatest luxury imaginable.

I would not normally have treated myself in this way, but two evenings ago the thought of wrestling my way on board was quite simply beyond me. Even dragging myself to the wharf in Khulna was a trauma. The crew at first refused to believe I was sick, and insisted I wait an unspecified time on the deck in the steaming darkness – a longer-than-usual power failure – for the boat to be loaded. Workers made quacking noises as I passed, or screamed in my ear. Their way of being noticed. An appropriate conclusion to this town; I have been finding Bangladeshis more and more difficult to like. Not until I collapsed on the wharf did the harbour master agree to smuggle me on board early. At least now, six days after the fever began and with a pale breeze in my face, I feel almost recovered.

The river before me is wide, brown and unlovely. Although I speak of it as though it were a single thing, in reality it is more a whole landscape than any well-defined course, a maze of turnings and journeys that renders my map laughable. If there is an end to the world, a place where all life and chaos and rubbish comes to die, this is it. I imagine this is what the river Styx must be like, dreary and endless. The dead would be right to hope for a coin under their tongues; nobody would wish to be forced to wait by these banks for a hundred years.

The water is strewn with all manner of flotsam – broken banana trunks, palm leaves, the occasional plank of wood – all churning to the surface, swirling, swirling. It is carpeted in places by a tangled kind of Sargasso weed, which breaks away in house-sized masses to join the sick brown soup. All motion is dead and slow. I think back to the funeral pyres of Varanasi, to the bodies of babies and those who died from disease, wrapped in cloth and tossed into the river. Their bodies were caught in this same weed, trapped at the river's edge by moored boats. Bloated figures; the yellow stench of human corpses. Can a body float a thousand kilometres? I scan the river for the dead, just in case.

Bangladesh is a true water world, a place where the presence of water is so inescapable, and on such a giant scale, that the rules of life are different. This river is over thirty kilometres wide in places – even wider further south – and the land around it is little more than silt it has deposited over the years. The land is thus constantly changing, silting, shifting, and with every flood Bangladesh grows a little, mutates a little. It is a process which has destroyed countless cities in the past, as the land has changed and sagged and vanished. Bridges are impossible, roads unreliable, and the only sure means of transport is on water. As a result, we are not the only boat, nor the biggest. We are accompanied on our journey by a cavalcade of vessels, all making their own way through the maze of waterways that lace the country. The boats are all either ancient rusted hulks or wooden handmade skiffs, large and small. Rotting cargo carriers lie almost submerged beneath their loads, balanced precariously in ways ocean-going vessels could never dare. The black skiffs are little more than giant canoes, with a single oar at the rear acting as both propeller and rudder. They play in the water under the control of lone men, who turn their oars slowly in the muck as though stirring an enormous pot. Venetian gondoliers spring to mind; their movement across our bow is just as slow.

The river banks here are fortified, a vain protection against titanic floods. People are everywhere. Balanced on the banks are men and women wherever we go, rice paddies and palms and tiny patches of jungle at their backs. Superficially, at least, I can see little in common with Pakistan. Women are forever in evidence, their colourful *shalwars* lighting the landscape of green. The men wear the long, collarless pyjama tops of Pakistan, but their lower halves bear brightly coloured check sarongs known as *longhi*. A length of cloth joined into a hoop and then tied around the waist, the garment imparts an air of ease and unhurriedness even stronger than that of the baggy pants of Pakistan.

Still a day before we reach Dhaka. I spend most of the journey sitting here, watching the days slink past, the monotony only broken by the terrible meals and the occasional chaos as we stop to pick up passengers. At least it gives me time to think. Time to consider what I know of Sufism before I try to find it for myself.

To an orthodox Muslim in the Eighth and Ninth centuries, Sufi mystics were bizarre, almost deranged figures. Their teachings were esoteric in nature, confrontational, and often seemed blasphemous. Some exhibited wild and unrestrained behaviour, while others deliberately flouted orthodox laws to demonstrate their contempt for human judgement.

The Sufis were primarily concerned with an inner sense of dislocation in the soul. They felt such a dislocation was present in all human beings, and came from separation from God. Their aim, roughly stated, was to heal this rift, to achieve a union, or reunion, with the Source of all things, the One. Many identified this One with Islam's al-Lah, though their view was a thoroughly mystical one, refreshingly free from the dogma and trappings of orthodoxy, and bound to offend the established religion.

'Intoxication in God', for example, was fundamental to the early Sufi mystics.

They approached God as one would a lover, sacrificing their own needs and desires in order to become one with 'the Beloved'. They longed for a gradual stripping away of identity until nothing stood between God and themselves, a state of annihilation of self, 'fana, in which true union with God could be found. The effects of such a union on the psyche were significant, and often dangerous – some Sufis might today even be classified as mentally disturbed. The state of union could only be reached through severe intellectual discipline, through meditation assisted by fasting, night vigils, and chanting the divine names of God as a mantra in order to induce a higher level of awareness. Not all were up to the task, but those who were claimed they had reached Paradise. After days of prolonged effort the Sufi could claim a personal encounter with God, who seemed so close to their soul that it felt like union with the divine. "Glory be to Me!" was the cry of Abu Yazid of Khurasan. It was a cry bound to be identified as idolatrous by the religiously conservative, but the Sufis did not care. The God they were seeking was no external reality, no identifiable being 'out there'. The Sufi God was present in all things, and nowhere closer to man than his own soul. God was within all of us, if only we knew where to look. The concept was enunciated in the Qur'an: "Wheresoever ye turn, there is the face of God". Indeed, the Sufis drew on the mystical overtones of the Qur'an in many ways, seeing Muhammad as a true mystic:

> We indeed created man; and We know
> what his soul whispers within him,
> and We are nearer to him than the jugular vein.
>
> *The Qur'an*, 50:51

This mystical union with God answered a yearning in many people, brought on by that sense of loss and loneliness, of being stranded in this existence, that most of us have felt at one time or another. It was a yearning which today psychologists might attribute to nontheistic sources, but which nevertheless remains part of the human experience. "The flight of the alone to the Alone" was how Sufis described it, a phrase which aptly demonstrated the Sufi view of the loneliness of the soul, one which echoed their belief that God created the world primarily from a sense of loneliness. The Sufis were turning away from dry, legalistic interpretations of religion and seeking enlightenment for themselves, in a contemplative experience familiar to both Hindus and Buddhists.

The Sufi approach to introspective contemplation often included a certain degree of asceticism; indeed, rejection of the world was a part of the Sufi ideal. Poverty was respectable, austerity desirable. The idea was an old one – Socrates had once stated "having fewest wants, I am nearest to the gods" – and it was one that made the establishment nervous. To the government it was a political message embodying a rejection of authority, while to the orthodox *ulema* it was but one of a litany of blasphemous Sufi ideas.

The orthodox reaction against the Sufi movement began early in the Tenth century. The figure of al-Hallaj, an Arab living in the Tenth century under the Abbasids, perhaps best represents the collision of Sufi practice with Islamic orthodoxy. Al-Hallaj preached the overthrow of the caliphate and the establishment of a new social order, and he was imprisoned by the authorities. It was his religious claims, however, that most aroused the ire of the *ulema*. Tradition relates that when asked to identify himself while knocking on his master's door, al-Hallaj replied, *"Ana al-Haq!"* I am the Truth! *Al-Haq* is one of the names of God; to a Muslim, such a claim is idolatry itself. One of his poems expressed what he meant:

> I am He whom I love, and He whom I love is I:
> We are two spirits dwelling in one body.
> If thou seest me, thou seest Him,
> And if thou seest Him, thou seest us both.

Accused of blasphemy, al-Hallaj refused to recant. He was executed for his extremist views, and crucified like his hero, Jesus. Yet death was hardly punishment for one who had sought union with God all his life. Like many Sufis, al-Hallaj believed he would at last be meeting the object of his love. He went to his death singing.

Al-Hallaj was not alone in seeing Jesus as an inspirational figure. To Sufis, Jesus was a true mystic, one who had simply approached God as a father rather than a lover. According to the Gospels, Jesus had made claims similar to al-Hallaj, such as when he said that he was "the Way, the Truth and the Life". He had embodied the same ideals of austerity, and of peace with all. Most importantly of all, however, the God of Jesus was a God reached through love. Love of all humanity had long been one of the hallmarks of Sufism, and their identification with the teachings of Jesus was thus strong. To Sufis, the error of Christianity lay not with Jesus, but with the interpretations applied to the religion after his death. The Christians were wrong to believe that a single man, however holy, could express the entirety of creation. What Jesus had simply been teaching was something close to the heart of Sufism itself: that God could be found within us all.

It was not until late in the Eleventh century that the crisis between mysticism and orthodoxy in Islam was resolved. Al-Ghazzali, an Iranian born near Mashhad and one of the greatest Islamic scholars in history, managed to present a unified view of religion. He combined the three elements of Islam which had been threatening to tear the religion apart: orthodoxy, mysticism, and the intellectualism of the philosophers. His work has been considered the greatest religious book written by a Muslim, second only to the Qur'an. Al-Ghazzali taught that al-Hallaj had not been blasphemous but merely unwise to proclaim that God is in all men, arguing that such an esoteric truth could be misleading to the uninitiated. Al-Ghazzali established that Sufism was not only valid, but that it was the most authentic form of mystical experience of God.

In the wake of al-Ghazzali's work, Sufism ceased being simply a minority movement. Sufism became the norm for Muslim spirituality throughout the Islamic world, and Islamic orthodoxy learned to coexist with mysticism as a complementary route to al-Lah. Indeed, the Sufi concept of God would remain the most widely accepted throughout the Islamic world until recently.

The Twelfth and Thirteenth centuries saw a great growth in the movement, and heralded the establishment of numerous Sufi orders, or *tariqas*, each with its own conception of the mystical faith. Poetry, already a well-established part of Islamic culture, fell under the sway of the mystics and a full understanding of the great poets of Islam – Sa'di, Hafiz and Jalal ad-Din Rumi – would be impossible without an understanding of the mysticism on which their poetry is based. Rumi's verses, in particular, echoed the Sufi obsession with the annihilation of self and union with God.

Rumi's great work, the *Mathnawi*, became known as the Sufi Bible. After his death, his followers – who knew him as *Mawlana*, the Master – established the Sufi order of the Mawlawiyyah, known in the West as the "whirling dervishes". Dancing was a feature common to many Sufi schools, who used both music and dance to enhance concentration and induce religious ecstasy. The whirling dance of the Mawlawiyyah was a means of concentration: as the Sufi spun, he or she felt the very definition of self dissolve into the dance, felt their identity fade as they progressed towards *'fana*. Dozens of schools proliferated – the Suhrawardian schools of Iran and Pakistan, for example – and before long the movement had millions of adherents.

By the end of the Thirteenth century Sufi sheikhs, or *pirs*, had come to have a profound influence over the local population, and were revered as saints in a way similar to the Shi'a Imams. I think back to the crowded scenes at the shrine in Lahore, to the hordes still clamouring to ask favours from Ali Hujwiri nine centuries after his death. Sheikhs were quite simply heroes of the people. The death anniversary of certain sheikhs, their *urs*, became times of pilgrimage and intense religious devotion. Their selfless devotion to God, their rejection of wealth, and their love for all humanity made them universally attractive figures. Everyone flocked to them: rich and poor, Muslim and non-Muslim alike.

This last point was especially significant. The appeal of Sufism to other religions was fundamental to its success, and nowhere was this more true than in India. In the Sufi view, all religions were equally acceptable paths to God – indeed, Sufis felt that there were as many paths to God as there were people. They spoke of "the God created by the faiths", a term meant to emphasise that all dogma is human creation, liable to breed intolerance and fanaticism, lying at the core of every sectarian dispute. Sufis realised that the rules and regulations governing organised religion were anything but divine. Ibn al-Arabi summarised their perspective when he wrote:

> Do not attach yourself to any particular creed exclusively, so that you may disbelieve all the rest; otherwise you will lose much good, nay, you will fail to recognise the real truth of the matter... Everyone praises what he believes; his god is his own creature, and in praising it he praises himself. Consequently he blames the beliefs of others, which he would not do if he were just, but his dislike is based on ignorance.

Sufi missionaries, with such flexible attitudes, were bound to prove popular in areas deeply attached to established beliefs and superstitions. The orthodox *ulema* were opposed to any tradition which did not spring from either the *hadith* or the Qur'an, but Sufis recognised all traditions as authentic paths to God. They were quite willing to permit hybrid forms of religion to develop, ones which involved beliefs taken not only from Islam but also from local customs, incorporating elements of magic, myth, superstition, music and dance alongside the more traditional aspects of Islam. The result was what theologians term *syncretised* religion, a mixture of Islam and local beliefs that would often have been almost unrecognisable to the orthodoxy of Arabia, but which would dominate belief on the subcontinent right up to the current century. It is this mystical tradition of Islam that I hope to glimpse in Bangladesh.

The river, as we move towards the capital, opens up before us, sighing out and down and away. I am left with an impression of a space that teases the infinite, a world of pale brown water still and silent in all directions. A despairing, empty colour. A great lawn of Sargasso heaves and swings to the right of the boat, meandering haphazardly to the horizon. The scale of the emptiness, of the broad expanse of water, is truly amazing. I cannot tell what parts of the world are normally river and what is flooded landscape. A patch of land to the right, a fragment to the left.

Decrepit trawlers, barges and blighted wrecks float across my vision. Late in the morning we pass a frightening region of the river, a ship's graveyard of mythic proportions, an area of dead and stranded boats. Those still functioning do not look much better: dark crowds swarm the decks of the larger vessels, resembling media images of unwanted refugees. Fishing canoes as dark and two-dimensional as silhouettes scoot back and forth across our path. A funereal hue to everything. The place is timeless, nameless, futureless; I cannot even be sure if it is real.

Dhaka delivers me from my drifting oblivion, if 'deliverance' can be considered an appropriate term. We dock with a grey and sepia world, a city hidden behind its own stagnant waterfront. White kites flutter randomly above iron roofs, the fluttering hopes of the city's children; most are unable to soar for long. The city itself is merciless, mad. I am stuck for half an hour in the dock area in my rickshaw, in a logjam of a thousand blue and white hoods. Later on the same journey, closer to my hotel, it takes twenty hot, carbon monoxide ridden minutes to travel a single block. The streets twist through wretched, leprous buildings, sad places rotted by time. They are filled with the noxious black fumes of auto-rickshaws, with the smell of human sewage, choking with a terrible mass of humanity, and every one is a sea of angry vehicles. Buses and rickshaws launch themselves into the vehicles in front, prodding them forward precious centimetres. Everyone is screaming or honking horns. The drains are blocked; the city has been flooded by the monsoon.

Over an hour from the dock, I climb from the rickshaw, sliding my foot into the sloppy human waste that mixes its terrible odour with the sickly smell of all the other rubbish underfoot. In every way, Bangladesh seems an exaggeration of the worst of India. Poorer and more crowded, dirtier and slower, more angry and frustrating. Only a week ago I would have sworn this would have been impossible.

Friday 6th October
to Kushtia

Today, after two days of loneliness amidst the noise and crowds, traffic and demonstrations of Dhaka, the illness still with me, things have shown a turn for the better. I have found a most remarkable man, someone whose sheer enthusiasm may mean I end up liking Bangladesh after all.

I first met Subroto – or perhaps I should say he met me – a week ago, on my way from Jessore to Khulna, and his utter insistence that I visit his home town is the reason that I find myself in Kushtia, at the end of a half-baked, looping route through the country, back almost to where I began. He is a slight, balding man, with eyes of an amphibian. He speaks the best English I have encountered so far in Bangladesh – although this isn't saying much – so it is lucky that he has been inspired by my investigation into Islam, and wishes to assume responsibility for showing me "Islam as it is lived in Bangladesh". He is somewhat demented, stricken by the twin demons of verbal incontinence and a desire to impart as much information as he can. It comes at me in a lisping, effervescent rush: "I cannot say how happy I am, I cannot say", "the proud history of Bangladesh Islam", "you must promise me that you feel a love for me as a brother, as a brother, not as a friend", "I only follow our Arabic traditions of hospitality", "I tell you now, Andrew, I tell you now of Kushtia's very own Sufi saint". It seems appropriate to the logic of Bangladesh that Subroto, the first person to speak to me of these things, should himself be Hindu.

The worst aspect of my journey to meet him was knowing that I must eventually return to Dhaka. The city's western bus station, when I finally made it through the political demonstrations which plague the city, was a swamp of mud and confusion. A place of miniature people and huge discomfort, packed with buses of tattered, rotting seats, seven across a row. The scale of humanity here renders me a giant.

The wrestle for seats on the bus – several buses, in fact, a result of being unable to get any to start – came as no surprise. Travel in the developing world knows no other way. What stays in my mind, however, is the image of an old man arguing vehemently with a young girl for the seat in front of me, spite and contempt tattooed into the expressions of both. It was an attitude I could see in everyone around me, one which seems to pervade everything in Bangladesh. Everything is a fight, everything a conflict. The crowd struggled with both each other and the conductor to remain on board, a scene no different from countless others experienced in other countries, other times. Unlike elsewhere, however, there are no smiles behind the grimaces here, no laughter at life's predicaments. I search for a shrug of shoulders, a wry smile of resignation: I can find none. Beneath the anger there is only resentment, not a laughing acceptance that all the strain is part of some huge joke. Beneath the struggle there is only despair. Perhaps desperation reaches a stage where humour is no longer possible.

For the first time I saw the limits of Dhaka by land, although we followed such a thin littoral that we might as well have been afloat. Coolies, both men and women, worked in ant-like teams loading rocks onto river boats on either side of our road. Dark bodies glistening, stark images of Bangladesh's abundance of human labour. Coolie – the name derives from the Urdu *kuli*, or slave. When the Raj was laying its railway lines across India, the coolies went on strike against the imposition of the labour-saving device known as the wheelbarrow, as they felt it would reduce the number of jobs available. The attitude clearly lives on; every job is made as labour-intensive as possible, and each head carries a wicker tray laden with rocks. The lines of workers, up and down the river, seem more insect than human.

I was hardly in the mood for absorbing any of the scenery we passed. My bag was on my knees, a woman's elbow in my face, and with every pothole we struck – and we struck many – my head hit the metal roof of the bus. I did, however, try. Our road followed a raised embankment, and the most common sight was of men, neck-deep in water, clearing weeds and soaking harvested jute on either side. Bangladeshis are as amphibian as human beings can get – most of these men seem to spend their entire lives in the water. They wade through borrow pits, dug to provide earth for the embankments, filling with water in the wet season to create a landscape of endless water, flat and still and eerie. At times the chimney of a brick factory would rise from the water some distance from the road: the land here is completely submerged.

Relief from the bus came only when we boarded a ferry to cross the Padma river, the main branch of the Ganges on its tired journey to the sea. The scene, in some senses at least, was captivating: black shapes everywhere on the water; grey-blue sky the colour of a drowned woman's lips; nets raised with bamboo; the slap of paddles against canoes. But the tranquil fishing scenes were shot through with images of decaying machinery and dead industry rotting in the water everywhere, littering the shores. No conquering scenic beauty on this river. I tried to imagine the mouth of the Amazon or of the Congo, to be like this, but I could not. Surely, there, the stench of humanity does not pervade everything in sight.

The journey may have been tiring, but it was no preparation for the rampage Subroto had in store for me this evening. From early evening to midnight – six long hours – we toured the town on his scooter, the dust of the day flapping at our tongues. A school. The telegraph office. The police station. A meeting with Subroto's associates, lawyers all. A technical college, missing all its windows. A visit to the town's mosque, where Subroto introduces me as a man who has visited every Muslim country in the world. A stay with Subroto's best friend, Kabloo, the head of a Muslim family. The law courts, visited in the darkness of a power failure. An odyssey of polite smiles and endless introductions.

Subroto's easy affection for his Muslim friends was refreshing, a welcome change from the hatred between Hindus and Muslims I experienced in India. As I watched him, the centre of all attention, drawing laughter from Kabloo and his daughters with irreverent jokes and lightning-quick conversations, I could only marvel at how *natural* it all was. The diatribes of sectarian hate I endured in Agra, in Varanasi, in Calcutta, suddenly seemed so strange. Subroto's animated mannerisms are thoroughly Indian – a waggle of his head when he is pleased; an outward scooping gesture with his hand to emphasise a point, finishing with his palm outward – but his heart most certainly is not.

Most importantly of all, Subroto has arranged meetings for my day tomorrow, to help me with my research. The list is impressive: religious scholars, heads of political groups, a doctor of divinity from Harvard, journalists, university lecturers. The most significant, however, is with the head of the Lalon Academy, a place devoted to the study and practice of mysticism. Lalon Shah is Kushtia's patron saint, a mystic born here early last century, and a figure exemplifying the syncretistic, mystical tradition of Islam in Bangladesh. Subroto's coup, one of which he is most proud, is that I shall be formally received at the Academy tomorrow evening.

Our final journey is out past the edges of Kushtia, to where Subroto's home village of Gobindapur huddles in the darkness. Occasional flashes of lightning light a purple sky in the distance: in Bangladesh the storms are never far away. It is a dangerous ride, swerving recklessly between the trucks and carts and buses and pedestrians that hide behind curtains of headlights and dust. Bicycle rickshaws meander along the road, their only light a single oil lamp suspended between their wheels just above the ground. The dim glows they cast, swaying gently through the streets, give Kushtia an almost medieval feel.

I am not sure which I value most, Subroto's assistance or his companionship. I do, however, know that the wearying evening has been a small price to pay for the entertainment he provides. As we fly through the night, Subroto's earnest voice lost beneath the sound of the motor and of the air thrashing at my ears, I realise I am beaming for the first time since Calcutta.

Suddenly a field opens up somewhere in the darkness to the left, absorbing all the quiet sounds of night. An empty, airy silence. I can see nothing, but the complete absence of noise conveys an impression of infinite space. Subroto turns to me and tells me his village is there, in the darkness, sleeping. We will visit it tomorrow before our appointment at the Lalon Academy.

"We go back to town now," he says, "to finish the evening. We must find you some food. To get through the night."

"Subroto, I really don't need anything. Usually I sleep right through until morning."

"But it is such a *long* night, a very *long* night. How will you get through such a long night?" Subroto's idea of caring for me, completely well-intentioned, has already tended to be rather stifling. He forces me to buy five bananas and promise to eat them.

A Sweet, Silent Rot

Saturday 7th October
Kushtia

> What makes the Sufi? Purity of heart;
> Not the patched mantle and the lust perverse
> Of those vile earth-bound men who steal his name.
> He in all dregs discerns the essence pure:
> In hardship ease, in tribulation joy.
>
> from *The True Sufi* by Jalal ad-Din Rumi

On one side of the courtyard a few candles flicker beneath a bare cement shelter. We walk slowly from the arched gate along the grass towards it. Two figures emerge from the silent darkness. A few muttered words, like a secret code, and we walk around a darkened shrine to the other side of the courtyard. Into a low building.

A lone red candle lights the room; its gravity has clearly affected those assembled. The room is long and thin; bookshelves on one wall, a narrow table in the centre. Posed against the walls like wax statues, their eyes on Subroto and me, are perhaps thirty people. I am introduced to the most important among them: Rezaul Hoque, advocate and Academy secretary; Assistant District Commissioner Sattar, administrative head of the district; Magistrate Goton, a former student of Lalon; eager young students and strange old men.

We sit. Dozens of flying ants are in the process of immolating themselves on the candle before me, and I find it difficult to concentrate. The secretary leans close across the table. His voice is low and slow, breathed with a sense of reverence, of some awesome secret about to be revealed. "Nobody knows the exact date of Lalon's birth. It was around two hundred years ago. He was born into an ordinary Muslim family in the village of Horispur in the Jessore district. His father and mother died when he was very young. His guardian and guiding influence became Shira Shah, a *faqir*. When Lalon was twelve, he became a *faqir* also." I take notes of all I am told; I feel it is what is expected of me. "He had many disciples – Moni Rudinshah, Banju Shah, Malon Shah – who are buried with Lalon here at the academy." The secretary points outside, to the painted shrine in the centre of the courtyard, its entrance guarded by several bare tombs.

"None of his songs or speeches were recorded at the time," he continues, "but Lalon Shah had a great spiritual power. His disciples recorded two thousand songs at a later time."

"Are these translated into English? Can I see any?"

"The translations into English are not nice. They are not popular."

"But they are popular in Bangla."

The whole gathering shifts and smiles and nods. "Oh yes. I would say... I would say that if someone owned five cassettes, then one would be Lalon."

"Even young people?"

"Especially young people. You listen, you will see. Always on radio and television. Very popular indeed." I am impressed. Few Christian hymns written two hundred years ago retain their popular appeal with Western youth today.

The secretary continues, leaning closer. Something in his look reminds me of a Van Gogh self-portrait: intense, perhaps even obsessed. And slightly deranged. His voice is now as low as a whisper, one I must strain to catch, yet I find its smooth cadence and rhythm mesmerising.

"Lalon has not been so popular in the past, not popular with some people of Islam. But we are trying to change this. We have now a school here to study the teachings of Lalon. In two weeks we will have the urs celebration, and over one thousand followers and *faqirs* will come from all over the country, on pilgrimage. You can see some of the *faqirs* are already arrived."

He gestures outside again, this time to the other side of the courtyard, to the cement shelter. The darkness is thick, but shadowy shapes twist through it, silhouettes outlined in candlelight. I look around the room. All faces gathered around the table are centred either on me or upon the secretary, frozen by the spell of his soft, secretive voice, the candle. Red light flickers upwards on our necks, lining the bones of our faces. A magic spell has been cast here, surely. I look back to the candle, the centre of our universe, and concentrate on the darkness pressing at it from everywhere.

"You know Rabindranath Tagore, the Bengali poet?" the secretary asks.

How could I not? Tagore is Bangladesh's favourite son. Awarded the Nobel Prize for literature in 1913 for his poetry, songs, stories and philosophies, his name is virtually inescapable. His house lies on the edge of Kushtia, and Subroto delighted in showing me his furniture earlier this afternoon. I nod my assent.

The secretary is clearly pleased. "Good. Then you should know that Tagore was a student of Lalon." His voice, the mesmerising liquid noise, becomes softer still, sucking us towards it. I can feel everyone at the table hunched forward. "You want to know about Lalon and Islam. Lalon was a Muslim, but he went beyond Islam. His followers follow something much larger and more spiritual than Islam. These people," – I am not precisely sure who he means – "mix Islam and Lalon together. His followers think of themselves as Muslims, but they know Lalon is separate. Lalon is special. Even Christian and Hindus follow Lalon. Lalon's God has love for everyone. We must follow the path to God, to love, not keep ourselves apart in different sects. Lalon is above religion.

"Of course, the Imams do not approve of Lalon. They do not accept Lalon as part of Islam. In the past, they have tried to *eject* him." Again, I am unsure what this means, but it is impossible to break the spell. "Now, they don't reject him so severely. They know that his songs are part of Bangladesh."

In Bangladesh, a country fired by its quest for identity, anything which differentiates it from the rest of the world, any fragment of cultural heritage like Lalon, has become sacrosanct. The aftermath of the War of Independence witnessed a backlash against the fundamentalists, who had supported Pakistan in the conflict as the true home of Indian Islam. Now it is virtually impossible for them to attack anything seen as synonymous with Bangladesh's own culture, no matter how unacceptable in the eyes of Islam. Lalon is protected, ironically, by his divergence from orthodox Islam.

The lights snap on. Emerging bleary-eyed as if from a dream or an anaesthetic, the group stirs, confused. Kushtia's idiosyncratic power supply has broken the spell, saved us from complete paralysis. The Academy's single globe lights only this room, suddenly revealed as a place of peeling paint and broken shelves, but within its reach we are protected from the world of sorcery and darkness and the dead. Our salvation, however, is short. The secretary coughs, discusses with the other dignitaries. We must go outside, he says, into the candlelit darkness for a tour of the Academy.

Across the courtyard to those flickering candles, an underworld of strangeness. The beings who wait on the bare cement floor could only exist in darkness, I am sure; with the day they will be gone. These are the *faqirs* of whom the secretary speaks, the men and women who have journeyed here for Lalon's *urs*, his death remembrance. Most wear long white robes, a fashion I have seen nowhere else in Bangladesh. Large wooden beads hang around their necks, and at first glance they seem to have far more in common with India's crazy-eyed sadhus than anything related to Islam. The first man, unwashed in weeks, has long dreadlocks and vacant eyes. His female companion is the same, her mud-coloured eyes flickering with little else than the light of the candles around her. Her frizzy hair is gathered into three huge silly lobes, two of them hanging in masses to the side and one mad cone extending vertically out of the top of her head. All the *faqirs* greet me with a small bow, their palms pressed together as they speak to me with the quiet breath of devoured phantoms, mumbling a single word – "guru" – before resuming their cross-legged meditation.

As we stroll through their midst, the seductive voice of the secretary begins. "Lalon followers do not *salaam*. He wanted a universal greeting, one not attached to any religion. *Salaam* is fine to say, but it is better to pray for love than peace. Peace comes from love."

We come to a woman, breathtakingly old, shrivelled almost to nothing. She grips my hands and smiles a smile without teeth. The candle glow lights the roof of her mouth. A skull yawning up at me, a mummified head – my sense of the underworld is stronger than ever.

We return to the courtyard, where a ring of chairs has been placed around a large white cloth. We sit, while a band appears from various parts of the darkness, their slow movements even more full of lassitude than the normal Bangladesh drift. They settle on the sheet. Each man bears an instrument: a single-stringed lute, several drums, an harmonium, a flute, finger cymbals. Apart from one or two exceptions, all embody those who have renounced the world. All have long, lank and greasy hair. Most are robed in white like the *faqirs*, adorned with heavy wooden beads, though one man is draped in coloured cloth, his body wrapped in heavy steel chains. A symbol of the way his soul is chained to his body, I am later told. The milky gaze of each wanders to me, over me, past me. Heedless. I may have found what I have been looking for. A place of *faqirs*, a place of Sufis, a place of mysticism.

The music begins. The band members, judging by their dreamy, mellow expressions, are all stoned. Drugs are not frowned upon by many Sufis. To them, anything is acceptable if it brings the believer closer to a state of ecstasy, whereby he or she may reach God. The chained one clashes a pair of tiny finger cymbals, his wrists and arms twisting absently as he closes his eyes, loses himself in the music.

The vocalist is a large man, with a thick greying beard and black hair greased back behind his head. He plucks at a guitar with a single string a few times, then launches himself into his performance. He beats his chest, he closes his eyes, he wails. His eyes fling open, fixing me with a punishing stare: it is clear he sings to me. They close again. The song builds, the music gets louder. All participants are clearly losing themselves in their song to God – their eyes half-lidded, their bodies swaying – but none more so than the singer. His arms fling wide, he poses, he dances on the spot, he whirls. The notion that this is a mere performance is misguided – his whole being is in the song. It deals with the demon of the body, how its needs weaken the soul, and it has both participants and crowd in a near trance. I am bewitched.

The music stirs the *faqirs* from their resting place, slack-limbed and slack-jawed. There are far more than I realised, and their variety is astounding. One man, naked apart from a grimy orange loincloth, is covered in ash like the holy men of India. Orthodox religion encourages respectability in its men of faith, but such a thing is impossible for a religion centred around renunciation of the world. Holy men in India, and clearly here also, look more insane than respectable. This man has shoulder-length dreadlocks as long at the front as the back, completely obscuring his face. The glow of a cigarette traces the movements of his hand as he twists and turns in the darkness. His movements are slow, retarded: he is as stoned as anyone I have ever seen. One arm writhes in the air up to a wrist that flips back and forth. He seems completely demented, and lost in joy as the music brings him closer to his God. Other faqirs dance, turning, together, but most simply stop and stare, open-mouthed, expressionless. A constant murmuring chant had flowed from them earlier; even this now stops as they immerse themselves in the music.

Eventually the singer lapses into silence; soon afterwards the music peters out. In devotional dances Sufis believe that once a dancer has started dancing the singers must not stop until the dancing does, "lest the sudden breaking of the dancer's trance may kill him." The band's attitude to their singer may well be the same.

The gaunt man in chains sings the second song, his eyes half closed. Subroto translates the words under his breath – "...what an unknown bird is kept in my body... the cage of my body... yet that bird is not mine..."

For the next hour the music continues, while the scene is brushed gradually with silver as the moon rises above the trees. Fireflies surge into brief luminescent glory in their branches. I am caught completely by what I am witnessing, by the ethereal world of these drifting mystics.

It is not difficult to see why an Arab might see Bengali Sufism as intolerably Hinduised. These *faqirs* look more like Hindu mendicants than pious Muslims, the ceremony more Indian than Arabic. When we return to the Academy building, to the reality of the light globe, the velvet voice explains.

"Oh yes. The Hindu *yogi* and Muslim *faqirs* were always very similar in Bengal. If a saint was very famous, it did not matter what religion he was. Followers of both religions would go to him and ask for miracles."

"Could Lalon perform miracles? Did he have the power of magic?"

"Of course. Lalon was a very holy man. He could cure sickness. He could make an empty woman have child."

Magic of this kind was one of the reasons Sufism was so popular in India. Capitalising on the blind belief in the miraculous that permeated Indian society, Sufi masters began, at least in the public consciousness, to use magic to combat the forces of evil. Not only the poor and dispossessed came to believe in their powers: the powerful in society often consulted Sufi masters to beseech favours, which extended from the supply of magical, holy amulets to the ability to influence major political events. Sufis in India had no problem reconciling these supernatural powers with Islam. Ali Hujwiri, the most revered saint in Pakistan, the Data Ganj whose shrine we visited in Lahore, explained the reasoning thus:

> God has saints whom he has especially distinguished by His friendship and whom He has chosen to be the governors of His kingdom... He has made the saints the governors of the universe... Through the blessing of their advent the rains fall from heaven, through the purity of their lives the plants spring up from the earth, and through their spiritual influence Muslims gain victories over unbelievers.

The Sufi did not possess powers of his own; rather, due to his particularly devout and holy nature, and his close connection with God, he was able to use the powers of God on earth. Magic was transformed from an individual power into an act of God.

Many *faqirs* were little more than travelling charlatans, claiming magical powers in order to make a living, but this was not always the case. Many were men of real faith, and the search for God was the most important thing in the life of a true Sufi master.

The other characteristic of Indian Sufism was its devotion to poetry and singing. Despite the deprecations of the orthodox, it was probably this tradition – originally derived from Persia – and the superstitious need to believe in magic that most helped Islam grow. Sufis bequeathed tomes of poetry and singing, and Sufi gatherings, *sana*, often focused on music as the primary means of connection with God. Apocryphal or not, some *sana* are famous for having emotions so charged, religious ecstasy so intense, that death has occurred.

Under the single bulb, the committee shifts. They wait for something important. Polite and weightless smiles until the secretary, uncertain for the first time, seems to decide the time is right. Awkward and fumbling, he pulls three cellophane-wrapped bunches of yellow flowers from a chair.

Earlier dignity suddenly vanished, he hands them quickly to me, to Magistrate Goton, and to the Assistant District Commissioner. "We are so very honoured to have you... attend our Academy. All of you. We are honoured..." He trails off.

Goton, who was once chairman of the Academy, takes up the thread. As a guest himself it seems odd for him to be the one to welcome me, but I cannot claim to understand the intricacies of Bangladeshi protocol. "We would also like to present you with this plaque," he says. He hands me a wooden carved relief picture of Lalon, set on black fabric. His body is twisted, contorted, his head thrust backwards; in his hand is a guitar with a single string. "We would also request that you take the message of Lalon to Australia. You must tell people about our school. We would very much like to have followers of Lalon in Australia. You must spread the message." Just how I am going to spread this message with little more than a carved picture and a memory of ecstatic singing is not clear, but I promise to do my best.

I look to Subroto, whose ecstasy seems more total than anything religious. His beam is impossible to suppress, and once the presentation is over, a gush of something – a mix of excitement, gratitude and servility – rushes from his throat. He astonishes me as we leave by attempting to brush the dust from the feet of the District Commissioner.

We walk down the darkened path. I am startled and honoured by the whole experience, and I feel dazed. Subroto, for his part, is lost in a kind of bliss. A soft rush of words comes from him as we walk. "The ADC was *early*, early! A huge gesture, you might not understand, amazing, the ADC never arrives early. Normally he doesn't arrive until very late, so everyone is talking, saying things like 'why are they not here', 'when will they arrive' et cetera, et cetera, so when he arrives he is the centre of attention, it always happens. So to come early..." He sighs dreamily.

It is now extremely late, and after a long and emotionally draining day I yearn for bed. Subroto, however, has one last surprise in store. We motor to a tiny corrugated shack in the centre of town. Its low roof is hung with cobwebs and lanky spiders, which brush my hair even as I stoop. This is the office of one of the local newspapers and after the requisite introductions, Subroto reveals that an article about me graced the front page today. I am astonished. I only arrived yesterday evening. The article recounts how a "famous" writer from Australia is in Kushtia to learn about Islam. The feeling is eerie. A whole community could be aware of me without my ever knowing. I cannot even make out my name in the Sanskrit-like Bangla script, which means this sort of thing might be happening all the time without me discovering it. Subroto certainly did not plan to reveal it; we are here instead so he can excitedly recount the night's events for tomorrow's edition. He babbles about the Academy, about the attendance of the ADC, about the presentation of the gifts I still carry, about my promises to spread the message of Lalon in Australia.

Finally, release. Subroto has installed me in the clean and spacious

"Government of Kushtia" guest house, an institution reserved for visiting dignitaries. I am only gradually beginning to realise that this is what I have become.

Indefinite Late

Tuesday 10th October
to Dhaka

Four days in Kushtia, each one crowded and unique. A second visit to the Academy, an interview with the chancellor of the region's Islamic University, love songs from a pair of Bangladeshi nymphs. Numerous newspaper appearances, despite my reluctance, with my views on religious interference in politics during the final interview being used by the ruling party to denounce its Islamic fundamentalist opposition. And yesterday afternoon, a procession of people I did not know arriving to have their photograph taken beside me in Kushtia's sole photographic studio.

Today, however, the adventure has come to an end. We stand on the platform of Kushtia's railway station, waiting for the train that will take me most of the way back to Dhaka. It is a stark place, as lost to decay as the rest of the country. Jungle lichens speckle the stone and cement; all metal is the colour of rust.

Subroto, melancholic about my departure all morning, is leafing through the notebooks I have given him; he claims he wants to keep them to "cherish" my handwriting. He has gathered a small crowd of friends to bid me farewell – Kabloo and his nephew, a pair of university lecturers, some business associates – but the number of faces crowded around me is far greater than this. They shuffle in close from everywhere, pressing, gaping, dull, their sluggish movements the signature of Bangladesh. Mouths hanging open and silent, bodies blocking my path. The wide eyes and gaping jaws, the expressions of astonishment, make them seem unnecessarily stupid. Most are poor, though several well-dressed gentlemen in trousers and Western shirts stand inches from me, mouths agape.

I smile heartily at the faces I meet, trying to elicit even a single smile. I fail. This kind of thing has been haunting me ever since I entered Bangladesh. It cannot be called animosity, yet there remains something impenetrable about it all, something wearying and discomforting. I am judged worthy of intense curiosity, but nothing more, nothing welcoming. The experience here is so different from Iran, where a smile could be the key to almost any face. Even the hard-edged men of Pakistan would return toothy grins when I smiled. In Bangladesh the stares remain brazen and blank.

It is intriguing how desire and experience can change. I remember reading of such scenes before first travelling to Africa, and the spell they cast over my imagination. Then, the thought of a white face generating such interest seemed more like fiction than reality, something that would have vanished generations ago, and I longed to experience it for myself. Surrounded by these faces now, I reflect that an earlier me would have marvelled at this scene, high on the rare thrill of a dream fulfilled. Instead I find it little more than a minor irritation, insignificant and common. Try as I might, I can no longer summon into my heart the joy I would have once felt. This disturbs me for it reminds me that, in some ways, the more one experiences the more one's capability for joy is diminished. It is dangerously easy to concentrate only on what one gains through experience, forgetting to mourn for what one loses.

Subroto looks up at the shriek of the train, arriving beneath brown-grey clouds that look like the underbelly of a wet sheep. He attempts a brief, if melodramatic, speech about the tragedy of my departure before rushing me on board, leaning in the window to harangue the other passengers into making room for me on their hard wooden seats. The carriage is as cramped as one would expect of the most crowded country in the world. My final goodbye to Subroto and his friends is as inadequate as all railway goodbyes, coming in a rush as the train begins to move away. I lean over thin brown bodies to shake Subroto's hand; he runs with the train while the platform slips past behind him. Then he too slips away, falling behind like the rest of Kushtia. The long hot journey to Dhaka has begun.

Wednesday 11th October
Dhaka

Dhaka, as noisy and polluted and unlikeable as last time, is a city of unrest. Demonstrations block the streets as the opposition parties attempt to bring down the government; the newspapers report pitched battles between supporters of the various political groups each evening. A killing in one district, a fire in another.

This afternoon I learn that the opposition has called a nation-wide strike known as a *hartal* in protest against the government. It is to be four days long, the longest one in Bangladesh's history. The *hartal* has been a tradition on the subcontinent ever since Gandhi instigated them as a peaceful, non-violent form of protest against the British. In today's Bangladesh, however, Gandhi's principle of non-violence seems long forgotten. The last *hartal*, two weeks ago, left over a dozen people dead. Now, with tensions rising even higher, preparing for a strike twice as long as ever before, nobody knows what to expect.

My plan is to journey to Sylhet, a town in the north of the country, to visit my final Sufi shrine before preparing to leave Bangladesh. I will fly to Bangkok from the south-eastern town of Chittagong in eight days' time. The *hartal*, however, has set time at a premium. I have only four days before it begins. I have to travel from one end of the country to the other to learn what I can of Sylhet's Shah Jalal, before I must be in Chittagong. I hope I have time enough.

Thursday 12th October
to Sylhet

> Sylhet thus became a district of saints, shrines and daring but virile people.

Bangladesh tourist brochure

I arrive at Dhaka's Kamalpur railway station early in the morning, only to be told that the train to Sylhet is "indefinite late". I must wait, they tell me – perhaps the three o'clock train will be running. I have little other choice. I have already been defeated by the hike from my hotel, and have no desire to see any more of Dhaka, so I decide to wait out my sentence at the station.

As I search the terminal for somewhere to sit, I am hounded by a constant chorus of "Bundhu, baksheesh?", by hands tugging at my body and bags, by the remorseless eyes of the city's beggar children. And not just children: deformed men, blind cripples, and desperate women all add to the crowd. They may be no poorer than those of India, but they are far more numerous, and as the only foreigner in the entire railway station I draw them like moths to a lamp. Hands gesturing to their mouths and stomachs, imploring gazes – two dozen tragic faces follow me wherever I walk. I adopt the look of indifference to human suffering I perfected in India, though it does me little good. I know it would be impossible to give anything meaningful to such a large crowd, but feelings of guilt cannot be ruled by logic. I think back to the railway platform at Lucknow, waiting for the train to Varanasi. I had been there for hours and had stopped seeing such people, so the black pain in my arm came as a complete surprise. I turned to see a legless woman burning a cigarette into my elbow. Hers was a lumpy, ugly, crazed head, and in her eyes was all the malice of existence. Her eyes remained with me long after she had gone, long enough to make me uneasy around these beggars even now. And on the stark floor of the terminal, I have no escape from their appeals.

The hours pass.

It is a relief when the time comes to find my train. I walk out to where the open concrete platforms lie in a row, towards the only train left at the station. Rats on the tracks and the smell of human shit, a vision of travel on the subcontinent. The arms writhing out the windows of the third class carriages, the bodies climbing up wire grills to claim some breathing space for themselves, all look like images of the Holocaust. I march past, briefly thankful for the hard wooden bench that will be my seat for the next eight hours.

We travel quickly out through flooded lands, the water around us a colour like the backing of mirrors. Strange arched bamboo constructions rise out of the water in places, men hauling up large nets that seem forever empty. A white mosque with faded peeling paint and grey jungle mould sits alone on a patch of land. It is surrounded on all sides by water, touched golden in the dying sunlight. Mice run at my feet, trying to nibble the rubber of my thongs.

The train stops amidst an eggshell evening for the Maghrib prayer. All afternoon I have formed a kind of focus for the train's beggars, so the added assault of those who have waited at this nameless junction is most unwelcome. A crowd gathers at the window, beseeching; the smaller children rush on board. One boy makes an incredible noise – like the loud cracking of billiard balls together – by waving his arms about to dislocate his shoulders again and again. And it gets worse. I can cope with women with hair lips, blind children and legless men, but the completely naked children with huge bulges of deformed flesh protruding from odd parts of their bodies, who clasp their genitals and oddities to my legs and refuse to let go – these challenge my fortitude. Emotional extortion.

I am forced to endure an hour of this before we move off into the unbounded night.

It is past midnight when we finally arrive in Sylhet. The air is heavy with dust, stirred by the crowds of rickshaw-wallahs and goods trucks waiting for our arrival. On now: push through: find a hotel. It all comes to me through a doughy veil of tiredness.

I am here to visit the shrine of Shah Jalal, another Sufi saint, one closer to the heart of Islam than Lalon Shah. To the people of Kushtia Lalon Shah is a major saint and fully represents many of the spiritual aspects of Sufism. But he also remains on the periphery of Islam, ostracised by the orthodoxy, seen as a dangerous heretic. Shah Jalal of Sylhet, on the other hand, is a Sufi accepted by the *ulema*, revered as a kind of warrior saint, and has long been part of the Islamic mainstream. In the Fourteenth century his fame was such that he even received pilgrims from as far as Morocco. He was known to live in a cave, to fast for ten days and drink cow's milk on the eleventh, to remain standing all night in prayer. He would say his prayers each morning in Mecca, although he remained in his cave for the rest of the day. It would seem he is cloaked in legend and superstition just as completely as Lalon, which leaves me with no explanation for their differing status within the world of Islam. I have two days to find out.

Saturday 14th October
Sylhet

> The unnumbered lives of the city,
> stunted and solid and brutal.
> Shining with sweat they crowd the bridge, with stares
> dark
> of labourers and the poor, the eyes of Bangladesh.
> *The blue fuse burns deadly between hands and burns clear.*
> Half a *taka*, a moistened coin, buys a push up the crowded slope,
> labour for the tangle of rickshaws jammed solid. A mess

blue
of canopies, and my tattered toy amongst black umbrellas;
the strangled heat comes.
A cloud began to cover the sun wholly slowly wholly. Grey. Far.
An air of 'British Raj flotsam' the guidebook would say,
a 'distinctly British feel' – no, Sylhet is pure
unadulterated
urban chaos and decay.
Tired rectilinear buildings have a taste of their own
that of the rotting Bangladeshi version of modern,
of the saffron rumblings of poverty.
A warm human plumpness settled down on his brain.
Sick I am of the smell of my sweat, not the smell
pink
of physical exertion; rather, the stale and swampy odour
of sweat produced all day every day
A grey smell
of stagnant water that cannot evaporate
in this wet, maddening air.

I set off towards the shrine of Shah Jalal quite early in the morning, past
buildings splashed with graffiti: CUST YOUR VOUT FOR TARU. The streets
are jammed with people, and the press of their bodies becomes thicker
the closer I get to my destination. At the end of Sylhet's main street, a
small boy directs me down a crowded alley, and it is immediately obvious
that Shah Jalal wields far more influence than Lalon could ever hope for.
The street is lined with stores selling flowers, incense, religious trinkets
and sweets, all intended as offerings to the saint. It was offerings such as
these, made to 'lesser Gods' in the pre-Islamic age of ignorance, that the
Qur'an condemned; the irony is not lost on me. Beyond the stalls at the
end of the street, lies a large white stone archway, while beyond this is the
dome of the shrine itself, tainted grey by the Bangladesh jungle damp.
As I walk the street towards the shrine, it begins to seem as though I have
stumbled on a Bangladesh beggars convention. Crowds of them line the
gutters on both sides of the street. Legless men lie face-down, cheeks
pressed hard into the dust as they cry "al-Lah, al-Lah," again and again.
Two white cows gaze on with the kind of impassivity that only bovines
can muster, while yards away a shrieking youth gives a very convincing
portrayal of utter insanity. Children small and bony and naked rub their
stomachs and pluck at my clothes. Blind old men, crippled women: I am
assaulted, and the sight of all these infirmities clouds my perspective,
scrambles my thoughts. I push through as quickly as I can, into the shrine
complex.
The scene which confronts me is a vision of pure chaos. Thousands of the
faithful fill a large stone courtyard, pushing against each other, drifting
across my sight, climbing the steps to the shrine to pray. In one corner of

the courtyard is a large square pond filled with stagnant water. It is an unhealthy green, the colour of paint, yet men and women crowd its edge to bathe in the holy water. Legend has it that Shah Jalal turned his enemies into catfish, who still swim in the depths of the pond. Birds the colour of sulphur flash in the trees above. Rag-robed mendicants plant their hands on my chest, shake my hand, or ask for alms. One small, Western-garbed man with green phlegm lodged in both corners of his mouth questions whether I believe in God. For convenience I assent and he grasps my hands, closes his eyes and meditates. A strange silence, a crowd pressed around me in awe.

I decide to inspect Shah Jalal's tomb before I begin the unlikely task of searching for information. An array of perhaps forty stone steps leads up to the entrance to the tomb. I leave my shoes at the bottom with dozens of others, and begin the climb up. At the top is an arched passage, an engraved black tablet, the entrance to the tomb. I cross to it, inhaling the cold smell of sacred stone: appealing: lost. I enter.

Inside is purple and grey, dim beneath the small fragment of ceiling open to the monsoon sky. Tumbled books crowd the walls, blue and mournful in the dead light, piled randomly with scrolls and ribbon, stones and tablets. Strips of coloured cloth reach down from the ceiling, swinging silently in the breeze. And amidst it all, in the centre of the room, is the tomb.

It lies in a recessed pit around which the faithful stand, draped in coloured cloth and scattered with frangipani petals. Several Muslims stand there now, gazing at it, mumbling prayers. I remain near the entrance, watching them. They are subdued, controlled, with none of the religious mystical passion of the Sufis at the Lalon Academy, none of the mourning torment of the Shi'a in Iran. The scene is evocative, but I remain disappointed. I had expected something more dramatic from the most popular Sufi saint in Bangladesh – something ecstatic, something close to the Sufi mystical ideal. More mad *faqirs*, perhaps. I follow the example of the Muslims around me and walk backwards out the arched doorway, bowing to the shrine as I do. Beside me is a huge black stone tablet, engraved with the names of Allah and Muhammad in Kufic script; a man caresses it gently and then rubs his hands over his face, massaging the scent of God into his soul.

Back in the courtyard I meet with success. I am ushered into one of the complex's inner sanctums, a cool place with walls of thick stone, where I am introduced to Muhammad Piara, one of the Imams of the shrine. He is clad in flowing longhi and a white kameez, and has – I hope I am forgiven for such a lame description, but it is true – soft, kind eyes. There is a kind of greyness about his face. His tangled beard is worn in a style common to devout Bangladeshis, with his cheeks and upper lip shaved smooth, leaving the hair to grow untamed from his neck and chin. It makes him look decidedly odd.

Muhammad speaks exceptional English, the best I have encountered since

Calcutta. He explains that before becoming a holy man he was an academic, a professor in the science faculty of the Dhaka Institute for Postgraduate Studies, and spent several years teaching at Britain's Reading University. With such formidable education and prolonged exposure to the West, what he has to tell me is surprising.

The first part of our conversation is straightforward enough. Muhammad warmly grasps my hands in his, offers me a seat, and tells me a little of Shah Jalal's history. He describes him as a peace-loving saint, a 'true Muslim', and tells me of Shah Jalal's journey to Bangladesh from Delhi, where he gathered converts along the way. My real interest only begins when he starts to describe the saint's arrival in Sylhet, and his 'holy war' against Gaur Govinda, the local Hindu ruler.

"His army was much, much smaller than his enemy," says Muhammad. "But this did not matter, because Shah Jalal had the power of Islam on his side, the power of God." I have heard this kind of thing many times before; Muslim victories on the battlefield have throughout history been attributed to the greatness of God. This is not, however, quite what Muhammad means. He continues, his voice steady and serious, his eyes afire with belief. "Shah Jalal has the power of magic, granted to him by al-Lah. The arrows of his enemies were turned back towards them, killing Gaur Govinda's archers. When Shah Jalal needed to cross the river – there was no bridge in those days, you understand – he laid down his carpet, and took three hundred and sixty disciples across the river to fight."

Muhammad fixes me with his grey gaze. He fits his role well, this bearded Muslim in flowing robes, speaking with passion about the mythology of Shah Jalal, but I keep trying to imagine him in England, teaching physics to the youth of the West.

"Shah Jalal," he continues, "could show us how to use the *eman*, the spiritual strength that comes with Islam. You can only truly understand what this means if you convert to Islam, but perhaps I can give you an example. One day Shah Jalal just tells one of his followers to say a single word. Not loud, not shouting, just a single, soft word. His follower says the word, and Gaur Govinda's palace falls down. Without Islam we can achieve nothing, no matter how loud we shout, but with *eman* you or I could have all the power in the world."

He lets me ponder this for a moment. I find it difficult to reconcile his smooth, well-educated manner with his belief in these stories; normally educated Muslims are far less likely to interpret mythology as literal truth. Even the holy men I have met on this journey normally reserve such things for the time of the Prophet, not for events only a few centuries old. I know only that I am confused. Holy men in Australia wouldn't speak the same way of such fables. Or would they? I am not sure if I know any more. How much of Christian gospel appears as superstition to outsiders?

Muhammad barks an order, and a young boy appears from the moist shadows at the back of the room. He is planed, angular, with the eyes of a bird; until now I had not even been aware of his presence. Muhammad sends him for tea, apologising to me for being so uncivilised to have not done so in the first place.

I glance around the room while we wait. It is spartan, bare, suited perfectly to the life of an ascetic, yet its brooding stone walls and dark shadows give it a strange sense of timeless faith. I feel transported to another age, hidden in the cold bosom not only of the building but of Islamic history itself, far away from the world outside, far away from anywhere I have ever been. The feeling is not entirely unpleasant.

The tea arrives, a sign that the conversation may resume. The boy remains by Muhammad's chair to listen, though his face is knocked so clean of interest I am convinced he cannot understand a word of English. I begin by asking Muhammad about Shah Jalal's role in Islam.

"Ah," he replies, "he was a great Sufi, a saint. So people come here to get solutions from God."

"Isn't that a little like the idol-worship that the Prophet condemned?"

"No, not at all. Shah Jalal is a great man in the eyes of al-Lah. He can get God to do much for you. If you have no son but come to pray to Shah Jalal, then al-Lah will give you a son. *Al-Lah*, not Shah Jalal. This does not mean that these people follow Shah Jalal. It is like when I am sick, and I go to a doctor for his help because he is an expert on these things. I am not a follower of the doctor; I just want his help. A saint is just like this: he is an expert for God, and these people come for his help."

"So do the faithful think of themselves as Sufis?" The question is an important one: Sufism can hardly be said to be alive in Sylhet if the only true Sufi in the town lies in the tomb outside.

"No, they are just *common* people, here to get a solution from Allah," Muhammad replies. "They can become Sufis if they want. The only thing that makes a Sufi is that he does not lust after worldly enjoyment. But in general most of the people are here only for Shah Jalal, to visit a great saint."

In this answer is the real key to Sufism in Bangladesh, and probably also to the Sufi shrines in Pakistan. These places are the focus of intense devotion, and attract thousands of followers, yet to take this to mean that Sufism is as alive as it once was would be wrong. The legends surrounding Shah Jalal are what makes him attractive, not his teachings, and superstition governs his followers as much as mysticism. To most of the people outside, Shah Jalal is little more than a symbol, one which offers a convenient focus for prayer, and easy access to Allah. I am struck by how far this is from the original spirit of Sufism, yet it seems is he who represents mainstream Islam, the approvable face of Sufism in Bangladesh.

This, of course, is due to his acceptability to the orthodoxy who dismiss true Sufi doctrine – such as that of Lalon, and even Rumi, Muhammad informs me over a second cup of tea – as far from the fundamentals of Islam. This is a common refrain. With the spread of orthodox Islam over the last century, much of the power of Sufism has been lost. Sufi traditions are kept alive, certainly – in the urs remembrance celebrations of major Sufi saints, in the singing and dancing at their shrines – but true Sufism has become difficult to find, the rigours of the mystic kept alive only by the rare few. When I eventually bid Muhammad goodbye, it is this thought I take with me. My feelings are mixed. I am grateful for the insight Shah Jalal has provided, but I am also saddened. I cannot shake the sense that something great has been lost, that it is unlikely ever to be retrieved.

Four Grey Walls and the Stench of Boredom

Monday 16th October
Chittagong

I walk out into near-deserted streets. A taste of threat on the air: the *hartal*.

The alleys around my hotel, so crowded and mad when I arrived yesterday evening, have become empty canyons framed by metal shutters and security grills. A gust of rubbish, a few straggling pedestrians, little else. For the first time I can walk the streets of a Bangladeshi city with ease, untroubled by the crowds, but it brings me no joy – I am far too worried by the lawless feel to it all. I think back to the fear and the anarchy of riots in Nairobi several years ago. Something just as heavy waits over Chittagong today.

Yesterday's newspaper informs me that restaurants are exempted from the strike – as are ambulances, garbage vehicles, medicine shops, newspaper carriers and newsmen – so finding food should not be a problem. What concerns me now is how I am going to occupy my time, and whether the streets are safe enough to walk.

I march off in search of a large hotel, somewhere I can change enough money to last the coming days, somewhere I can find out how, in an environment where rickshaws are banned, I will be able to get to the airport on Thursday. I pass a group of street children attacking a rickshaw which is defying the *hartal* by carrying a woman. Despite their tiny size, there is nothing the rickshaw-wallah can do – he cannot fight them all at once. They beat and kick at him from behind, they tear at the woman, they let down his tyres. They are a horde of ants; they are invincible. The woman walks away in tears.

A kilometre away I find the Hotel Rose, where I change money with the hotel concierge. As he counts out my money I ask him whether the streets will be dangerous during the *hartal*.

He looks at me as though weighing my chances of survival. "You should try not to get caught by these crowds," he says. "Bad people are very many now. Most people are OK, but if you should meet one of these groups..." – he shrugs noncommittally – "well, there are no police to save you. That is why the *hartal* is bad."

"So what do you suggest?"
He thinks for a moment. "I think this is best. If they catch you, you say them you are a reporter. An observer. You say them to leave you alone."
It does not sound promising, but at least it is something. The safety of the streets, however, is only part of my problem. I am just as concerned about how to get to the airport. I ask him whether rickshaws are allowed to run at all.
"Rickshaws? Not rickshaws. Not *auto* rickshaws. Bicycle rickshaws, after three o'clock they run."
"So nothing can take me to the airport on Thursday morning?"
"No."
It is my greatest worry. I long to find someone with access to a car, even though the chances of doing so in Bangladesh are virtually nil. Private transport is not prohibited by the strike, and I harbour the vain hope that if I keep pressing the issue somebody will eventually offer to take me. "Do you have any solution to how I can get there?" I ask.
"No, I have no solution. No, I have no solution. How can I have a solution? It is a *hartal*." From the expression on his face he might as well have added, "you are doomed."
"So what would you do in my position?"
"Maybe you can go to the airport on Wednesday night."
Suddenly it seems there may be hope after all. "Are there hotels near the airport?" I ask.
"No."
"Oh. So could I sleep at the airport itself?"
"No."
Perhaps he is right: perhaps I am doomed. My only hope is that the *hartal* becomes less potent as it wears on.
I return to the sombre streets, the city vacant and ominous. Groups of youths gather on street corners, some menacing, some carefree, part of an atmosphere midway between a holiday and a war. People gather around an entertainer with a cobra; a truck carrying riot police thunders past. Yet there is a dirty, angry feel beneath everything. Children taunt adults, the entertainer looks ready for his audience to turn nasty; at every gathering there are men on the point of blows. I pass one group dragging a struggling fellow down the street. Presumably he is being punished for attempting to work: people's political convictions are beginning to collide with the desperate need of others to make a living. The day is only going to get worse. A permanent nasty feel is sewn into the wind.
The chanting in the distance loudens. A crowd of marchers, supporters of the hartal. From a distance I watch them confront a rickshaw driver, seizing his body and utterly destroying his vehicle. Loudspeakers on every corner blast forth political diatribes, their tones of hatred reminiscent of mosque sermons I heard in Islamabad. A voice can carry so much hate, even when one doesn't understand the words. The longer I am out in the streets the more uncomfortable I feel.

Inside my hotel room, I realise I am going to be seeing a lot of these four walls. I may very well go mad with boredom. It is evening now, the first day of four. My timing is impeccable, arriving just in time for the longest *hartal* ever.

Tuesday 17th October
Chittagong

Two dead and one hundred injured in bomb blasts around the city. The story is the same all over Bangladesh. The violence is building with the political tension, with the stand-off between government and opposition that is killing the country. In one article alone, I count ten reports of bomb blasts. Add to that the stories about arson, gun fights, looting and clashes between rival political groups. Meanwhile, here I sit, with no contact with the outside world, and no idea what might be happening. Just my daily dose of newspaper.

Wednesday 18th October
Chittagong

Today I am accosted in the street by a group of well-dressed youths, probably university students. I am searching for one of the town's Chinese restaurants, sick of my daily staple of rice and stew (in almost a month, Bangladesh has not been able to supply me with a single green vegetable – the vegetables dish I have been living on is coloured green but it really only contains potato, so it is little wonder I haven't been full of spark). The group is eager and arrogant and frightening. They surround me, grab my wallet, laugh and taunt and spit, kick at my legs. They fill me with a dull thudding fury, yet I know there is nothing I can do. Their mood is that of the nation. A place gone mad.
For the rest of the day I write, I read, I dream. I can only vaguely hear the chanting from a demonstration outside, the sounds drifting up to me as diffuse and ephemeral as rain. At least here I feel safe, if excruciatingly bored. Devoured by the thick air. I sit. I wait.
Outside, a rat scrambles through the gutters in broad daylight, made desperate by the sudden lack of food.

Thursday 19th October
Chittagong...

I wake early in the hope of sneaking silently out of the city, surreptitiously avoiding the clutches of the *hartal*. I must find myself a rickshaw in the deserted streets, and convince its driver to take me all the way to the airport, a destination normally considered too far for a bicycle rickshaw even without the added concern of the *hartal*. The distance is too far for those frail brown calves, the danger too great.

I need not have worried. The owner of my hotel has understood my anxiety of the last few days, and a rickshaw-wallah waits nervously for me in the hotel foyer. This final act of kindness could not have come at a better time.

We move off into silent streets that are dripping dawn from everywhere. I feel like a fugitive. We are assaulted almost immediately by a small boy, trying to alert the few people about to our presence, but there is nobody to hear him. We sail off feeling more conspicuous than ever, the only sound the *fzzz* of our rubber wheels on the wet roadway. The sky has closed completely, sinister and dark, and when a light rain begins to fall I am reminded more than anything of the day I crossed into Bangladesh from India, sitting behind a similar struggling brown frame as the soundless rain came down all around us. The days could be almost identical: the weather, the heavy cloud, the purple light. I am not sure if the omen is good or bad.

The ride to the airport is a long one, through pustulous buildings and waking slums, tainted by a perpetual fear that we will not make it. I do not think much during the journey: as in the last few days I seem trapped in an eddy of thought. I am aware only of the quiet symphony of my own nerves, of the pit of worry in my stomach.

On the edge of town we turn through industrial and shipping districts to follow the river. It is the same grey as the sky, the colour of navy ships. The world is encased in a huge gun-metal barrel of water and sky, grey upon grey. Towering ships lie idle at their docks: Chittagong is the nation's largest port, but for the last four days its docks have been empty. The stillness is complete, save for the occasional jangle of the rickshaw's bell.

When the wide open field of the airport appears I feel something hard inside me shift, and I feel a huge sense of relief. The journey has taken ninety minutes.

Chittagong International Airport is a low, poor place, reminiscent more of a suburban home than of international tourism. Its domestic lounge is a glass-walled room with a bare linoleum floor and a handful of plastic seats, while the international terminal is used so rarely it doesn't even have chairs. But it does give me the most joyous news of the week: my flight will be running, despite the *hartal*. I have nothing to do for five hours apart from sit and wait – precisely the sort of thing that the last four days have made me good at – while dozens of rickshaw drivers press their noses to the window to stare at me.

When I finally cross the tarmac towards my flight, I feel curiously empty. I am dimly aware of a kind of indignation swelling inside me, a feeling of protest I cannot define. It seems such a wrong way to leave the country, such an inconclusive end to the story of Bangladesh. I have found my Sufis, yet it all seems incomplete. Is it because I actually want to leave, that I feel lost without the usual feelings of regret? Or is it because I feel I am sneaking away, like a defeated dog with my tail between my legs? I do not know. I only know that another day in Chittagong would have driven me insane. Inside the plane I find a toilet drowning in shit and urine, its sink blocked with stagnant water and its light broken, with passengers trying to force their way in because the engaged signal does not light. I cannot think of anything more appropriate for Bangladesh's national airline: the entire country is in exactly this state of disrepair. Other tourists are already on board; they are the first I have seen for a month. They have not travelled in Bangladesh – few would be so mad – but are merely transiting through the country from Europe to Thailand. I smile at them all but receive no response. Perhaps something has happened to my smile – perhaps I am, in truth, grimacing. Or maybe, like the people of Bangladesh, like the countless brown faces that have stared unsmiling at me the last few weeks, they know there is nothing worth smiling about.

PART FOUR
EAST

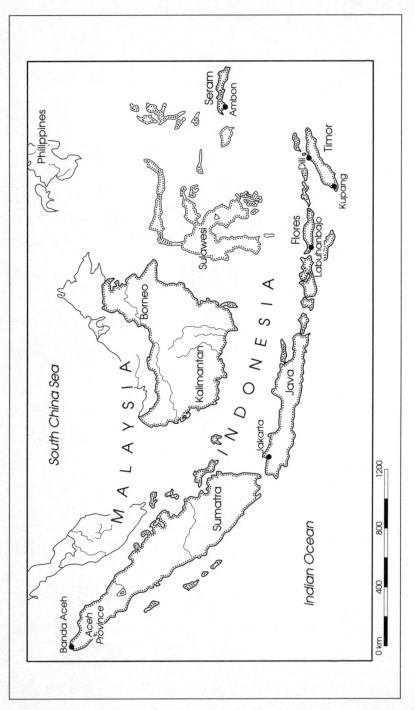

INDONESIA

Two Different Faiths

Tuesday 24th December
Jakarta

Having spent the last thirty-six hours on a bus, upright and denied sleep, life has started to feel a bit blurred at the edges. I now wait, bedraggled and somewhat forlorn, on the floor of Jakarta's international airport for Kirst to arrive. I have five hours ahead of me – her flight is delayed, I am overjoyed to discover – so for the first time in days I have the opportunity to put pen to paper.

This is my last day alone. I suppose it marks the end of a minor chapter in my life. I have only these few hours of solitude left before Kirst arrives, and I imagine I should be spending the time in introspective contemplation, in an appraisal of the last four months spent on my own. I find it difficult, however, when I know that the magnitude of the change will not really dawn on me until after she arrives. I am only aware in an abstract kind of way that my freedom, my complete independence, will vanish; I cannot truly imagine it. This blindness on my part, my inability to see what Kirst's arrival will bring, means I feel unable to fully consider what the last four months have meant to both my journey and myself. I find it much easier to consider instead what I have learnt in my time in Indonesia, ever since crossing the Strait of Malacca from Malaysia three weeks ago.

As the most populous Muslim country in the world, Indonesia cries out for inclusion in any book about Islam. It is a fascinating nation, occupying a unique position midway between a secular state and a religious one. It offers freedom of religion, for example, but only within a circumscribed set of faiths chosen by the government. Its constitution is entirely secular, tied neither to Islam nor any other religion, yet belief in God is one of the foundations of its identity. It has more Muslim inhabitants than Saudi Arabia, Iran, Iraq, Egypt, Syria and Jordan combined, yet millions of orthodox Muslims view the Indonesian version of Islam as corrupted and profane. It is a country of contradiction – complex, distinctive and important.

I have read a lot, therefore, about Indonesian Islam both before I arrived and during the last three weeks. And as a result of both what I have read and what I have experienced, I have come to feel that what distinguishes the Indonesian variety of Islam from what I have found elsewhere is both its variety, and its extreme flexibility. Much of this stems from the history of religion in the region. Islam came primarily to Indonesia as an idea, not a conquering force, brought here by traders instead of armies. As an idea, it was able to mingle with the ideas that existed before it. In many areas it did not replace existing beliefs, but merely transformed them, and in the process became transformed itself. It is estimated that only ten percent of the population adheres to a pure form of Islam, untainted by either Hindu influences, mysticism or animism. In Java, for example, the *Wayang*, or puppet shadow theatre, existed long before the coming of Islam. Its plays were immensely popular, and had been adapted from the Hindu epics of the *Ramayana* and *Mahabharata* which grew out of the island's ancient Hindo-Buddhist traditions. Islam did not extinguish the theatre; instead, new Islamic characters were simply incorporated into its stories. The Prophet's uncle Hamzah was a favourite character for this kind of treatment. And as new characters were introduced, the old ones were updated for the new religion. It is a tradition amongst the Tengger people of east Java to depict the Hindu character Ajisaka, a figure famous for his beauty and wisdom, visiting the Prophet in Mecca to seek spiritual knowledge. Significantly, Ajisaka does not become a Muslim. Instead he impresses Muhammad with his ability to make himself invisible. Muhammad declares: "You will be my equal... when you walk the night, I walk the day." In many other Muslim countries, such a declaration would be heresy.

An even better example of how Islam in Indonesia has been transformed, however, is with the people of the Minangkabau in Western Sumatra, where I have spent the last two weeks. The Minangkabau are Muslims, yet their society is both matriarchal and matrilineal, at odds with most of what one naturally assumes about Islam. All inheritance passes through the female line, and at the head of every household sits a woman.

The Minangkabau are aware that their traditions put them at odds with most of the world of Islam, but they make no apologies for this fact. In 1820, the religious orthodoxy tried to impose the rule of Islam upon the people of the region, but failed. Since then the Minangkabau have defended their rights to retain many of their pre-Islamic traditions, and to follow their own unique systems of inheritance and authority, of which they are fiercely proud.

My time with the Minangkabau was both illuminating and delightful. The locals happily recounted that when the word of the Qur'an conflicted with their traditions, then they would generally follow their traditions. In the words of one local, "Sometimes Islam just doesn't make sense." The Minangkabau were a perfect demonstration of how flexible Indonesian society can be, and even of how adaptable Islam itself can be when required. They were showing how it is possible to take only those aspects of Islam a society needs, that the relentless march of fundamentalist orthodoxy still has a long way to travel, and my experiences with them cheered me enormously.

As fascinating as they were, however, the Minangkabau made me realise that I didn't want to focus on Indonesia's version of Islam as the final chapter in this story. As an archipelago of over thirteen thousand islands, with a greater variety of tribal groups than any political entity in the world, the best I could hope for would be the merest representation of its incredible diversity. But even more importantly, I realise that while Islam may be central to Indonesia, Indonesia is far from central to an understanding of Islam globally. I hope to use these final days to look at the long history of interaction between Islam and Christianity. Kirst and I will be spending most of our time on the predominantly Christian islands of Flores and Timor, which makes Indonesia the perfect place – of all the countries on this journey – to consider this interaction.

I can only guess at what we will find on these islands, tiny areas of Christianity surrounded by a sea of Islam. I will be interested to see if the distrust between the religions is anything like what I encountered in the ultra-orthodox region of Aceh, in Western Sumatra, where Islam is at its uncompromising best, strict and pure. In an interview with the Imam of the region's largest mosque, I was stunned by the vehemence with which Christianity was denounced. *Christianity has three Gods; Islam has one. Al-Lah! Not three false Gods, but one great true God! Jesus may be a prophet of Islam, but Christianity is a bad religion. Christianity is very different from Islam.* After hearing of the closeness between the two religions, even in Arab states like Syria and Jordan, such animosity came as a surprise. I wonder whether it might come from being in a nation where the two religions must live together side by side, very often in quite significant numbers. Aceh's neighbouring province of North Sumatra is predominantly Christian, and contact between different cultures can breed friction just as often as it breeds harmony. Other religions, after all, present the ultimate challenge to any faith, the possibility that truth may not be absolute but relative.

I am going to have to sign off now. The customs-waiting purgatory is over: I can see Kirst's head through a tiny gap in the customs barrier as she waits in line, surrounded by the muttoned faces of her fellow travellers. She can't see me – by the look of the line she won't be through customs for a while yet – and it feels strange writing about her when she is so near. The stain of an emotion I don't recognise has given her the face of a stranger. Here's hoping the readjustment to each other's presence isn't too difficult.

Monday 25th December – Friday 5th January
Through Java to Labuhanbajo, Flores

Days a blur,
mind muffled, activities curtailed:
not Kirst, just the bleary tourism.
Woman.
She marvels at Indonesia with the untouched vision of one fresh to travel,
sees the shanties and slums I ceased seeing long ago.
And laughter once more, her companionship a gift.

Two-day ferry, belly of the boat.
Eastwards ho,

Christianity ahoy,
deliverance at midnight.

(A sudden sense of space, infinite.)

Saturday 6th January
to Ruteng

The night is filled with the immense, pounding fury of a monsoon storm, with the scream of lightning close above. Outside my room I listen to the mad combat of the trees, thrashing like seaweed in heavy surf. A bad night measured by eruptions of thunder.

The rain has lifted by the time we leave in the morning. I look back at the roiling mass of white clouds that have gathered over the dark hills behind the village. They crouch low on everything, and are potent and alive, so different from the monsoon sky of the subcontinent. Here they are heavy, massive, a bright white that is almost dark by virtue of the mass of the cloud alone. A treacherous white. Photographs can never capture the sense of such clouds: they hold far too much light. Indeed, something of their presence is beyond sight. It is left to the remaining senses to absorb them.

Our day today is one of travel, heading inland to Ruteng, and it is only on our bus, red and tight and noisy, that I begin to absorb the fact that we are now surrounded by Christianity. Above the driver is a plate-sized sticker of Jesus in a glittering white robe, his arms raised in supplication beneath the metallic golden orb of his halo. "TUHAN YESUS," reads the caption around its border. Below it is a second sticker, declaring, "FOLLOW ME I HAVE JESUS SAVIOUR OF THE WORLD", while scattered across the dash are brightly-coloured crosses, prayer beads, icons of a Caucasian Mary. I feel a sudden sense of dislocation, a mild kind of cultural panic. Perhaps I have simply become too accustomed to the trappings of Islam, rendering my cultural bearings as much Muslim as Christian. Such stickers strike me as odd in ways that their Muslim equivalents do not. I ceased seeing the Quranic quotations, the holy names in glittering gold, and the tiny replica Qur'ans hanging from dashboards long ago. All such things became part of my environment; it now takes Jesus to catch my attention.

Peering over our journey is one of Indonesia's thousands of volcanoes, this one so completely conical it is almost parody, rising from the landscape the way the pyramids rise over Cairo on the way out to Giza. The land it presides over becomes progressively less like jungle, more Australian, as we push eastwards. I finally begin to feel I am coming home. On the plateau of the island's interior we strike grassy hills for the first time. A strange sight, land that could be devoted exclusively to grazing, when I have become so used to livestock squeezing its existence out between dwellings and crops. The landscape is still wild and overgrown and tropical, but I get a sense here of the land having been used up, lived in, that I didn't find in the rainforests of Sumatra.

We arrive in Ruteng late in the afternoon, high in the crisp mountain air. I am keen to find out what we are going to see of Christianity while we are here.

Sunday 7th January
to Ruteng

> Believers, take neither the Jews nor the Christians for your friends. They are friends with one another. Whoever of you seeks their friendship shall become one of their number. God does not guide the wrongdoers.
>
> *The Qur'an*, 5:51

> Be courteous when you argue with the People of the Book, except with those among them who do evil. Say: 'We believe in that which is revealed to us and which was revealed to you. Our God and your God is one. To Him we surrender ourselves.
>
> *The Qur'an*, 29:46

> As for the unbelievers, their works are like a mirage in a desert... Or like darkness on a bottomless ocean spread with clashing billows and overcast with clouds: darkness upon darkness.
>
> *The Qur'an*, 24:38

The Qur'an varies considerably when it comes to Islam's relationship to Christianity. Many of its revelations depended on Muhammad's relationship with the Christian and Jewish communities of Mecca and Medina at the time he received them, and on the changing fortunes of Islam itself. It was not, however, Muhammad's revelations that would pave the way for the conflict between the two religions in the coming centuries. The collision between Christianity and Islam may have had its foundations in the Qur'an, but the most important and long-lasting divisions between the two religions were shaped by events which happened long after Muhammad's death. To understand those events one must understand Islam's changing perception of Christianity and the West, and the West's perception of Islam, as Islam grew in the early years of Arab expansion.

In terms of speed and permanence, the Arabic Islamic expansion was greater than any other in the history of the world. Hot and malleable from the crucible of Arabia, Islam was forged as much by the process of expansion as by Muhammad's original vision. As it met with success after startling success, Islam became no more the religion of the weak, of the outcasts from Meccan society. It became a faith working the conquering will of God, convinced of its importance in the world, confident and strong. It had only to look to its own ascendancy for evidence that it was, indeed, the one true faith.

With such rapid growth, Islam was bound to collide with a far greater diversity of peoples and religions than it had done in the backwaters of Arabia. In the Byzantine provinces of Egypt and Syria, Islam encountered entire communities of Christians and Jews, not just the minorities it had tolerated in Arabia. But by this stage Islam had moved a long way from Muhammad's inconstant rejection of the "People of the Book". The Umayyad Empire was well and truly in the ascendancy, and the Arabs found themselves living in the midst of an enormous variety of peoples differing in race, language and religion. In an exceedingly short time, the Islamic world had become a cosmopolitan one, striking in its diversity. And just as significant was its tolerance, a tolerance astonishing when compared to Islam's contemporary societies in the medieval Western world. Muslims, confident in their faith, felt no need to impose their religion by force on everyone subject to their rule. They knew that all unbelievers would eventually burn in hell, and that there was no need to anticipate divine judgement in this world. Tolerance became a hallmark of Muslim society.

At this time the Islamic view of Christianity was based purely on religious lines, rather than political or regional ones. To the Muslims, Islam was a religion, a region and a polity, whereas Christianity was simply a minority religion of the Empire. Christianity was not associated automatically with Europe, certainly not in the way the Europeans of the time felt it to be.

The historical literature of the Arabs makes it clear how utterly uninterested they were in the religious and cultural heritage of Europe. It was seen as a dark land of barbarism, a place from which Muslims had nothing to fear and nothing to learn. The Tenth century scholar al-Mas'udi wrote:

> The peoples of the north are those for whom the sun is distant from the Zenith... cold and damp prevail in those regions, and snow and ice follow one another in endless succession. The warm humour is lacking among them; their bodies are large, their natures gross, their manners harsh, their understanding dull and their tongues heavy. Their religious beliefs lack solidity... Those of them who are farthest to the north are the most subject to stupidity, grossness, and brutishness.

And an Eleventh century Qadi from Toledo could only concur:

> Their bellies are big, their colour pale, their hair long and lank. They lack keenness of understanding and clarity of intelligence, and are overcome by ignorance and foolishness, blindness and stupidity.

The Arabs were only interested in regions with something to offer them, be it knowledge or wealth, and Europe could provide neither. To the

Arabs, Europe was not a land of Christianity, but of barbarism.

The attitudes of the Christian West to Islam, however, could not be removed so easily from politics or regionalism. From the Islamic perspective it may have been possible to discuss purely the relationship between the Islamic empire and the Christian religion, but from the western European perspective the conflict was between governments, between empires, between societies, as much as it was between faiths.

The reason for this was that the West was under threat. Quaking before the Muslim juggernaut, it was impossible for it to judge Islam purely on religious terms. Twice, Islam almost conquered Europe, through the Arab invasions of Spain and the Ottoman advances into the Balkan peninsula. Further east, the Tatars would launch a third attempt, when they swept into Europe as far as Poland, conquering Russia and establishing the dominion of the Golden Horde. In the face of such a continued threat, beginning with the first Arab expansion in the Seventh century and only ending fully with the demise of the Ottoman Empire this century, it is little wonder the Christian world saw the relationship differently.

To European Christians fighting for survival, Muhammad could never be viewed in the respectful way the Muslims saw Jesus. Muhammad was nothing but an agent of the devil, an arch-heretic. Dante, in his *Divine Comedy*, constantly cleft Muhammad in two as eternal punishment for the sin of religious schism. Pope Innocent III declared him to be the Anti-Christ. Jaime Bleda, the Royal Chaplain and Father Confessor of Spain, described Muhammad in a work which became a standard history as "the deceiver of the world, false prophet, Satan's messenger." Even language betrays the West's attitude to Islam, and to "Mahomet", its prophet. From Muhammad's name, in the Fourteenth century, sprang both *Mahound* and *maumet*, the first meaning "a monster, a hideous creature, the Devil", while the second, "a contemptible or hateful person; a false God."

It was only after the Reformation in Europe that the West's attitude to Muhammad changed. He became less an agent of the devil than a cunning, self-seeking impostor. His life was dissected in extraordinary detail as European historians searched for anything with which to discredit him. He was denounced frequently as a sensualist, a man with depraved ideas regarding sex and love, a man who took wives as he pleased. Muhammad, to the repressed Europeans, with his teachings that the pleasure of sex was a gift from God, was a shocking figure. It is highly ironic that we should now applaud his more liberal teachings, using them to criticise the sexual repression in Islamic society today. What once offended the West is now considered the norm, and Muhammad's worst qualities a hundred years ago are now often viewed as his best.

Today, while the threat Islam poses the West may be seen as considerable, it remains far less potent than it once was. The West is no longer the conquered but the conqueror. Our distrust of Islam, however, has remained with us; centuries-old attitudes are difficult to erase. Moreover, now it is Islam under threat, and it is not the confident, conquering Islam it once was. Today, many Muslim societies have developed siege mentalities of their own, returning to religion in an assertion of their own divine strength, denouncing the ethical bankruptcy in Western society. Islamic revivalists condemn the moral decay of the West just as the West once denounced the morals of Muhammad.

The intriguing thing about the division between the West and Islam is that it remains, in many ways, a religious one. One might ask how religion could possibly be important when the West, difficult enough to characterise politically, can hardly be viewed as a religious entity. The answer is that the clash between Islam and the West is a clash between two cultures, and for Muslims culture and religion are one. To a Muslim, any cultural conflict is perforce a religious one. The collision between Islam and the West will remain, to many Muslims, religious in nature, a collision between Islam and Christianity.

Flores and Timor provide perfect metaphors for this collision. The two islands must be considered in tandem, however, as they have both responded differently to the Muslim domination they have had to endure. In the case of East Timor the situation is hopelessly politicised, a microcosm of essentially political conflict based on religion. Its history of oppression has been brutal, with the result that the distrust existing between Christian and Muslim groups in the region is almost total. In Flores the interaction is far more peaceful, with hardly any of the inter-religious tension that characterises other areas of the archipelago – not only Timor, but also places such as Ambon. After today Flores has come to symbolise, for me, the strong connection between Islam and Christianity. This afternoon we attended our first Catholic mass in Ruteng's cathedral, where we learnt that the Christian word for "God" in Indonesian is "Allah". I find the thought extremely symbolic, a kind of linguistic affirmation of the closeness of the two religions, a reminder that the Gods worshipped by Islam and Christianity are essentially the same. It is often lost in translation that the Muslim "Allah" or "al-Lah" is not a name but a description, one that can be equally used for the Christian God.

We spend the evening with Muslim friends who have adopted us, bemused by the sound of church bells which have now replaced the once-familiar call to prayer.

Monday 29th January
Kupang

> "My son," the Master said, "the City called Dis
>   lies just ahead, the heavy citizens,
>   the swarming crowds of Hell's metropolis."
> And I then: "Master, I already see
>   the glow of its red mosques, as if they came

hot from the forge to smoulder in this valley."
Dante Alighieri, *The Inferno*

A week in Flores, black sand beaches and outrageous volcanoes. Two more in Timor, both east and west. The monsoon heavy as ever, smothering and relentless. Animists, Catholics, the tension of Dili's streets, the welcome of the mountain villages, and then the long road out again. Goats balanced on gravestones; the rich, ripe smell of somebody else's sweat.

Which brings me here, on a break-wall overlooking one of Kupang's beaches, on the day before the journey ends. Kirst is back at the hotel, writing a diary of her own; I felt I needed to be by myself to figure out exactly what I wanted to write.

Everything around me is a reminder of the last five months in the tropical monsoon. Black trees covered in moss finger the air. Here a coconut palm, there a frangipani; here a banana tree, there a pine. The whole world has been toned a rich grey, smothered by the sullen, asphalt-coloured mass that stretches across the sky, potent and dramatic. Even the light is dark. The beach lies at the end of the street, and beyond it is the ocean, now meek beneath the imposing sky. Chickens peck at the sand and black rocks at the water's edge. After the bald red earth of the hills near Dili, it is a relief to experience this tropical world one final time.

There is little I wish to write about East Timor. Our experiences there were powerful, but were of little consequence to Islam as a whole. The region is too politicised, too full of the injustices of thirty years. Our experiences were extraordinary, but they belong to another journey, another story. Another book, not this one.

I spend the afternoon here, crouched on the break-wall, gazing at the sea. I don't know why, but I have the strong sense of having reached a significant moment, and it feels good just to sit here, watching, drifting, dreaming. Kupang is an Indonesian – and thus Muslim – city on an otherwise Christian island; it feels somehow appropriate that the journey should finish here. I try to send my mind skating out across the water, away from me, away from Indonesia, searching the distances I have travelled. Should I be able to comprehend such scales? The feeling that I should nags at the edges of my mind, and in brief moments I feel I can. It is a marvellous sensation.

I suddenly realise that for the first time, and almost certainly the last, I am facing backwards, back towards where the journey began. I think of the places I have been in the last nine months. I think of the day spent staring into waters just as enigmatic, though much dirtier, on the Persian Gulf in Iran. Or the day we crossed the Bosphorus in Istanbul, stepping into Asia for the first time. I see the waters of the Ganges, the floating bodies, the funeral pyres. The powdered waters of the Indus, the flooded fields of Bangladesh. All these places feed the quiet grey-blue before me; can I truly remember any of them? Some of it comes to me in vivid fragments, but the rest has crumbled, scattered, leaving nothing in my memory but random litter and a face or two. It seems to me now that the frailty of memory, its inability to truly reproduce experience, must be one of the true tragedies of life. These experiences will only ever happen to me once. Once gone they are lost forever, and this is something no written word can possibly prevent.

I have with me a copy of Dante's *The Inferno*, given to me by a Canadian tourist about a week ago. I would like to finish it before we leave, as it is exquisitely appropriate to any chapter about the relationship between Islam and Christianity. Symbolising all the distrust and animosity between the religions, the buildings of Dante's Hell are mosques of red-hot iron.

In Dante's time, of course, the mosque was seen as sheer perversion, a twisted counterpart of the church, just as Satan in his underworld was seen as the corrupted equivalent of God in heaven. To Dante, and to thousands of Christians of medieval Europe, there was no more apt portrayal of Hell than as a place of mosques. I cannot help wondering if many East Timorese would find a certain resonance in such an image. We encountered enough hatred, towards Muslims, not just in the children of slaughtered parents but in many people we met, for me to think that many would.

I am going to sign off now. With incredible timing, the call to prayer has started, strangled and foreign, from a mosque nearby. A reminder that I should probably start my final assault on the lower depths of Hell. I will read with the timeless sound of the *muezzin* ringing in my ears. To hear it again, even after this short time, brings a smile to my face. *Allahu Akbar.*

A SENSE OF LOSS

Tuesday 30th January
Kupang

> Travelling is not just seeing the new; it is also leaving behind. Not just
> opening doors; also closing them behind you, never to return.
>
> Jan Myrdal, *The Silk Road*

In *The Heart of the Matter*, Graham Greene mentions the unreality one feels
when leaving a country to which one knows one shall never return. We
leave for Darwin tomorrow, and I know the feeling. The dislocation I feel
now, the sense of nothing around me being real, is even stronger than it
was the day we left Australia. The world around us is a sham, without
substance. We are moving closer to that half-life between two countries,
between disjointed chapters of a life, when neither past nor future seem
real, and the present is a blur suspended between the two.
I yearn for home, for that great big brushstroke of sky, for the empty
spaciousness of summer. I have wearied of the stares and the constant
chorus of "hello, mister". I long to say goodbye to having my belongings
inspected by strangers, to the sneers and harassment of the transport
touts. Goodbye to the lack of running water, to ill health, to crushing
humidity, to roosters and chickens, to sleep broken by the dawn call to
prayer, to filth and dirt, to malarial mosquitoes, to bedbugs, to the creak
of geckoes in the night, to an inability to communicate... the list goes on.
Yet I find myself midway between relief and regret. I know that the fact I
am finally leaving it all behind really is a delight, but at the same time the
thought seems unbearably sad.
The strange thing is that I cannot truly picture Australia any longer. I
cannot picture home, even though I have been dreaming of it for months.
I cannot even really picture Indonesia, or the journey just completed. I
want to. At some stage I shall have to. I need to be able to sum it all up,
to conclude, if only for the fact that I want to turn these experiences into
a book. I do not want to simply explain Islam, if indeed it can be *explained*.
I want the reader to experience it. Description and explanation, in the
end, is no substitute for experience. How wrong were my preconceptions
of Iran? I want the reader to experience the journey for themselves.
    But right now
    I am
        cut
            free
    from the journey,
    a journey (in some senses)
    already over
    because of the way I feel. And with this feeling of detachment comes
the sense of loss I have so long waited for. It's over. The thing I have lived
for nine months is over. I feel hollow. I feel devastated.
I lie down beneath the tired fan in our Kupang hotel room, forcing my

mind to go down flat. I try to remember the journey, to get a sense of the billowing, ribboned experience that stretches backwards into my life. I try to imagine the self I once was, the self I have become as I have learnt about Islam. Something I write today, after all, should reflect what I have learned of the religion, what I wish to impart to others.

I think back, then, to Iran. To the shock of religious ecstasy, of women and men weeping for their God. The surprise of a country completely unlike my idea of it. The realisation of how naive it is to describe the Shi'a as a fundamentalist sect, that doing so is like labelling all Germans neo-Nazis. A place of kindness and extremism, of peace and terror, a place where God is as present as the desert. And a place I will remember as having given us a deeper understanding of Islam – beyond Shi'ism, beyond Iran itself – than I could have possibly expected. Names: Ali, Abu Bakr, Umar, Uthman, Fatima, A'isha, Mu'awiya. In many senses, our entire understanding of Islam – the *hadith*, the experience of the Qur'an, the incredible sense of faith – came more from Iran than anywhere else.

I drift onwards, to Central Asia, steeped in history. The Abbasids and Seljuqs, the Mongols and the Turks. And a completely different version of Islam, one barely recognisable after eighty years of Soviet occupation and cultural destruction, seen through the fractured lens of alcohol.

Pakistan was cruelty and kindness, sexual repression and sexual anger. Guns and drugs and crime and corruption. The worst side of misogynist Islam. Bangladesh was Sufis and saints, syncretism and superstition. It was an encounter with the mystical experience of Islam, one I had been unable to uncover anywhere else. And Indonesia, of course, had many faces: ultra-orthodoxy in Aceh; complete flexibility in the shape of the Minangkabau; religious collision in Flores and Timor.

All these encounters, all these experiences, have taught me what I know of Islam. I feel, in some way, that I must conclude, must find a unifying thread which binds them all together. Yet I know that no single conclusion can be gained. The variation of experience is too great. Each stage of the trip so far has yielded its own version of Islam, has offered its own particular view of the religion. I swim through the memories. Do any of them represent Islam? Taken as a whole, they are one idea of it, as incomplete and as biased and as varied as the real world. Like the Sufi conception of God, Islam is beyond a single description. My memories are beyond description in the same way, beyond the realm of categorical fact. But they are Islam. They are my Islam. And, taken as a whole, I hope that they give some idea how many things the word 'Islam' can mean.

A simple condensation of experience and knowledge thus seems insufficient when it comes to Islam. The subject is too varied, too complicated. If it were not so, I would not need to write a book about it. If Islam could be given a summary, distilled to anything coherent, then a simple essay would suffice. One would certainly not need a nine-month trip, a set of diaries, a book. Indeed, there can be no single thesis when it comes to 'Islam' in its entirety, and such a fact makes concluding impossible. The only conclusion that can be offered is the journey itself. To summarise would be to diminish the details, to ignore the multitude of impressions that have made Islam more than just a word, that have made Islam real.

The journey is the only possible expression of itself; all I can do, when I put down my pen, is reflect on the journey. And when I do, I will hope that it was neither a sensationalised view of fanaticism and cruelty nor a sanitised one of an idealised faith, but somewhere between the two. I will hope that this journey, this patterned mosaic of experience that belongs only to me, provides a tiny glimpse of the infinitely varied reality that is Islam.

NOTES AND ACKNOWLEDGEMENTS

I would like to make a brief comment about the method of transliteration used within the book. It is particularly difficult to reconcile the transliteration styles of Arabic, Persian, Turkic and Russian words and personal names. The system I have adopted is obviously imperfect. No standard method of transliteration from the Arabic script to the Latin one exists, not least because of differences in regional pronunciation, and in differences between Persian and Arabic. I am of the opinion that the method used by Orientalists such as Bernard Lewis, while no doubt as accurate as possible, detracts somewhat from readability, and for a book such as this is of very little benefit. My system of transliteration is my own, designed to approximate as closely as possible the sound of the particular language concerned. The few exceptions to this rule are all names with an English equivalent, such as Mecca, or names and words whose translation is already well established.

Finally, I have a number of people I wish to thank, without whom the book you hold in your hands would not exist. Unfortunately, this will always remain the part I like least about writing. The fear I have missed someone, that my words inadequately express the gratitude I feel, always paralyses my hand when the time for thanks arrives. In advance, I apologise to those I should thank but haven't, which includes anyone who influenced, either directly or indirectly, the writing of this book.

More than anyone, I would like to thank Kirst, not only for her companionship during the journey but for her support and encouragement afterwards; for the many stimulating conversations in which she bounced my ideas and hopes, my thoughts and dreams, back at me. Words can scarcely express how much it has all meant to me, something I feel more strongly now than ever before (which makes writing this section incredibly difficult). The same is true for the gratitude I feel towards my parents, who never receive the thanks they deserve, but keep on giving all the same. It is for these reasons that I have dedicated the book to them, and to Kirst, although this is a mere gesture when compared with how important all three of them are to me.

My enormous gratitude goes out to Mack Cameron, Peter Davis and Mark Dunn, for not only giving me the opportunity to take the journey, but to support me as I wrote the damn thing. Thanks also to Robert and Libby Albert, without whom I would often be lost, and who managed to sell more copies of the last one than anyone else; to Stu and Jon for being themselves; to Laura for her unbridled enthusiasm. Thanks to all my proof readers, including those already mentioned as well as Paul, Marty, Tiff, La, Mel, Jane and Phil - without your input I would never have come up with anything vaguely readable.

For having the foresight to see the potential in the book when it landed on her doorstep, and the faith to take it on, I give my most sincere thanks to Sheila Drummond. Thanks also to Sheena Dewan and Caroline Jory at Vision, for their assistance and support, but most of all their sheer enthusiasm about the book, which is something I have treasured.

My task in thanking those who assisted me during the journey, particularly in Iran and East Timor, is made especially difficult. Many names and circumstances have been changed, for reasons I should hope are clear. To those people, I can offer only my genuine gratitude, in the belief that they know who they are. I sincerely hope this is the case. There is someone who needs thanking in almost every place I stayed - Subroto, Mehrdod, Nasser, Farzaneh and Mahsoud, Ahmad and more - the list goes on. Whether their names have been changed or not, I hope they recognise who they are, because they all, in their own way, managed to teach me something of their own, and to show me that with the wealth of kindness and generosity there is in the world, there is probably still hope for it yet.

GLOSSARY

Abbasids The most durable and most famous Islamic dynasty, whose rule over much of the Islamic world lasted five centuries. The Abbasids were descended from the Prophet's uncle, Abbas, and overthrew their predecessors, the Umayyads, with the support of a combination of Shi'ite, Iranian and other Muslim and non-Muslim groups dissatisfied with the regime.

Abu Bakr First of the four "righteous Caliphs" of Sunni Islam. His young daughter, A'isha, was one of Muhammad's last and most influential wives.

A'isha Muhammad's youngest and probably most influential wife. A'isha is revered as the "mother of the faithful" by Sunnis, and the fierce enmity between her, and Fatima and Ali, was in part responsible for the Sunni-Shi'a schism which would sunder Islam.

Ali In Arabic, Ali ibn Abi Talib, fourth of the "righteous Caliphs" of Sunni Islam and first of the Shi'a Imams. Ali was Muhammad's nephew, and was one of the first and most faithful converts to Islam. He married Muhammad's daughter Fatima, who bore him two sons, Hassan and Hussein. In 632, when Muhammad died, Ali claimed the right of succession. His claim was bitterly opposed by A'isha, and he was preceded in the Caliphate by Abu Bakr, Umar, and Uthman.

Ali Hujwiri Pakistan's holiest Sufi saint, the Data Ganj, whose shrine is located in Lahore.

Amu Darya Large river in Central Asia formerly known as the Oxus, which separates present-day Turkmenistan and Uzbekistan.

Ashura Religious festival that commemorates the martyrdom of the third Shi'ite Imam, Hussein.

Atatürk, Mustafa Kemal Turkish soldier, nationalist leader, and statesman, who founded the republic of Turkey and was its first president. The name Atatürk (Father Turk) was bestowed upon him in 1934 by the Grand National Assembly as a tribute for his unique service to the Turkish nation. Atatürk sought to transform Turkey into a secular nation, abolishing the Caliphate and banning attachments to the past such as the fez.

Avicenna (Abu ibn Sina) Regarded by many Muslims as one of the greatest Islamic philosophers. Avicenna's philosophy was based on a combination of Aristotelianism and Neoplatonism. Contrary to orthodox Islamic thought, Avicenna denied personal immortality, God's interest in individuals, and the creation of the world in time. Because of his views, Avicenna became the main target of an attack on such philosophy by al-Ghazzali.

al-Azhar Mosque Islamic institution established in Cairo by the Shi'a Fatimids. Al-Azhar was converted to Sunnism upon re-establishment of the Sultanate of Egypt, and remains the most important centre for Islamic learning in the world.

Bismillah ar-Rahman ar-Rahim "In the name of God, the Compassionate, the Merciful".

Bosphorus Strait connecting the Black Sea and the Sea of Marmara, separating Turkey in Asia from Turkey in Europe.

burqa Face mask and cloak made of extremely thick and heavy fabric worn in the tribal areas of Pakistan around Peshawar.

chador Tent-like piece of fabric worn in Iran and among Lebanese Shi'ite women which covers the body completely and which is held in place with the teeth or underneath the chin.

din The religious aspects of Muslim life.

dunya The worldly aspects of Muslim life.

Eid Muslim feast or holy days forming the two most important religious occasions in the Muslim calendar. Eid ul-Fitr, the Minor Festival, breaks the fast at the end of the month of Ramadan, while Eid ul-Adha, the Major Festival, is the feast of sacrifice which takes place during the *hajj*.

eivan Arched portal sculpted with stalactite moulding common in the architecture of the mosques of Iran.

'fana Sufi concept of the state of annihilation of self, a stripping away of identity until nothing stands between God and the Sufi mystic, and hence a state in which true union with God may be found.

Fatima Daughter of the Prophet Muhammad and wife of Imam Ali. Fatima developed a profound animosity to Muhammad's last and youngest wife, A'isha, and their resulting enmity was in part responsible for the Sunni-Shi'a schism which would sunder the religion.

Fatimids Dynasty established in Tunisia during the decline of Abbasid power in the tenth century. The Fatimids were Shi'ites, claiming descent from Fatima, Muhammad's daughter and Ali's wife. At the height of its power, in the latter half of the tenth century, the Fatimid caliphate constituted a serious threat to the Abbasids in Baghdad, ruling most of northern Africa as well as Sicily and Syria.

Five Pillars of Islam The pillars of Islam are the elementary rules by which Muslims can claim to follow the path of Muhammad. The five pillars are: the shahadah, faith in the existence and unity of God, and Muhammad as his Prophet; salah, the five daily prayers; sawm, the fast during the month of Ramadan; the annual zakat tax to re-distribute wealth to the poor; and the hajj, once in a lifetime, the pilgrimage to Mecca.

al-Ghazzali Islamic philosopher and theologian, Latin name Algazel. Ghazzali's work *The Revival of the Religious Sciences* presented a unified view of Islam, incorporating elements from all three sources previously considered contradictory: tradition, intellectualism, and mysticism. The work has been considered the greatest religious book written by a Muslim, second only to the Qur'an. Later, al-Ghazzali set out to refute the Neoplatonic ideas of other Muslim philosophers, most notably those of Avicenna, which were opposed to orthodox doctrines such as creation and immortality of the soul. Al-Ghazzali's attack on philosophical theory and speculation, set forth in *Destruction of the Philosophers*, was in large part responsible for the eventual decline of rationalism in Islam.

hadith The body of traditions concerning the sayings and doings of the Prophet Muhammad, now considered to be second in authority to the

Qur'an and to embody the *sunna*.

Hafiz Iranian mystical poet.

hajj The fifth "pillar" of Islam, the pilgrimage to the Sacred Mosque at Mecca undertaken in the twelfth month of the Muslim year.

hajjah Muslim woman who has successfully completed the *hajj*.

hajji Muslim man who has successfully completed the *hajj*.

al-Hallaj ("the wool carder") Prominent figure in the early centuries of Sufism, who aptly represented the collision of Sufi practice with Islamic orthodoxy. Al-Hallaj was accused of having asserted his identity with God, and was executed in Baghdad.

Hanafi One of the four major sects of Sunni Islam, established by Abu Hanifa in the eighth century.

Hanbali One of the four major sects of Sunni Islam, established by Imam Hanbal in the ninth century.

Hashim Clan of the Quraysh tribe in pre-Islamic Arabia to which the Prophet Muhammad belonged.

Hassan Imam Ali's first son, who ceded rights to the Caliphate to Mu'awiya upon Ali's death.

hartal Organised strike used in the Indian subcontinent as a mark of protest or an act of mourning. Popularised by Ghandi as a peaceable protest against British rule.

Hezbollah Literally, "the party of God". Party associated with the rise of Imam Khomeini, and which rules in Iran. Also extremely influential among Lebanese Shi'ites.

hijab Both the veil worn by Islamic women and the act of veiling itself. Literally, "curtain".

Hijaz Literally "the barrier". Mountainous coastal region of Arabia between the central peninsula and the Red Sea.

hijra The emigration of Muhammad and his followers to Medina (formerly known as Yathrib).

Hussein Imam Ali's second son, who was slaughtered with his family on the field at Karbala, and whose death is mourned by Shi'ites as part of Ashura.

Ibn Khaldun Full name Abu Zayd Abd-Ar-Rahman Ibn Khaldun (1332-1406), the greatest of the medieval Islamic historians. Ibn Khaldun outlined a philosophy of history and theory of society that was unprecedented in ancient and medieval writing and that is closely reflected in modern sociology. Societies, he believed, are held together by the power of social cohesiveness, which can be augmented by the unifying force of religion. Social change and the rise and fall of societies follow laws that can be empirically discovered and that reflect climate and economic activity as well as other realities.

Imam Literally, "leader". The term is generally used for spiritual leaders, and can be used to refer to the leader of a congregation, important members of the Shi'a ulema, Shi'a or Ismaili saints, the Aga Khan, and so on.

Insha'allah "If God wills it".

Ismailis Sect of Shi'ite Muslims, followers of the Shi'ite Imam Isma'il. Ismailis are found mainly in India, Pakistan, Yemen and East Africa.

jahiliyya Pre-Islamic era.

Jinnah, Muhammad Ali Indian politician, leader of the Indian Muslim League, who became the founding father of Pakistan and its first governor-general.

Ka'ba The central shrine of Islam, the "house of God" where divine touches the mundane, the Ka'ba is a cube-shaped, one-room structure in Mecca, Saudi Arabia. The Ka'ba is the focal point of the yearly hajj, the pilgrimage to Mecca, which all Muslims must attempt to make at least once in their lives if they are able.

Kameez See *Shalwar Kameez*.

Karbala Plain in southern Iraq where Ali's son Hussein, along with his family and supporters, were brutally slaughtered. The event came to take on extreme significance to the Shi'a faith.

Khadija Muhammad's first wife. Muhammad acquired wealth and social position by marrying Khadija, the widow of a rich merchant, several years older than himself, shortly after she hired him to manage her businesses.

Khurasan (also Khorasan) Eastern Iranian province centred around Mashhad. Khurasan once denoted a far larger region, encompassing both Herat in Afghanistan and Merv in Turkmenistan, and has been politically and strategically important throughout Islamic history.

Komité The Revolutionary Guards of post-Revolutionary Iran, renowned for their brutal methods, and responsible for both the maintenance of Islamic values in the Islamic republic and for the elimination of any opposition to the regime.

madrasa Religious school or centre of religious learning.

Maghrib prayer Nightfall prayer, conducted just after sunset. Maghrib literally means "place of the setting sun".

magneh Wimple-like veil worn mostly by young women in Iran.

Mahdi Messianic figure of Islamic mythology, representing the righteous common man who will appear to usher in an era of truth and justice.

Mahmud of Ghazni

Majlis Originally the council of elders forming the basis for authority in tribal Arabia. Today used more widely, such as for the parliament of Iran.

Maliki One of the four major sects of Sunni Islam, established by Malik ibn Anas in the eighth century.

Mamelukes Sultanate which ruled Egypt from Cairo nominally under Abbasid authority until 1517. The Mamelukes represented the height of power for Turkish mamluk slaves in the latter centuries of the Abbasid empire, and established their authority through the complete emasculation of the Caliphate.

mamluk Literally "owned". Turkish slaves renowned for their military prowess who came to occupy positions of great power within the Abbasid empire.

manteau Heavy coat worn by the women of Iran.

Masjid Mosque.

mawali Non-Arab converts to Islam under the Umayyads, whose discontent over their treatment by the empire led to its eventual overthrow.

Mawlawiyyah The Sufi order known in the West as the "whirling dervishes".

mihrab Niche built in a mosque or prayer-hall to indicate the direction of Mecca.

Mu'awiya Governor of Syria during the reign of the Caliph Umar, Mu'awiya became the greatest opposition to the rule of the Caliphate when he challenged the authority of Ali. Upon Ali's death he seized control of the Caliphate, moved the empire's capital to Damascus, and established the Umayyad dynasty which would rule for the next seventy years.

Mughals Muslim dynasty descended from Timur which ruled an empire in India, based in Delhi, from the 16th to the 19th century.

mullah Islamic cleric.

Najd Great inland plateau of the central Arabian peninsula, consisting mostly of desert.

NWFP North-West Frontier Province. Northern area of Pakistan bordering Afghanistan.

Omar Khayyam Persian mathematician, astronomer, and author of the Rubáiyát, one of the world's best-known works of poetry.

Pancasila The "five principles" originally proposed by Sukarno which form the philosophical backbone of the Indonesian state. The first and most important of the five principles calls for faith in God. governing almost all political and social activity in Indonesia, the most important of which calls for faith in God.

Pukhtun Ethnic group of Afghanistan and western Pakistan, also known as Pashtun.

Purdah Tradition of seclusion of Muslim women in Pakistan and India.

Qadi Muslim judge.

Quraysh Most powerful tribe in pre-Islamic Mecca, of which Muhammad was a member. The Quraysh were composed of various clans, such as the dominant Umayya, and Muhammad's own clan, the Banu Hashim.

Rafflesia Genus of various parasitic leafless plants, distinctive for their putrid, carrion odour. The large, pink flowers are pollinated by carrion flies. The blossom of one species, the corpse lily or *Rafflesia amoldii*, is recognised as the largest flower in the world.

Ramadan The ninth month of the Muslim calendar, during which a month-long fast, the fourth "pillar" of Islam, takes place.

Rumi Perhaps the most famous of the Iranian Sufi poets, founder of the Mawlawiyyah order of Sufis, and whose great work, the *Mathnawi*, became known as the Sufi Bible.

Sa'di Iranian mystical poet.

Saffavids Iranian Islamic dynasty, based originally on a radical Sufi religious movement, which established independent rule in Iran in 1501. The Saffavids were responsible for the exquisite mosques and architecture of Esfahan.

salaam wa leikum Ubiquitous Islamic greeting meaning, "peace be upon you."

Sassanids Pre-Islamic Persian empire, known for its well-organised social structures and dynastic succession. Rival of the Byzantine empire.

Savak Secret police of the Shah before the Iranian Revolution, known for their brutality.

Seljuqs Turkish dynasty which established control over the Caliphate in 1055.

Shalwar Kameez Muslim dress found primarily in Pakistan, but also in India and Bangladesh. It generally consists of an overlong shirt (*shalwar*) and large baggy pants (*kameez*) of an identical colour. They can be worn by both men and women, but in general the *shalwar kameez* of Pakistani women are brightly coloured and often decorated, while the men choose more drab, conservative colours.

Shari'a Islamic law.

Shi'a, Shi'ites Sect of Islam which arose in the seventh century after a split over who should succeed Muhammad after his death. The *Shi'atu 'Ali*, or "partisans of Ali", believed that the Prophet's nephew, Ali, was the rightful successor.

Sufism Islamic mysticism.

Suhrawardiya One of the most important schools of Islamic mysticism on the Indian subcontinent.

sunna The traditions of the Prophet.

sunnat A commendable act in the eyes of God.

Sunni The main sect of Islam, named to denote those who follow the traditions of the Prophet, the *sunna*.

surah Chapter of the Qur'an. Each *surah* begins with the phrase, "In the name of God, the Compassionate, the Merciful." The *surah* are arranged arbitrarily in the Qur'an in order of length, the longest chapters first and shortest ones last, some of which are no longer than a couple of lines.

tariqa Sufi order.

Timurids Dynasty established by Timur in the Fifteenth century, and which ruled from Samarkand for a brief period following his death.

Tughluq Muslim dynasty which established control over central and southern India from the Sultanate of Delhi. The dynasty was short-lived, but its effects were significant in encouraging Muslim settlement in southern India.

Turkestan Area of Central Asia stretching from Western China to the Caspian sea, home to numerous Turkic peoples, such as the Uighur, Turkmen, Kyrgyz and Kazakh.

Uighur Indigenous Muslim people of the Western Chinese province of Xinjiang.

ulema The Islamic religious clergy. Used to indicate both individuals within the clergy and the organisation as a whole.

Umar Second of the four "righteous Caliphs" of Sunni Islam, who presided over massive expansion of the Muslim territories.

Umayya Dominant clan of pre-Islamic Mecca. The Umayya resented the fact that Muhammad's rise robbed them of much of their power, and worked hard to regain it. Their influence increased strongly with the appointment of Uthman to the Caliphate, but was only fully cemented when Mu'awiya successfully challenged Ali's authority, eventually establishing the Umayyad dynasty which would rule from Damascus for seventy years.

Umayyads see Umayya.

ummah The global community of Islam. Originally a term used to refer to the local Arab community, it is now used to indicate all followers of Islam.

urs The death anniversary of a Sufi saint or sheikh.

Uthman Third "righteous Caliph" of Sunni Islam.

Wahabism Extremely strict, puritanical form of Sunni Islam predominant in Saudi Arabia.

Whirling dervishes Western name for the Turkish Sufi order of the Mawlawiyyah, followers of the poet Rumi. The whirling dervishes are famous for their spinning dancing, through which they claim to be able to become closer to God.

wudu Both the act of washing before prayer and the state of Quranic grace it achieves. A Muslim should only pray or handle the Qur'an whilst in a state of wudu.

Xinjiang Chinese province in the extreme West of the country.

Yathrib Former name of the Arabian city of Medina.

Yaweh The Jewish God.

zina Sex out of wedlock. Of particular importance in Pakistan, where laws relating to zina were introduced by General Zia-ul-Haq, drastically reducing the rights of women.

Zoroastrianism Religion founded in ancient Persia by the prophet **Zoroaster**. A fundamentally monotheistic religion, Zoroastrianism is based largely on the conflict between a spirit of light and good and one of darkness and evil, and is still practised in Iran and India.

BIBLIOGRAPHY

It should be clear to anyone who has read this far that *Godless Pilgrim* is a work of literature, not of academia. It was for this reason that I chose to omit footnotes and page references in the text.

The following list of texts represent, to the best of my knowledge, the great bulk of writing responsible for my view of Islam. It not only includes works on the religion itself, but on Islamic history, on the countries through which I travelled, and anything which assisted in the production of this book in any way.

With a topic as vast and eternal as Islam, I have been unable to avoid a repetition of many ideas, and I gratefully acknowledge these sources.

Adshead, S.A.M. *Central Asia in World History* (Macmillan, 1993).

Ahmed, Akbar S. *Discovering Islam: Making Sense of Muslim History and Society* (London, 1989). Highly recommended.

Arabshah, Ahmed ibn. *Tamerlane or Timur the Great Amir* (translated by J.H. Sanders, London, 1936)

Arberry, A.J. *Muslim Saints and Mystics*. A translation of the *Tadhkirat al-Auliya'* of Farid al-Din Attar.

Armstrong, Karen. *A History of God* (New York, 1993). Erudite and inspiring look at religion itself: essential reading.

Ayliffe, Rosie, Dubin, Marc and Gawthrop, John. *Turkey: The Rough Guide* (London, 1994).

Basgoz, I., "Religion and ethnic consciousness among Turks in the Soviet Union" in Pullapilly, C.K. (ed.), *Islam in the Contemporary World* (1980).

Bennigsen, Alexandre A. and Wimbush, S. Enders. *Muslim National Communism in the Soviet Union*.

Bray, John. "Pakistan in 1989: Benazir's Balancing Act" in *The Round Table*, April 1989.

Brooks, Geraldine. *Nine Parts of Desire: The Hidden World of Islamic Women* (New York, 1995). A well-presented examination of the plight of women in the world of Islam.

Brown, Lesley (ed.) *The New Shorter Oxford English Dictionary* (Oxford, 1993).

Dante Alighieri *The Inferno*, (translated by John Ciardi, New York, 1954).

Dawkins, Richard. *The Blind Watchmaker* (London, ____).

Dawood, N.J. (trans.) *The Koran* (London, 1993).

Farmaian, Sattareh Farman. *Daughter of Persia* (New York, 1993). An excellent insight into the development of modern Iran.

Fierman. *Soviet Central Asia*. Extract by Teresa Rakowska-Harmstone appears in the foreword, page ix.

Friedman, Thomas. *From Beirut to Jerusalem* (London, 1993).

Goodwin, Jan. *Price of Honour: Muslim Women Lift the Veil of Silence on the Islamic World* (Little, Brown and Company, 1994). Another valuable look at women and Islam.

Greene, Graham. *The Heart of the Matter* (London, 1971).

Grey, A.J. "Islamic Script" in *The Australian Financial Review Magazine* (May 1996).

Haeri, Shaykh Fadhlalla. *The Elements of Islam* (Brisbane, 1993).

Hick, John (ed.) *The Myth of God Incarnate* (London, 1977).

Iqbal, Zubiar and Mirakhar, Abbas. *Islamic Banking* (Washington, 1987).

Israeli, Raphael and Johns, Anthony H. *Islam in Asia Volume II: Southeast and East Asia* (Boulder, 1984).

Karim, A. *The Bauls of Bangladesh: A Study of an Obscure Religious Cult* (Kushtia 1980).

Karim, A. *The Myths of Bangladesh* (Kushtia 1988).

King, John and St Vincent, David. *Pakistan: A Travel Survival Kit* (Melbourne, 1993).

Khomeini, Ruhollah. *Islam and Revolution* (1981).

Lewis, Bernard. *The Arabs In History* (Oxford, 1993). Essential reading, from one of the most well-respected Islamic scholars of this century.

Mace, John. *Modern Persian: A Complete Course for Beginners* (London, 1971). Where would I have been without it?

Mahmoody, Betty. *Not Without My Daughter* (London, 1987).

Maqsood, Ruqaiyyah. *Teach Yourself Islam* (London, 1994). A good introduction to the religion.

Mesbahi, Mohiaddin. (ed.) *Central Asia and the Caucasus After the Soviet Union* (Florida, 1994).

Microsoft Encarta Encyclopaedia 1996.

Microsoft Encarta World Atlas 1996.

Mills, C.W. "The Cultural Apparatus" in *Power, Politics and People: The Collected Essays of C. Wright Mills*, ed. Irving Louis Horowitz (Oxford, 1967).

Mumtaz, Khawar and Shaheed, Farida. (eds.) *Women of Pakistan: Two Steps Forward, One Step Back?* (London, 1987).

Murray, Jon. *Bangladesh: A Travel Survival Kit* (Melbourne, 1991).

Naipaul, V.S. Among the Believers: An Islamic Journey (London, 1981).

Newberg, Paula. "Dateline Pakistan: Bhutto's Back" in *Foreign Policy*, Summer 1994 (Washington DC, 1994).

Nicholson, Reynold A. (trans.) *Rumi: Poet and Mystic 1207-1273* (London, 1950)

Olonabadi, Ahmad Ahmadi. *A Study of the Relationship Between Iranian Counsellor's Values and Philosophical Orientations and Their Counselling Functions and Activities.*

Roy, Asin. *The Islamic Syncretistic Tradition in Bengal.* (Princeton, 1983).

Said, Edward W. *Covering Islam* (London, 1981). As valuable and thought-provoking as all of Said's work.

St Vincent, David. *Iran: A Travel Survival Kit* (Melbourne, 1992).

Sluglett, Peter and Farouk-Sluglett, Marion. *The Times Guide to the Middle East: The Arab World and its Neighbours* (London, 1993). A valuable resource.

Smart, J.R. *Arabic: A Complete Course for Beginners* (London, 1986).

241

Taylor, Jennifer (ed.) *The Traveller's Quotation Book* (London, 1993).

Thomas, Dorothy Q. and Gossman, Patricia. *Double Jeopardy: Police Abuse of Women in Pakistan Asia Watch and the Women's Rights Project* (1992).

Turner, Peter. *Indonesia: A Lonely Planet Travel Survival Kit* (Melbourne, 1995).

Vermes, Geza. *Jesus the Jew* (London, 1983). A fascinating study of Jesus as an historical figure.

Walsh, Mary Williams. "At the Mercy of Men" in *The Wall Street Journal*, May 3, 1989.

INDEX